STOIC WISDOM

OTHER BOOKS BY NANCY SHERMAN

Afterwar: Healing the Moral Wounds of Our Soldiers

Untold War: Inside the Hearts, Minds, and Souls of Our Soldiers

Stoic Warriors: The Ancient Philosophy Behind the Military Mind

Making a Necessity of Virtue: Aristotle and Kant on Virtue

The Fabric of Character: Aristotle's Theory of Virtue

Aristotle's Ethics: Critical Essays (Editor)

STOIC WISDOM

ANCIENT LESSONS FOR MODERN RESILIENCE

NANCY SHERMAN

OXFORD
UNIVERSITY PRESS

Oxford University Press is a department of the University of Oxford. It furthers
the University's objective of excellence in research, scholarship, and education
by publishing worldwide. Oxford is a registered trade mark of Oxford University
Press in the UK and certain other countries.

Published in the United States of America by Oxford University Press
198 Madison Avenue, New York, NY 10016, United States of America.

© Oxford University Press 2021

First issued as an Oxford University Press paperback, 2023

Library of Congress Cataloging-in-Publication Data
Names: Sherman, Nancy, 1951– author.
Title: Stoic wisdom : ancient lessons for modern resilience /
Nancy Sherman.
Description: New York, NY, United States of America : Oxford University
Press, [2021] | Includes bibliographical references and index.
Identifiers: LCCN 2020052426 (print) | LCCN 2020052427 (ebook) |
ISBN 9780197501832 (hb) | ISBN 9780197673072 (pb) |
ISBN 9780197501856 (epub)
Subjects: LCSH: Stoics. | Resilience (Personality trait)
Classification: LCC B528.S2993 2021 (print) | LCC B528 (ebook) |
DDC 188—dc23
LC record available at https://lccn.loc.gov/2020052426
LC ebook record available at https://lccn.loc.gov/2020052427

DOI: 10.1093/oso/9780197501832.001.0001

Paperback printed by Sheridan Books, Inc., United States of America

To Marshall
For his love (and humor) always

"Some things are up to us and some are not up to us."

—Epictetus

"I am no longer accepting the things I cannot change. I am changing the things I cannot accept."

—Angela Davis

"If you want to be a true professional, do something outside yourself."
"Who will take responsibility for raising the next generation?"

—Ruth Bader Ginsburg

Contents

STOIC WISDOM

Eduardo Rosales, *Seneca*, 1836–1873.

LESSON 1

———— ✸ ————

THE GREAT
STOIC REVIVAL

A NEW ZEN

Stoicism has made a comeback—and a huge one at that. There are Stoic self-help books, digests of Stoic quotes, websites with Stoic wisdom to kickstart your day, podcasts, broadcasts, and on-line crash courses—some to learn how to become manly, others to become calm, some to learn to meditate Roman style, others to practice abstention, some to learn to take more control, others to take less. Tim Ferriss, the well-known author of *The 4-Hour Workweek* and popular Silicon Valley thought leader and podcast host, touts Stoicism as the "ideal" philosophy "for entrepreneurs." It's the right "operating system," as he puts it, to help train people who dream big to learn when and how to contain their egos. Stoicism has become the "new Zen." It's a philosophical practice for reducing stress and cultivating goodness. Beyond the online Stoic community is "Stoicon," an international, annual meet-up to help learners of all walks incorporate Stoic practices into their daily lives. The fervor has spread to the alt-right, too, with Stoic enthusiasts championing the great works of Western civilization as a bastion of whiteness and masculinity.

It's fair to say that Stoicism has become the darling of many. But why? For a start, it's an accessible philosophy with pithy wisdom. Among its Roman authors and sympathizers were emperors and political advisors, the likes of Cicero, Seneca, and Marcus Aurelius, who had power and class and the gift of letters. In Seneca's case, his most famous student was Nero, in need of daily lessons in controlling rage and anger. The political climate then was ripe for Stoicism—a philosophy of calm in the face of imperial power and intrigue. There are parallels today.

But Stoicism never was just for the elite. It was also for enslaved persons, such as Epictetus, who in a remarkable irony of history went on to inspire an emperor, Marcus Aurelius, to write his own Stoic meditations. The *Meditations* were meant for Marcus's eyes only, private reflections written at nightfall in a tent along the Danube during the Germanic campaigns. The nighttime journaling was to remind himself, as emperor and general, of the importance of humility and reason-based virtue in the face of his unlimited power. Marcus embraced Epictetus's message that we have power over our own minds and not outside events. Our well-being hangs on our judgments about what affects us and not on brute, uninterpreted objects or events. We are, by default, interpreters of the world. There is no unfiltered experience. In this the Stoics were prescient.

But why is Stoicism the new Zen of the West *now*? In part, the need for finding calm is ever pressing in Western culture. In the start-up tech world, work weeks can be manic, the lead-up to new funding rounds even tougher, and the pressure to design products that are both user-friendly and examples of smart engineering leads to stress and burnout at all levels. Life-hacking, or creating shortcuts for living efficiently and well, has gained a new attraction. Stoicism appeals to many as offering time-honored workarounds. For the alt-right, it has the additional badge of being a philosophy of "dead white men."

The Covid-19 pandemic added a new layer of anxiety for everyone as people faced new stresses from social isolation, job losses, massive death, and basic fear. The pandemic made it abundantly clear that we need ways of preparing ourselves, emotionally and psychologically, for worst-case scenarios. In short, we are hungry for ways of dialing down anxiety and tempering despair. There is a call for self-help and for self-calm. For those looking for counsel and wisdom in the traditional Western canon, Stoicism's Greco-Roman roots give it a seal of approval. Its recognizable imprint in much of the Western thought that followed makes it all the more approachable. On top of that, it's a philosophy (at least the Roman school of Stoicism) that is and always has been not just contemplated, but practiced. Its pivotal idea is not to get rid of self, as Zen Buddhism teaches, but to strengthen self-mastery, while still recognizing its limits. Practicing Stoicism was for the ancients, and is now for so many moderns, a way to build resilience. Its methods are psychological but also philosophical and normative, tied to living a life of virtue and character. The goal is inner strength, woven through and through with goodness rooted in reason. The merger is unbeatable: ancient virtue ethics meets modern life-management skills.

It is hard not to be attracted to some aspects of Stoicism, especially its core idea of strengthening self-control while abiding by hard limits set by forces outside ourselves. The applications are ubiquitous. You don't have to be Seneca in the court of Nero, or the US Navy pilot and Vietnam era prisoner of war James B. Stockdale, who embraced Epictetus's philosophy as a survival method during seven years in captivity. The challenges of pushing the boundaries of personal control are part of all of our lives, whether as a parent trying to figure out how to influence a grown child yet worried that too much control will alienate, or as a life-hacker wanting to beat death while realizing that it's an inflated attachment to self that is probably driving the urge. In much of life's pursuits, we want to have more control, don't quite know the limits, want to push hard until they're reached, and then want to accept what must be with equanimity. In short, we want control where we can have control, and want to accept limits in due course so we don't succumb to anger or crippling disappointment. We want to be masters of our fate, captains of our soul, to paraphrase the Stoic-inflected poem "Invictus" by English poet William Ernest Henley.

But the challenge to the Stoics, both ancient and modern followers, is to figure out just what is subject to our mastery and finesse. If, as Stoics, we draw the boundaries too narrowly, Stoicism looks like a way of playing it safe, a way of being in charge because so much is left beyond our will, in the hands of luck or the universe. If others draw the line for us, an appeal to Stoicism can overburden us as individuals and create a myth of an indomitable will that can and should do battle whatever the conditions and systemic structures, however adverse. It leaves out the collective work of changing those systemic structures. The image of the sage tortured on the rack who still can thrive is one that Aristotle rejects as "outrageous" and that orthodox Stoics resuscitate as the paragon of virtue sufficient for happiness.

But most of us, and Stockdale certainly included, experience distress when we push against boundaries to no avail, or undermine the goodwill of those we're trying to influence. Unimpeded exercise of cultivated or natural abilities brings pleasure. The reverse is also true: we experience pain when, despite our best efforts, we are thwarted, even if we see growth opportunities down the line.

In short, resilience as invincibility is a misguided notion. Epictetus, one of our sources, often appeals to the notion of resilience, as well as to the idea of moral training as a kind of athletic sport, where you are always ready to pick yourself up and get back in the ring. Willpower and grit know no limits. But Epictetus is a hyperbolizer. And he makes too little mention of the social supports that can sustain us or fail us.

Other Stoic writers do a better job of appealing to our connectedness and vulnerability to love and loss. A lesser known Stoic writer, Hierocles, visualizes a series of extended, concentric circles with the self at the center. "To be at home" in the world requires striving to bring the outermost circles toward the center. The Scottish Enlightenment philosopher Adam Smith, himself influenced by the Stoics, would go on to call that identification process "changing places in fancy," honed through exercises in empathy and imagination. Marcus Aurelius paints a more visceral image in his *Meditations*: Picture a dismembered hand and head lying apart from the rest of the human trunk. That's what "man makes of himself . . . when he cuts himself off" from "the world" of which he is a part. Marcus was writing while on a military campaign. Presumably, he had in mind intimate killing and dismemberment that he had seen on the battlefield earlier in the day. Body parts can't function cut off from the organic whole to which they belong. Similarly, we can't thrive cut off from the political and social whole of which we are a part. The implications are critical in a world witnessing the rise of corrosive forms of nationalism and rampant hatred fed by tribalism. The pandemic has made clear that we are a global community, like it or not. The reduction of fear and risk is essential not just for our own survival, but for the welfare of distant others with whom we are connected by virus, food supplies, transportation, medicine, and technology.

The Stoics were our first serious cosmopolitans. It is not surprising. They are of a political world that had begun to extend its borders beyond the small Greek city-state or *polis*. The Roman Empire advanced into vast swaths of land of many continents. The actual coinage of the term "cosmopolitan" predates the Stoics. Diogenes the Cynic, the fourth-century BCE immediate Stoic predecessor from Sinope (likely near Corinth, Greece), famously replied, when asked where he came from, "I am a citizen of the world," a *kosmopolitēs*. Zeno of Citium (Cyprus c. 335 BCE), the founder of the Stoic school, developed the idea and taught that social and political engagement in that global universe is necessary for flourishing. We share common reason and depend upon bonds of social support and cooperation to live a good life. What the ancient Stoics meant by sharing in the reason of the cosmos is likely not ours. But one thing the Stoic notion of cosmopolitanism suggests is that resilience is not a matter of just doing your very best, with individual effort and stamina the marker of survival. Quite to the contrary, being "at home in the world"—another pivotal Stoic notion which we will explore—is a matter of being connected to others who invest in you and who sustain and support your goodness. That richer Stoic story of cultivating virtue by extending circles outward needs to be part of a critical guide of how to thrive as a Stoic. That's part of the story I shall tell.

This book is a field guide for a *credible* Stoic practical philosophy. It corrects distortions in recent popularizations of ancient Stoicism and argues for Stoic tenets and practices worth following. It offers a kind of app for how to live a good life. It explores the reason for Stoicism's revival in the tech world, in the military, in the alt-right, in self-help circles, and even in psychotherapy. It explores its appeal for all of us, in all walks around the world, as we search for calm in the face of the pandemic of a century.

A PREVIEW OF LESSONS

The Roman Stoics engaged in philosophy as practical discourse. They taught, and wrote letters and meditations, as a way of giving counsel. They gave lessons for "the art of living," as they would put it. In that spirit, here is a synopsis of Stoic lessons.

In Lesson 2, I introduce readers to the Stoics—who they were, their ideas in historical context, and their legacy. The arc of Stoic influence is long and strong. Stoic DNA is embedded in Judaism and Christianity, medieval and Renaissance thought,

Enlightenment philosophy, and American intellectual thought, as in the works of Ralph Waldo Emerson. Emerson refashioned the Stoic notion of self-mastery with a notion of self-reliance meant to challenge convention through authenticity and a commonality of mind disclosed in nature. The Stoic themes of inner mastery dependent on sociality and nature resonate throughout history.

I can only gesture at some of the intellectual trends in this book, but the key is that the Stoics are a bridge between the ancient and modern worlds. They sit at the cusp of the first millennium, and they usher in the Judeo-Christian era and the Western philosophies that follow. What's more important to bear in mind in reading this book is that the Roman Stoics were quintessentially public philosophers. They advocated a practice of philosophy—Stoicism was a household philosophy, taught and practiced. That is precisely the appeal of Stoicism today—a philosophy for everyday living that is not the stuff of the ivory tower. But popularizations bring exaggeration and distortion. It did then—the Stoics were famous hyperbolizers, out to convince young men, their primary target, of the attractions of their school. History may be repeating itself in the ways in which Stoicism is misrepresented today. Tracking that pattern, then and now, is a critical feature of this book. In our attraction to Stoicism, are we picking up a balanced picture of Stoic teachings?

In Lesson 3, I turn to the question of Stoic practice. How does it work and what are the Stoic techniques of self-control? Are the Stoics control freaks? Or do they give us healthy ways of regulating our complicated emotional lives? The Stoics are inveterate neologists, eager to coin terms that aren't tainted by old ways of thinking. The aim is to carve up the inner and outer world at different joints from their predecessors. The practical upshot of the new conceptual map is that it pinpoints areas for greater self-control and techniques for strengthening that control. Monitoring the impressions and evaluations that we assent to as we take in the world will be key. But equally important will be rehearsing in advance the kinds of losses and failures we may face in order to cushion the shock of what's unanticipated. Separating striving from successful outcome will also be key for finding the calm that comes from knowing the limits of our control. Rehearsal and exposure to stressors bear striking resemblances to contemporary methods of trauma relief, though in today's settings, exposure techniques are used more often after the fact, therapeutically, rather than as prophylaxis, before. Here, the Stoics have something important to teach us about how to train ourselves to diminish physical and psychological stress before we are overwhelmed by it.

How do the Stoics counsel us in managing our emotions? And which emotions? In short, does Stoic practice allow you to have emotional skin in the game? This is the subject of Lesson 4. The Stoics have a highly sophisticated and prescient account of emotions as cognitive. And they posit various levels of emotional experience, from near autonomic responses to cultivated emotions expressive of virtue and wisdom. A critical question to ask as we examine emotional regulation is if the Stoics can teach us how to limit stress in life without flattening the feelings that give life meaning—whether as lovers, caregivers, teachers, dancers, theater goers, novel readers, or engaged citizens. How do you hold on to interest, commitment, motivation, and "stick-to-it-iveness" without the kind of passion that can occasionally unhinge you? I'll raise these questions as we think about emotions in general, and specifically about anger and grief.

Many Stoic adherents are attracted to a program of self-mastery, rooted in hard endurance and grit. Stoicism has become shorthand for a time-honored way to build tough resilience. But as I argue in Lesson 5, resilience is a notion that is easily distorted. It's one thing to adapt well in the face of trauma and adversity. It's another to over-idealize the power of an individual to endure and tough it out whatever the resources. More critically, that notion of rugged self-reliance misuses ancient Stoicism. While Epictetus, one of our sources, often talks of invincibility, he is a popularizer, known for his epigrammatic bullets, and not our best representative of more nuanced Stoic thought.

I explore Stoic techniques for building resilience in light of contemporary notions of resilience. Most current psychological studies no longer view the resilient individual as "invulnerable," but rather look at the social and cultural protective factors that promote risk and adversity adaptation. This, too, is what some of the Stoics suggest we train: protection from risk and adversity; adaptiveness, not invincibility. If a modern Stoic model of resilience is to be plausible and not simply attractive to those wanting to tough it out at all costs, then it needs to be a model for healthy resilience. Otherwise, Stoic enthusiasts are advocating models that pose potentially serious mental health risks. As I have already suggested, the social dimension that is part of our well-being is central to Marcus Aurelius's *Meditations*. It is also a recurrent theme in many of Seneca's writings—in his letters and essays, and most vividly, in his tragic play, *Hercules Furens* (*Hercules Raging*). Here, Seneca showcases the idea that even Herculean courage requires the healing overtures of a father's soft touch and a dear friend's compassion to show him what, in his compulsion for heroic action, he can't show himself. Reliance on another is critical for even a Hercules.

Stoicism has long shaped the culture of the military, as I detail in Lesson 6, drawing on my own experience teaching at military institutions. For those who serve, "to suck it up and truck on" is just to be Stoic. For many in the service academies, "stoicism" has an implicit capital "S," with a strong nod to Greco-Roman teachings. The writings of Epictetus and Marcus Aurelius are standardly taught at the military schools in the United States and abroad. A naval admiral, venerated American hero, and military educator, James B. Stockdale famously credited his survival for seven and a half years as the senior prisoner of war in North Vietnam's famed "Hanoi Hilton" to internalizing Epictetus's *Handbook*. Yet Stoic doctrine is in tension with what is increasingly recognized in military circles as a psychological cost of war and a hazard of being a morally conscientious fighter: that is, moral injury. Moral injury is an extreme form of moral distress. Some of its symptoms overlap with those of post-traumatic stress, but its trigger is typically not overwhelming life threat but a sense of having committed, suffered, or witnessed moral transgressions. So, for example, a soldier may kill a young child in a car at a collateral incident at a checkpoint when the car, approaching a military base, failed to stop after repeated warnings. The soldier, himself a father, is racked by overwhelming guilt and shame, not lessened by the fact that the shooting was permissible, in accordance with just war rules and the specific rules of engagement. Can the Stoics leave room for moral injury in a training bent on eliminating stress? If they can, do they also tell us how to learn from moral injury and grow? In Lesson 6, I argue "yes" to both questions. I show how the Stoics leave space for the possibility of "good" moral distress and healing through self-compassion. That is critical if injury is to open the way for moral growth and the calm of repair.

In Lesson 7, I ask: Why is Silicon Valley so smitten by Stoicism? If Stoicism teaches the wisdom of humility and knowing the limits of self-mastery, then how does it resonate with those who want to push the boundaries of control to the point of hacking life to beat death? Are Stoic-inspired lifehacks always about me, or are they sometimes about better ways to see others without bias and irrational fear? Can instant global connection through Twitter or other social media itself be a modern Stoic "collective" lifehack for facing fears bound up with racism? Relatedly, how does the modern Stoic answer worries about misappropriation of Greco-Roman "dead white men" to construct social institutions that are whiter and that exclude women, minorities, and other marginalized groups? Were ancient Stoic philosophers themselves misogynistic in their writings?

In Lesson 8, I compare Stoic and Eastern meditation. The Roman Stoics meditated at the end of each day. Seneca details his own practices. Marcus wrote his journal at the end of a day of battle. The meditative tone is moral: strengthen reason-based virtue and analyze what is in accord with nature; let go of reputation, wealth, and honor; place ultimate value in the cultivation of your goodness; practice gratitude and humility. These are paths to equanimity. Eastern meditation practices, various forms of which I have practiced, offer less moral suasion. Vedic meditation is a practice of calming the mind by a gentle anchoring in a repeated mantra. It's not about virtue or goodness or moral perfection. Indeed, it's not discursive practice. The idea is not to talk or scold, but to quiet the babble. Buddhism emphasizes a notion of emptiness by letting go of illusions associated with the ego. Given that meditation is part of the appeal of the Stoic revival, just what does that meditation practice look like? If the mantras are not chants of "Om," but moral maxims, then how do those maxims create calm when their very point is to remind us of our shortcomings so that we can resolve to do better? Is moralizing ever a viable way to find equanimity? In this lesson, I reflect on my own meditative practices, Eastern and Stoic, and those of others who draw on Stoicism in their professional lives.

I draw some conclusions about Stoic life in Lesson 9. If you still want to be a Stoic, can you be a psychologically healthy modern Stoic? Can a modern Stoic support and be supported within a life of vibrant social connections? Is Stoic resilience something more than individual rugged grit and endurance? I argue "yes," throughout this book, to all of these questions, but it will require going beyond some of the public caricature of Stoicism and drawing on the richer reality of Stoic texts. It also requires a reckoning with the Stoics on enslavement. Epictetus was an enslaved Roman who turned to inward freedom because outward freedom wasn't possible. Seneca wasn't enslaved, though he was a political exile. He pleaded a powerful case for the humane treatment of enslaved Romans, but his motives were complicated and often self-serving. The weave of human connection isn't always benign or grounded in respect, even if that is the promise. Texts are framed by history, and the reality of lived lives are morally messier than the pure aspirations expressed in writing.

Still, those texts and their aspirations give us an abundance of wise counsel, including prototypes of lifehacks for how to find healthy calm in a world swirling with widespread fear and anxiety. The lessons are about virtue writ large, not just about me and managing desire or risk, but about us, and tools we can use together to serve a higher goal. The Stoics are exhorters. And at their best, they exhort us to rise to our potential through reason, cooperation, and selflessness.

NOTE ON TERMINOLOGY

Texts are framed by history, and so, too, language and terms. Lived lives are messy, but so too is moving in and out of time periods. Stoicism applies to us, not as ancient Greeks or Romans, but as moderns, living in our own times, with our own challenges and honest reckoning with our past. Our past includes the enslavement of African Americans and our present the legacy of that enslavement. The Black Lives Matter movement, reignited in the wake of George Floyd's death in the summer of 2020, reopened a national conversation about race, including the language we use to talk about it and the conditions of marginalization. "Slave," to my ear, suggests that this is a person's whole and enduring identity. "Slavery," in turn, conceals the institutions and agency of those who are the enslavers. I'm uncomfortable with both terms, and have avoided using them in my own voice, whether I'm talking about modern or ancient times.

The Greeks and Romans bequeath a history of enslavement to us. Persons were enslaved by birth, by capture in war, and by sales at auctions. But the Stoics famously distance themselves from institutional enslavement. They turn real enslavement to a condition of the soul. Philo captures the Stoic paradox with a pair of treatises: "Every Good Man Is Free," and another (unfortunately lost) "Every Bad Man Is a Slave." The powerful and free swindler, scoundrel, and enslaver can be enslaved. The bought and beaten enslaved person can be free. It's a retreat that distances morality from social and political reality.

Wisdom requires learning from the past, but also avoiding its sins and errors. Only then can we move forward morally, politically, and socially. And so, in my own writing, I have used the term "enslaved" persons and institutions of "enslavement" to signal that enslavement is a political and social condition imposed on a person. We need constant reminders that all persons share in humanity. If they are turned into mere tools, property, or objects, as in the case of torture and enslavement, it is imposed from outside. In a similar vein, I refer to Philo, not as "Philo Judaeus," but as "Philo" or "Philo of Alexandria." "Judaeus" swamps his identity.

That said, I use texts translated by others whose deep scholarship I am indebted to and respect. If they translate a text from Seneca or Epictetus or others using "slave" or "slavery," I preserve that. I have no interest in eviscerating the past and its record. We need to see it in order to know what a better future for all of humanity might look like. The enduring Stoic promise is to empower us in our common humanity. We need to remember that as we turn to Stoicism for guidance.

Top row, from left to right:
Zeno of Citium, Cleanthes, Chrysippus.

Middle row, from left to right:
Cicero, Philo of Alexandria, Seneca.

Bottom row, from left to right:
Musonius Rufus, Epictetus, Marcus Aurelius.

LESSON 2

———— ✦ ————

WHO WERE
THE STOICS?

THE STORY of the Stoics begins with **Socrates** (470–399 BCE). His simple style of life, gathering of disciples in the marketplace, and his fabled death all establish him as the progenitor of the Stoics. His image and influence loom large in Stoic thought.

The Socrates most of us know is the creation of his pupil, Plato. Socrates was an oral philosopher only—he left behind no written texts. In his early dialogues, Plato paints a vibrant portrait of his teacher as a philosophical innovator committed to the health of the soul (the psyche) and practices that will promote it. Socrates's famous method is to cross-examine those he meets in the marketplace in order to see if their sincerely held beliefs about justice, courage, temperance, piety, and the like hold up to scrutiny. Conventional views inevitably come up short, and Socratic inquiry ends in impasse. But the process of examining a lived life, through the bite and sting of Socratic cross-examination (*elenchus*), established a powerful model for honest scrutiny about how to live a good life. The Stoics perpetuate that model.

Socratic practice is embodied in a persona. That persona becomes central in the diffusion of Socrates's influence. Socrates is the epitome of self-restraint. We learn from Plato that he could go for long periods without food or sleep, he could endure the cold, he wore only a single cloak in both winter and summer. He could take in good food and wine at drinking parties without getting either sated or drunk. Via these stories about Socrates, the ideal of self-mastery becomes essential to the Stoic story of how to achieve inner freedom. The turn inward is also helped by the fact that Socrates was, by most accounts, no handsome man. He cut an odd appearance and manner. The snub-nose and flaring nostrils were hardly his fault. But he used what nature endowed to cultivate an image of strangeness. Aristophanes satirizes him in the *Clouds*:

You waddle in the streets and cast your eyes
     sideways,
and go barefoot, enduring a great deal of suffering,
     but put on
a hoity-toity expression . . .

If Socrates's strange appearance was for many contemporary Athenians hard to stomach and a painful critique of their own ordinary conventions, for generations that followed it inspired an image of real beauty being inner and not outer. The goodness of conventional goods and the inheritances that come with luck and good looks were challenged by Socrates's very person.

This challenge becomes central in Socratic irony. It's spoofed again, now by Xenophon in his comic portrait. Socrates's pushed-in nose and flaring nostrils are what's really beautiful—not as fashion model noses go, but as a prototype of "a more efficient vent." In being wide open and not pointing to the ground, those nostrils allow him to "better . . . catch scents" from all around. And too, if beauty is not just a matter of shapely contour but function, then his bulging eyes are really more beautiful than most because Socrates can see peripherally and not only straight ahead. The Socratic nose-eye combo is simply unbeatable: a snub nose "doesn't put a barricade between the eyes" but allows for "unobstructed vision" that has a full 180-degree range.

Socratic irony is a subtler and more serious matter in Plato's hands. Socrates famously admits in the *Apology* that although he is wise, his knowledge is actually quite limited. Or as Plato has him say with ironic twist: "I do not think I know what I do not know." That famous untangling of the Delphic god's oracle—that no one was wiser than Socrates—is what launches Socrates on his quest to examine claims of knowledge—his own and that of others. The irony isn't feigned ignorance, but a sincere belief that he doesn't have *real* wisdom, the kind of gold that boys like Alcibiades and other followers are so eager to find in him.

Still—and this is important for the Stoic legacy—Socratic irony comes with a tacit endorsement of a philosophical method that inverts meaning: ignorance becomes a form of knowledge. Ugliness becomes a superior form of beauty. Words keep their familiar sense but change what they stand for. This swap becomes part of the Stoics' philosophical method as they begin to relabel experience and our evaluation of it. What we thought to be good may be false goods (or at least lesser ones) and other goods more deserving of the name. Stoic training is, in no small part, a re-education of attitudes and emotions so that experience lines up with these new evaluations. Moreover, while Socrates acknowledged that he didn't have flat-out ignorance, he also didn't think that the kind of knowledge he or others had could guarantee that a rational and happy life was attainable.

The Stoics don't take Socrates's resignation at face value. Nature must have so constructed us to be able to attain the knowledge necessary for happiness, even if it is only a rare sage, one who rises only as often as the phoenix, who can achieve that kind of infallible knowledge. Even if Socrates is the model for many Stoics of a Stoic sage, it is not in his embrace of ignorance as wisdom.

Diogenes the Cynic is the pivot between Socrates and the Stoics. The Stoics liked to publicize a line of succession that went back to Socrates: Socrates taught Antisthenes. Antisthenes taught Diogenes. Diogenes taught Crates. Crates taught Zeno. And Zeno was the first head of the Stoa. But it was Diogenes whose influence after Socrates was the greatest, and the most colorful. In the Stoic hagiography, he is often part of a duo with Socrates as quasi-sages. Diogenes, like Socrates, subscribed to a simple life of minimalist needs. But he's an eccentric and exhibitionist. And his irreverent but austere asceticism made for political street theater. When he couldn't secure a cottage, he took an earthenware tub as his homeless home and parked it in the heart of the Athenian agora. In summer, he rolled the tub over hot sands, and in winter, he hugged cold statues, in order to inure himself to hardship. Following the Cynic rule on dress, he folded his cloak, his sole garment, so it could double as a bedroll and accessorized with only a staff and a wallet to carry his belongings. He wandered streets, famously lighting his lamp in daylight in search for an honest man. "Deface the coinage" became his signature slogan, shorthand for "flout political convention." He was a countercultural figure, a Yippie of his day. His anti-money sloganeering brings to mind Abbie Hoffman's famous targeting of Wall Street in 1967 by dropping hundreds of dollar bills from the galleries of the New York Stock Exchange, effectively closing down the trading floor as brokers scampered for the bills.

When asked where he came from, Diogenes famously replied that he was "a citizen of the universe," and likely meant that "he was at home nowhere—except in the universe." He was a citizen unbound by the borders of a city—a citizen of the cosmos—hence, a "cosmopolitan," the origin of the term. He spurned marriage as a convention and the business of power and politics. With other Cynics, he championed unisex clothing and liberally showing off body parts, not only in the gym. He condemned hypocrisy— whether in those who insisted honest men were superior to the rich while themselves envying the rich, or in those who would sacrifice to the gods for health while gorging like gluttons at the sacrificial feasts. It is the Cynics' general break from regressive norms of marriage, gender, dress, and money that opens the way for a Stoic notion of moral authority rooted not in convention, but in following nature and its purported rational order. Inner virtue, under the Stoics, becomes virtue in accord with nature.

Diogenes spouted black humor zingers to drive home the point that psychic health depended on inner freedom and self-mastery. His witty repartee is a biographer's dream. And our biographer,

Diogenes Laertius (probably living sometime around 250 CE), revels in the retelling. It is a retelling, for he probably was copying and quoting wholesale out of library manuscripts which ended up preserving what otherwise would have been lost to history. Still, Diogenes's gossip can be juicy and makes for a good read in the absence of other biographies. And so we are obliged to turn to him. He tells us that as an enslaved person and up for sale, Diogenes the Cynic was asked about his skills. He wasn't really joking when he told the auctioneer that he could "rule men" and to give notice to potential buyers that they might be getting someone who was the real ruler of the house. Real mastery was inner, whether you were an enslaved person or an enslaver. He called "demagogues the lackeys of the people," and misguided those who thought they could clean up their acts just by a little ritual purification: "don't you know that you can no more get rid of errors of conduct by sprinklings than you can of mistakes in grammar." "An ignorant rich man" he dubbed a "sheep with the golden fleece." Legend has it that upon being asked by Philip II who he was and why he was being brought before him as a captive, Diogenes brazenly told the king to his face, I am "a spy upon your insatiable greed." Impressed by his bravado, Philip freed him. On another occasion, upon seeing temple officials hauling away a petty thief for stealing a bowl, he quipped: "The great thieves are leading away the little thief."

Diogenes was uninhibited, "shameless" as a dog, hence his moniker, the "cynic," *kunikos*, (meaning "doglike"). He's "Socrates gone mad." The gadfly of mad comedy. But like Socrates's stinging cross-examination, Diogenes's comic gibes were meant to sting and shock listeners into questioning their norms.

Few Stoics can mimic the antics of Diogenes. But the substance of his teachings—questioning the authority of culture and custom, adapting to circumstance and the vagaries of fortune, finding happiness in self-mastery in highly adverse circumstances, being a global citizen, inverting meanings and accenting the new inversions with hyperbole, all become Stoic inheritances. So too is teaching by a strenuous mental training that parallels and pairs with athletic training of the body—hard toil, steady striving, incremental building of endurance and strength. With those weapons, as Diogenes taught, you are "capable of outright victory over anything." The Stoics let up on some of the harsh austerity of Cynicism. But they develop Diogenes's seed idea of cosmopolitanism, and the notion that self-mastery is supported by affiliation in a community that extends to all humans. We are social, as Aristotle insisted. The Stoics don't relinquish that insight, though it gets interpreted in new ways.

Zeno (334–262 BCE) was a student of Diogenes's student, Crates. And it is Zeno, a native of Citium or Cyprus, who founds the Stoic school in Athens. The Zenoians soon came to be called the Stoics, after the *Stoa Poikilē* (a painted, or better, fresco-lined colonnade) in the central Athenian agora where followers—"the men from the Stoa"—met to talk philosophy and get exposure to the new conceptual tools and lingo Zeno was developing. Philosophy had been a public affair since the time of Socrates—its topics abuzz in walks, gardens, gymnasia, and the agora. Stoicism continued the tradition.

Stoicism wasn't the only school that had followers. Aristotle's influence in Athens was waning. Aristotle himself had gone to Macedonia in 343 BCE to teach Alexander, who would become

Alexander the Great. With Alexander's Hellenization of the Mediterranean, and excitement about all matters Greek, foreigners, like Zeno, came to Athens to do philosophy and set up shop. Others, some Greek and some from more distant shores, also set up schools, with doctrines and loyal adherents, such as those who came to be the Skeptics (largely taking on the Stoics and their "orthodox" doctrines) and Epicureans and more. Philosophy at this time was still a street subject, but it came to be specialized and far more technical, its schools narrowly philosophical in a way difficult to imagine in the time of Aristotle, whose research program at the Lyceum reflected who he was—a practicing scientist (a marine biologist) as well as philosopher. The breadth of his knowledge and academic competence was truly remarkable.

It is no surprise that casual readers don't know Zeno's work in the way that they may know the Roman Stoics, such as Epictetus, Marcus Aurelius, or Seneca. Zeno's work comes to us only in snippets told and retold by editors and expositors. Still, we are fortunate that among our own contemporary scholars, Malcom Schofield has engaged in breathtaking, sleuth-like work in assembling a jigsaw-puzzle of pieces from disparate sources to recreate a picture of Zeno's political tract, the *Republic*. In that treatise, Zeno lays the foundations for an ideal cosmopolitan city of the human and divine, a critical reply, of sorts, to Plato's *Republic* that mixes the communal theme of Plato's city with the Cynic belief that the norms of morality are grounded not in convention, but in reason and the rational order of nature. The universe is the home of that city—a city that knows no borders or walls and is administered by a providential nature that is "beneficent, kind, well-disposed" to humans. Political authority becomes vested not in the state, but in reason—the *logos* of the universe.

This Stoic ideal of a cosmic city is a reminder to modern Stoics that the Stoic founder tied the ideal of self-regulation to a system of global social cooperation. However sketchy the picture, the core idea is that universal reason unites us, and a community based on that reason, with respect for persons in virtue of shared reason, must be nurtured and cultivated. We depend on that community for our own strength. Any Stoic who severs self-reliance from a sense of belonging to that community is missing an essential element of Stoic doctrine.

Working through Zeno's *Republic* is not something, thankfully, we need to do here. But it's important to stress that its themes of looking at things from the point of view of the whole and not our individual selves, of making politics not local but global in a habitat where humans and gods can mingle, get taken up by later authors, from political leaders, such as Marcus Aurelius, to moral theorists, such as Immanuel Kant. Our deep sociality is not a new theme for the ancients. We are by nature social and political animals, Aristotle famously said. The Stoics' departure point is in neither restricting community to those who happen to be our neighbors nor the excellence of practical reason and its functioning to human nature. Gods are in our community.

Zeno is no eccentric in the mold of Diogenes. But his biography, again as retold by Diogenes Laertius, has comic notes. Apparently Zeno knew that he was destined to study philosophy once the oracle told him that the way to achieve the best life was to "take on the complexion of the dead." To a student who talked too much, he was said to have told him his ears had slid down and merged in his tongue; to another who denied that a sage could fall in love, he told him that if he really thought that, no one was a more hapless youth than he. The tip is that teaching, then and now, has always required some wit to keep an audience entertained.

Zeno systematized three areas of philosophy that came to be central in Greek Stoic thought: logic, physics, and ethics. It is ethics that is our concern, and ethics as the ancients understood it: how to live a flourishing life with virtue or character excellence at its center.

Virtue, for all the ancients, is guided by the perfection of our cognitive capacities, and especially, our practical reason. In pioneering work, Zeno lays out one of the most sophisticated and prescient accounts of the cognitive basis of emotions in the history of philosophy. Despite the popular idea of Stoicism as a wooden philosophy that bowdlerizes emotions from human experience, Zeno never argued that we should get rid of all emotions, but rather that we should manage those emotions that are debilitating and that lead to uncontrollable cravings, fears, or distress. Much of the shock and awe of Stoic management of emotions comes with later Roman Stoic writers, especially Epictetus. Though Zeno is less of a practitioner than a theoretician, when he sketches certain emotions, we know them by his concrete descriptions: Grief can be a "heaviness that weighs us down." Annoyance can come with a sense of feeling "cooped up," a kind of emotional stenosis—a constriction, an obstruction—that makes it hard for things to pass through us or let us move beyond them. Distress is a feeling that can come from over-"ruminating." Distraction colors grief in a way that distorts judgment and "prevents us from seeing the situation as a whole," in a balanced way. These are emotions that are palpable, described by a Stoic who seems to know just how they feel.

We'll have much more to say about emotions, what they are and how to regulate them. But to appreciate Zeno is to appreciate, in part, a philosopher who understands how intimately virtue is tied to our emotions, and thus, why we are owed a sophisticated account of emotions and their regulation as the underbelly of virtue training.

Also critical to Zeno's legacy is the refinement of Socrates's view of the sufficiency of virtue for happiness. For the Stoics, that comes to mean that all other goods are "indifferents," though as Zeno taught, this doesn't mean that they are indifferent in our lives: they are just not proper components of our happiness. To select or reject them wisely becomes a matter of living in "accord with nature." How to understand that cryptic phrase sets in place an agenda for generations to come, focused on natural law and its place in human governance.

Cleanthes (331–232 BCE) of Assos (Modern Western Turkey) is Zeno's colleague at the Stoa and successor as Stoic head. Apparently, he wasn't the sharpest knife in the drawer. As Diogenes Laertius tells us, his renown was more for brawn than brain. A pugilist as a youth, and impoverished upon arriving in Athens, he supported his daytime activity of studying philosophy by a nighttime shift of drawing water from a local well. Built like an ox, he stood up to his peers' gibes about his intellect by insisting "he alone was strong enough to carry the load of Zeno." Few of his writings remain, though the titles of his works suggest a wide range of subjects in ethics that become central to Stoic thought— on what is fitting, on impulse, on gratitude, on envy, love, honor, and deliberation, to mention just some of them. His tenure at the school was shadowed by the third and final head of the Stoa.

"In industry," **Chrysippus** "surpassed everyone," writes Diogenes Laertius. But Chrysippus of Soli (in Southern Anatolia) also surpassed most in brilliance and creativity. Along with Zeno, he is responsible for the enormous influence of Stoic thought on most of Western philosophy. His output was voluminous (we have more than 705 titles) and included works in logic and fallacies, grammatical mistakes and blunders in speech and ordinary language, ethical works on the virtues, character states, and arguments against pleasure as the ultimate good. He even weighed in on art conservation in "Against the Touching up of Paintings." He trained early on as a long-distance runner, and stamina and endurance were part of his intellectual profile as well. For many, early Stoicism has come to mean the philosophy of Chrysippus. He figures heavily in Cicero's account of the Stoics on emotions and the final good, and his arguments show rigor, sophistication, and acumen.

The scanty snippets of Greek Stoic writings contrast with the volumes we have from the Roman Stoics. And it is these that have been read and reread, and refashioned in some degree, as part of the European intellectual tradition of the Renaissance and Enlightenment, and now, the current Stoic revival. Some of the more negative Stoic views about the unruliness of emotions have become encrusted parts of modern thought.

We owe much to **Cicero** (106–43 BCE) for the transmission of Greek Stoic ideas to the Roman world. Not himself a Stoic, he was nonetheless sympathetic to many of its views. He labored to translate into accessible Latin some of the more arcane Greek terms that were part of the Stoic machinery, and was committed to making Stoicism, and in general Greek philosophy, accessible to a non-Greek-reading lay audience. Many will know the rough details of his public life: Of humble origins, he rose meteorically through the ranks of the Senate to become consul at the young age of 43. He was a well-known Roman political orator, military leader, and ally to Pompey. He devoted his energies to philosophical writing at the end of his political career, after Caesar's assassination and while in hiding from his own future assassins, Antony and the other triumvirs. Philosophical writing became profoundly personal after the death of his beloved daughter, Tullia, in childbirth. In his grief, he turned to the Stoics, though, as we shall see, in *Tusculan Disputations*, he argued with the Stoics as much as swallowed their tonics. His works *On Moral Ends* and *On Duties* were to become indispensable in European political thought for their statements of Stoic positions.

Seneca the younger, the Seneca most of us know (3 BCE–65 CE), was from an eminent family that groomed him early on for a political career. A sickly youth felled by several bouts of tuberculosis that resulted in a suicide attempt in adolescence, Seneca knew setbacks and rebounds from an early age. Trained in rhetoric and philosophy—Seneca's father was a famous teacher of rhetoric—the young Seneca was a prize tutee of the Stoic Attalus. By then, in part thanks to Cicero, philosophy had gained considerable credibility in elite Roman public life, even as an alternative to politics. But many mixed philosophy and politics, and in particular Stoicism and public office, however awkward the fit of Stoicism's more austere Cynic teachings with the decadence of imperial Rome. The tension is a recurrent theme in Seneca's lived life and writing—craving and managing craving, whether of oysters and mushrooms, anger and drink, power and well-connectedness. Roman life, especially for those in power, gave wide ambit for the need to rein in the passions.

Seneca is, in many ways, the flawed protagonist of this book. He is an important source for modern Stoicism, and one we should read more often. He is full of nuance, even if not without hypocrisy. He may offer fewer pithy quotes than Epictetus, but he is a masterful writer with dazzling rhetorical skill. And he is a moral aspirant living in a complicated, messy world. He yearns for self-freedom in an ecosystem larger than himself. Indeed, he's a pragmatic philosopher who knows well the muddy waters of politics and power. He swims in those currents, as Nero's tutor, political advisor, and speechwriter. Nero, the 16-year-old boy emperor, didn't necessarily want to repeat the reign of Caligula, but he didn't hold back when the dynastic succession was threatened. Seneca thought he could help him and restrain his more wanton ways. But as history tells us, he wasn't so successful, ultimately.

A few historical details should suffice: Seneca came to the court through the interventions of young Nero's mother, Agrippina, who sought him out as a tutor with the most famed reputation in the empire for rhetoric and public speaking. She became his patron, bringing him out of exile in Corsica (41 CE) where her husband Claudius had banished him for eight years for his alleged adultery with his niece, Julia Livilla. Getting Nero closer to the throne through the powerful pen of Seneca was part of Agrippina's motive. Seneca's own motives then became keeping the boy in power, even though it soon involved keeping the mother out, who had fallen out of favor with her son. There is no shortage of intrigue in this palace where Seneca lurks in the background. There was the poisoning of Claudius's biological son, Britannicus, when he became of age to take the throne, a plot of which Seneca, as a palace insider, was likely aware. Though Agrippina was his benefactor in getting him to the palace, he showed her limited gratitude in defending Nero's murder of her in a speech which records suggest didn't go down well with all. What comes around goes around, and while Nero's anger may have been restrained on occasion, it was by no means ever managed. Seneca must have been well aware of the threat against his own life, given his repeated attempts to retire from public life in his later years and his general preoccupation in his writings in those years (in the *Letters*), once he did retire, with issues of mortality and the transience of power. In 65 CE Nero orders Seneca's suicide on charges that he was involved in the Pisonian plot to have the emperor assassinated.

This mini-bio reminds us that when Seneca writes about clemency, grief, anger, or constancy or rails against the evils of materialism, he writes as no moral or political naïf. He knows the pull of wealth and power and the perils of trying to escape it under the eye of a watchful and vengeful tyrant. He takes up his pen and well-trained Stoic stance, in part, to calm his own fears about political power and to aspire to something purer. As he often says, he writes from the perspective never of a sage, but from that of the moral doctor who is at once a patient, in need of Stoic medicine and healing. His famed nighttime meditations are meant to quiet himself and give moral suasion. But the mirror sometimes turns outward, and his pointed finger aimed at less urbane folk who may have cast an insult his way. He rose from a modest equestrian background in the provinces, and never, like some other Stoics in

Rome, stayed clear of Nero's inner circle. Once in it and wanting out, he opted for his own suicide rather than being forced to it. In this regard, he writes not as an Epictetus, who was a freed but formerly enslaved person, living well outside the halls of power and poor all his life, with no aspiration to write polished prose that would earn him renown through the ages. In short, Seneca is a pragmatist who has been in the political trenches, suffered its glory and infamy, and yearns for some personal moral change and a reset of what counts as glory. That, at least, is a way to begin to read some of the moral essays, letters, and tragedies which I take up in these pages. His writings are important for our own politically troubled and tumultuous times.

The list of Roman philosophers typically omits **Musonius Rufus** (30–101/2 CE), a Roman senator and Stoic who taught at various times in Rome. The omission is a pity, for he is the teacher of Epictetus, probably the most oft-quoted Stoic, and Musonius's own writings are themselves important records of Roman Stoic thought. Part of the reason that he has fallen into recent obscurity is that selections from his work have not been anthologized. But he was well known in antiquity as a major figure: the Christian theologian Origen paired him with Socrates as a moral exemplar. The historian Tacitus pictures his followers as a stern, serious bunch, among them statesmen and politicians, who, as one scholar writing in 1896 put it, were "waiting quietly through the wild riot of the court in Nero's time till their turn might come." Turning to Stoic lessons in finding calm while preparing for better political times might be a prescription for our own times. Indeed, Musonius was willing to work with the politicians if through their voice and influence they could promote greater public improvement. Of those who weren't politicians, they came because they were serious about the state of their soul. Epictetus was among them.

Musonius wrote tracts that should be read by more modern Stoics, such as "Should Daughters and Sons Get the Same Education?" and "That Women Too Should Do Philosophy." His debt to Plato's *Republic* on the equality of women can be traced. And he seems to be following closely the theme of Cleanthes in his lost work, "On the Fact That the Same Excellence (or Virtue) Belongs to a Man and a Woman." While Musonius's feminism is dampened at times by concessions to Roman custom, his commitment to the excellences of a flourishing life as the same for all humans is decidedly Stoic.

Epictetus (50–130 CE) was enslaved; he was a native of Phrygia, a Greek-speaking province in Anatolia. He was acquired (and later emancipated) by Epaphroditus, a wealthy freedman and secretary of Nero. While still enslaved, he studied philosophy in Rome with Musonius Rufus and once freed, established his own school in Nicopolis on the Adriatic coast of Western Greece. Like Socrates, whose style Epictetus may have modeled, he was exclusively an oral philosopher whose audience was primarily boys between the ages of 18 and 23. We know his work through his student Arrian, who ghost-wrote the detailed teachings in what come to us as *The Discourses* (four extant of the original eight volumes), and in the popularized short manual, the *Encheiridion*, or *The Handbook*. The writings are informal and are penned in the common Greek that Epictetus would have used to lecture.

The suffering of an enslaved Roman permeates Epictetus's writing. He was a cripple, as a result of disease, according to some accounts, and according to others, as a result of beatings under enslavement. Even as a freed person, he chose an ascetic life, with a pallet and a rush mat as his furnishings. Enslavement leaves indelible marks on Epictetus's teaching: real freedom is inner freedom that can be sustained even in bondage. He may not be a Stoic on the rack, but physical pain and adversity guide him.

Part of the popular appeal of his writings is that they are brimming with pithy and quotable epigrams sprinkled generously with hyperbole. Though a popularizer, his views are rooted in the systemic doctrines and arguments of earlier Stoics. Epictetus goes in for shock and awe tactics in part to wake up his listeners—young men on the cusp of adulthood—hooked on material goods or fearful of loss and irreversible bad luck. The style is meant to entertain and exhort, and set out a program for coaching discipline. Indeed, his work is replete with tests of mental drills in worst-case scenarios—what a person *would do* in a hard case. Counterfactual reactions to tough cases become rehearsals for real life. They are a form of virtual training. The tests are tough, and so was his love. Here he took a lesson from his teacher Rufus. Epictetus tells us, "It is not easy to gain the attention of young men who are soft, for you cannot get hold of soft cheese with a hook; but the naturally gifted, even if you turn them away, hold all the more firmly to reason." Rufus, for the most part, tried to turn them away, but the gifted ones couldn't be easily repelled. Discipline in disciples requires testing firmness, just as in cheese!

In an irony of history, the Roman Emperor **Marcus Aurelius** (121–180 CE) turns to an enslaved Roman, namely Epictetus, for enlightenment. Written as "reflections to himself," what has come down to us as *The Meditations* are essentially diary entries (written in Greek), never intended for teaching or distribution. They are rambling meditative notes jotted down at the end of a long day of battle during the Germanic campaigns while Marcus was camped along the Danube (170–174 CE). A breviary, of sorts, they reflect a ruler taking counsel with himself, with compassionate reminders about how to reckon with the possibility of lost power and title, how not to get seduced by gold and glitter, how to find satisfaction in simplicity. A massive golden effigy of himself would likely have been wheeled out by day as the battalions lined up. At night, he needed to remind himself of the vanity of it all. Soft-pedaling the contradictions of power and abstinence was not his game. That's Seneca's style. Despite his power, Marcus is a humble supplicant, aware of the Heraclitean flux that takes what it gives, and our connected status with each other and god through shared universal reason.

In popularized modern Stoicism, Marcus is the ideal of masculine strength and self-reliance, epitomized by the monumental, equestrian statue whose image is front and center on many Stoic websites and books. But Marcus is no lone horseman. Nor would he have us think that we are either. His battlefield imagery, as I noted in the previous lesson, underscores the need for social connection and the perils of isolation. We are incomplete without others and are interdependent parts of a whole. In the wake of a pandemic, his views about global interconnection are more relevant than we ever could have imagined. His view of interdependence reflects Stoic doctrine that human and cosmic nature are parts of the same whole and allies. We are members of a community that unites humans and our better selves, or gods; our fulfillment is in working out that collaboration.

Philo of Alexandria (c. 15 BCE–50 CE) is not an oft-mentioned actor in the Stoic cast of characters. However, his work represents an important aspect of Hellenization in the Jewish world and, specifically, an attempt to interpret the Old Testament in light of Greek Stoic teachings. Philo draws on Stoic teachings about layered emotional experience to explain how Sarah, who on his reading of Genesis is on the cusp of being a sage, could laugh when God tells her she is going to have a child at the ripe old age of 90. If laugher is an emotional disturbance, then as a near sage, she should be able to control it a bit better. But she did, in a way, argues Philo: For she only "laughed within herself." It was a nervous laugh, we could say. Once she caught it, she was ready "to be filled with joy and divine laughter." And so, too, Abraham, when he goes to Sarah's grave to mourn and weep, catches himself before he gives in to uncontrolled wailing. He was only *going* to weep, but *caught* himself before the onset. And so, in these Stoic interpretations of Genesis, Philo provides lessons on how emotions can be controlled and regulated. Pre-emotions can be nipped in the bud before they become full-blown ordinary emotions. And ordinary emotions can become cultivated, good, and virtuous emotional states befitting a sage, or in this case, a biblical matriarch and patriarch.

Philo draws from other ancient sources, including Aristotle's *Nicomachean Ethics*. Here, Philo mimes Aristotle closely on our social nature: "nature has made man not like the solitary beasts but highly social like the gregarious animals that graze together, so that he might live not for himself alone, but for his father and mother and brothers and wife and children and his other relations and his friends and his fellow citizens and his tribesmen and his country and those of the same race and all men . . ." It is only at the end of the passage that Philo tags on a distinctively Stoic note— that the boundary of social connection extends outward beyond the *polis* to all of humanity.

The Stoics had a major influence on Christian thought. Like Philo, early Christians also turned to the Stoic notion of pre-emotions in thinking about how to control emotions and avoid temptation. With some twists and turns and concept blurring to suit a new religious agenda, they made Stoic pre-emotions your own fault, and advanced the idea that "bad thoughts" now accompany the body's emotional arousals, its tears and nervous shudders, its shrinkings and swellings. In this way they could allow for intermediate degrees of sin. With Christianity also comes the idea that bad angels or the devil could induce the bodily agitation that leads to temptation.

Much later, the Dutch Humanist and theologian Erasmus (1466–1536) will refashion Epictetus's idea of a handbook in writing his own handbook, or *Enchiridion of a Christian Knight*. Written at the turn of the sixteenth century, it's a book intended for the lay reader, instructs Erasmus, to prepare knights for war against the Turks. As a handbook to carry into battle, it takes pain "more in exhorting . . . than in teaching" "not with threatening epistles" but with a method "taught in few words" that shows clearly "the manner of living." Missionizing the gospel is the "cause" or purpose of the knights' wars. The "conduct" of war, teaches Erasmus, hangs on chivalrous behavior. And those lessons in chivalry have a better chance of sticking, he tells his readers, if they are delivered with punch and brevity. That said, his handbook is brief, but it has little of Epictetus's punch.

Still, it is Stoic in many of its doctrines, as in the view, again, of sudden pre-emotions or "first motions" that don't necessarily impugn a wise warrior: a "perfect wise man should lack" ordinary "motions," even if he still is subject to those "first motions" that come as impressions that he may experience but not act on. The sage's example is meant to set a standard for warriors of all ranks. Emotional restraint, whether outlined in a code of chivalry, as in Erasmus's era, or in just war theory, in our times, is a permanent feature of the conduct of war. It is also crucial in the conduct of policing, as we shall see in later lessons.

The overall impact of Stoicism on later European moral and political thought is too wide and deep to summarize here. The Stoics, and especially the Roman Stoics, were read, re-read, cited, and quoted by most who considered themselves educated. The natural law tradition in Christianity, for example, and through to the modern secular works of Grotius and Pufendorf in the sixteenth and seventeenth centuries, owes an especially strong debt to Stoicism.

Montaigne in the mid-seventeenth century draws from many of the ancients, but notably the Stoics, in exhorting readers to endure hardship and penury and develop the virtues necessary "to defy pain." "It's our opinions that give value to things," not the things themselves, he pens with a clear nod to the Stoics. Montaigne is a colorful writer and his Stoic advocacy is, at best, a mixed bag. He appeals to the Stoics in their view that "vices are all alike," despite their variety. But drink, he then insists, shouldn't be on that list. Well, again, maybe it should be for the Germans "who drink almost indifferently of all wines with delight." But why should a Frenchman give up wine, given his sophisticated palate? If drunkenness is a vice, he sums up, then it is "less malicious and hurtful than the others, which almost all, more directly jostle public society." Whatever Stoicism is for Montaigne, it is not undiluted asceticism.

In his correspondence with Princess Elizabeth of Bohemia, **Réné Descartes** (1596–1650) turns to Seneca to paint a portrait of the Stoic sage and the happy life. He counsels the Princess to cultivate "a firm and constant resolution to carry out whatever reason recommends without being diverted by passion or appetite." What impedes happiness is "desire, regret and repentance." Still, Descartes adapts Stoic tenets to modern principles, showing how faith and Christian religion, and not only "natural reason," must enter in this new modern account. He also famously ushers in the doubt and fallibilism of the modern era: "it is not necessary that our reason be free from error"; a conscience testifying to resolution and "best judgment" suffices. So here we have Stoicism propelled into modernity through a model that includes guidance from a monotheistic God and human fallibilism in place of wisdom that never errs.

Immanuel Kant (1724–1804) is undoubtedly the philosopher who develops in the most original and revolutionary way the Stoic seed idea of the moral law as inseparable from our rational natures. The view is revolutionary in that it now is *autonomous* human reason, free of the pushes and pulls of nature or divine guidance, that is the foundation of our morality. Still, the idea of a shared universal reason across all persons is decidedly Stoic. Kant's famous idea that all persons are due respect in virtue of their common humanity, as ends in themselves in a "kingdom or realm of ends," is a direct descendent of the Stoic notion of sharing humanity in a cosmopolitan moral and political order.

Kant, like many of the moderns, exploits the Stoic view that emotions can be excessive, hard to curb (or "pathological" as Kant says), and, as a result, unreliable moral motivators. Acting from duty and not emotion becomes a signature Kantian theme. But it's an oversimplified picture of Kant's view of the role of emotions in morality. He tells us that emotions help us "do what duty alone cannot do" whether it's recognizing others' needs through sympathy, or showing a face of human kindness in ministering to others. They are a "garment that dresses virtue to advantage" and so we have a moral duty to make them allies of duty. Some emotions, says Kant, are more responsive to reason than others. They are "practical emotions" and bear a striking resemblance to what the Stoics call the "good emotions" cultivated with full virtue.

That said, Kant never embraced the Stoic view that all emotions are cognitive. He rejected it. But he wasn't alone among moderns in hiving off desire and emotion from reason. The Stoic view of emotions got sidelined historically. That's all the more reason to turn to Stoic texts now for insight into how emotions are and can be intelligent.

The legacy of the Stoics obviously does not stop with Kant and the Rational Enlightenment. It continues, as I suggested in the previous lesson, with Emerson, and before that, with the American founding fathers. Jefferson read the Roman Stoics. So, too, did Washington. What they didn't read, they absorbed. Ancient Stoic virtue was in the air then, and it is now.

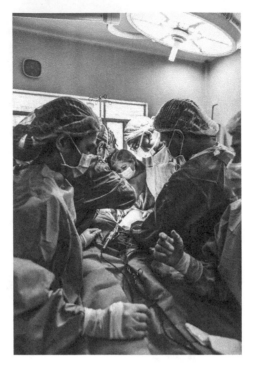

Doctors and nurses treating a patient.

Aart van Oosten, Firechief Arnemuiden, The Netherlands.

LESSON 3

---- ★ ----

FINDING CALM

STOICISM IN THE TIME OF A PANDEMIC

I am writing in the midst of a raging pandemic. We are under siege. When it will end is hard to predict. But one thing is certain for me: it is a time to test the full promise of Stoicism. Covid-19 has lurched us into worldwide war against an invisible enemy for which we have little armor. I have written about war for over three decades as a noncombatant. But this is a war in which we are all combatants with an enemy. We are in this war together, the global community that the Cynics and the Stoics augured. We are interlocking pieces of a larger puzzle, in terms of protection and social behavior, enlightened leadership and clear messaging, financial markets, travel, supply chains, and crucially, testing, treatment, and the race to develop an effective and safe vaccine that can be equitably distributed. We want outcomes, but day to day we want ways to lower our anxiety as we worry about exposure to the virus, how to break out of loneliness, the vulnerability of healthcare workers and others on the frontlines, the limits of access to hospitals, and the availability of life-saving equipment. We face our mortality squarely in a way many of us have never done before. It is a moment, if not to be Stoic, to use Stoic tools wisely.

We do what we can to be prepared. The public message from the chief infectious disease doctor of the National Institutes of Health, Anthony Fauci, is that preparation has to be strategic. Fauci, with his plain-speaking Brooklyn accent, is a consummate communicator, who, not unlike Epictetus, knows he has to reach a lay public with memes that catch: "When you are dealing with an infectious disease, you know, you always have that metaphor that people talk about. That Wayne Gretzsky, he doesn't go where the puck is, he's going where the puck is going to be. Well, we want to be where the infection is going to be, as well as where it is now." That is, we need now to be acting as if we are already facing the future. We have to be proactive, not just reactive. We have to anticipate.

"Pre-rehearsal," "anticipation," learning how "to dwell in advance," vividly imagining future evils as if now present are key to the Stoic approach of mitigating anxiety. Know the enemy you *might be* fighting. Don't be caught off guard. Applying these tools to the Covid-19 scenario: run simulations, understand the potential trajectory of a pandemic, and then heed the warnings. The Trump administration's Department of Health and Human Services actually ran such a simulation from January to August 2019, code-named "Crimson Contagion." The warnings were not heeded. In Stoic terms, there were extensive high-level pre-rehearsal exercises, but they were not taken seriously by those in power. The bottom line is that we failed to be prepared at both an individual and systemic level.

A pandemic is a colossal crisis. It is hard to anticipate something of its magnitude and hard to coordinate an enduring effective global response. Still, one lesson it has taught is that surviving is a coordinated community project. Yet part of the popular appeal of Stoicism, especially in the online community, is in its treasure trove of lessons for self-sufficiency. Here's popular advice from Epictetus: "Yes, my nose is running. And what have you hands for, then.... Is it not that you may wipe your nose?" Epictetus's surface point is: don't complain. Some put the stress note on self-reliance: take care of wiping your own nose and don't wait for someone else to do it for you. Many generalize the point as a univocal Stoic theme that is all-purpose.

But human self-sufficiency, on any honest conception, is relational, dependent at all levels on support from those whose help we often don't acknowledge or whose dignity we don't always properly respect. The notion of interconnectedness has deep Stoic roots, as deep as any themes of self-reliance. Marcus Aurelius puts it this way: "Beings endowed with reason, constituted for one fellowship of cooperation, are in their separate bodies analogous to the several members of the body in individual organisms. The idea in this will come home to you more if you say to yourself: 'I am a member of the system made of rational beings.'" California Governor Gavin Newsom, in his early "shelter-in-place" order to all state residents, put forth a message that echoes not just Marcus's sentiment but words: "A state as large as ours, a nation-state, is many parts, but at the end of the day, we're one body. There's a mutuality, there's a recognition of our interdependence. . . ." He went on to say that we have moral duties anchored in our sociality.

The lessons in this chapter are about Stoic techniques for mitigating anxiety. But Stoic insistence that we are socially interdependent will always be in the picture, as foreground or background. We are "woven together" by a "common bond," with "scarcely one thing foreign to another," Marcus writes, telegraphing Zeno's image of a cosmic city. Our preparedness to face the present and future depends on our own will and the will of others in coordinated, well-informed, and cooperative efforts.

A More Stable Happiness

Still, it is hard to square the Stoic idea of social connectedness with their view that our vulnerability rests in things precisely outside our own virtue. The Stoic promise is to stabilize happiness through stable and reliable good character. That, too, was what the Stoics' great intellectual predecessor Aristotle was aiming for. But Aristotle insisted that good character alone was not enough for happiness. We need, in addition, resources, opportunities, means, and friends for exercising virtue in the world. Otherwise, as Aristotle put it, happiness would be compatible with passively "being asleep" for the rest of your life and "with the greatest sufferings and misfortunes." Yet if happiness is virtuous *activity* and thus depends on things outside your control both for its exercise and full promise—on luck, children who don't predecease you, good political leadership, and more—then as Aristotle himself admits, "you entrust to chance what is greatest and finest," and that would be a "defective arrangement." Still, to deny common sense and hold that you can be happy tortured on the rack, or lose some 13 sons, as Priam supposedly did during the Trojan War, without suffering a reversal of happiness, is pushing matters too far. And so Aristotle, it seems, had an unstable position. Happiness included both inner and outer goods. But just how to order them in a good life so that things outside your control don't derail your happiness was never fully resolved. Aristotle likely held that the matter couldn't be formally resolved. "The decision rests with perception." We "discern the particulars" and take up matters case by case. We settle with how things are "for the most part." It is "foolish," he insisted, to look for the kind of precision in ethical theory that you would demand from the "demonstrative proofs of a mathematician."

But this didn't stop the Stoics from wanting more precision and brighter stripes. At very least, they wanted to secure happiness and tranquility for the fully virtuous and provide guidance for a path of progress. If it required forging new concepts and coining new terms, so be it. Clunky machinery wasn't an obstacle if the end goal was tranquility.

External goods, the Stoics go on to argue, are categorially different kinds of goods from virtue. In fact, they are not real goods. Here, the Stoics appeal to Socrates, who argued that virtue alone is necessary and sufficient for happiness. Possessing such things as good health, stable and sufficient income, good friends and family, enlightened political institutions and communities, social esteem and respect—all these are not themselves part of happiness, the Stoics teach. They grant common sense and say these are things that, in general, we are naturally attracted to as human beings. They are "preferred." Their opposites are things that, in general, we naturally avoid. They are "dispreferred." But they insist that their presence or absence can't make or break happiness. They are not just externals. They are "indifferents"—they do not make a difference to happiness positively or negatively. The rub, as we shall see, is that they still play a substantive role in our lives. Indeed, virtue involves wisely selecting or rejecting them.

The view is challenging, no less in ancient times than now. But one thing crucial to remember is that the term "indifferents" (*adiaphora*) does not mean "indifference." We are by birth and breeding neither indifferent to these goods or bads, nor should we harden ourselves to become so. Still, learning to live in a Stoic way requires fundamental recalibration of values. In particular, we need to learn behaviorally and not just intellectually that preferring or dispreferring goods or bads involves going for them or avoiding them in a way that isn't filled with restless yearning or panicky aversion. So not only do the Stoics have a different valuation system for what we might loosely call inner and outer goods. They also carve out a distinctive kind of approach and avoidance behavior that is meant to inculcate calm—we go for things without sticky, acquisitive attitudes; we reject things without fearful avoidance or anxious dread. Learning how to cultivate those new attitudes is part of Stoic training. And the striving critical to stabilizing that new value scheme is itself a Stoic way of life. So while the sage may be too exalted a model—the human turned divine—the sage arrived where she is through strategies for minimizing what's outside her control. And those are strategies, the Stoics teach, for all of us to adopt.

"Some things . . . are up to us": Assent to Impressions

Still, what do we say about our clutch on life, or fear that our children might predecease us, or worry about a pandemic and a death toll that has taken more American lives than lost in battle in all of World War Two? What do we control when we act with disciplined Stoic self-control? What do we let go of?

Stoic self-control begins by drawing a line between our psychological faculties and what lies outside. Epictetus famously opens the *Encheiridion* this way: "Some things in the world are up to us, while others are not. Up to us are our faculties of judgment, motivation, desire, and aversion—in short, everything that is our own doing. Not up to us are our body and property, our reputations, and our official positions—in short, everything that is not our own doing." Many of us would protest right off the bat at where the line is drawn. Even if we can't fully avoid disease, penury, ignominy, loss of career or office, many of us can do some things some of the time to protect our health, material means, and so on. Epictetus grants that. But at some point, he argues, our armor and efforts, even that of the most privileged of us, will be no match for natural or human-made misfortune. That is Epictetus's core claim: We are all hostages of fortune in some way or other.

Fine. We can grant him that. But we still might object that there is no hard line between controlling what is outside and what is inside. What's inside is vulnerable. Our capacity for judgment might be impaired by traumatic brain injuries or an aging brain, our cravings not in line with what we want to want, our fears pathological phobias rooted in psychological syndromes we wish we didn't have. Equally, there are epistemic biases. What we see may be tainted by implicit bias, and what we judge to be the case may be less "our doing" than the product of privileged standpoints and access. This is, of course, a modern view of the psyche and of knowledge. The Stoic view, by contrast, is radically volitional. And their claim is that the range of our willpower is expansive and its work empowering: with effort and choice we can turn our gaze inward to monitor stubborn patterns of attention. Through a modern Stoic lens, these might include cognitive or epistemic biases. I explore this application later.

The locus of control on the Stoic view is our assent to impressions, or how things seem to us from the sensory input from outside and from within. Assent is the mechanism by which we tacitly say "yay" or "nay" to that input. It is the moment of basic control in judgment, motivation, desire, or aversion. So we may assent to a perceived insult as an evil that is distressing, or to disease as a perceived threat to be feared, or wealth as a perceived good to be desired and acquired. Each of these is an evaluative judgment—an acceptance that what appears is a good or a bad. In the case of evaluative judgments that are emotions, such as anger or fear, the evaluations are "umphy"; they engage us affectively and impel us (through "impulses" or *hormai*) to action. They are motivational. *Hormē* is the cognate of our word "hormone," and like that organic substance, it stimulates action. But it does so through the mediation of the mind.

Seneca explains it this way: "Anger is undoubtedly set in motion by an impression received of a wrong. But does it follow immediately on the impression and break out without any involvement of the mind? Or, is some assent by the mind required for it to be set in motion? Our view is that it undertakes nothing on its own, but only with the mind's approval." Emotion is thus a kind of voluntary action. Through assent we implicitly frame and grasp the world propositionally and act on the resulting opinions or judgments. Emotions involve agency.

Epictetus insists that with agency comes responsibility: "It is not things themselves that trouble people, but their opinions about things. . . . So whenever we are frustrated, or troubled, or pained, let us never hold anyone responsible except ourselves, meaning our own opinions." The idea is intuitive. We are inveterate interpreters at the most basic level of perception, seeing a penny, to take a simple example, as having three-dimensional depth when we really only see its two-dimensional face. We wear lenses of all sorts to sort and shape, and construct and categorize the world—and so, too, when it comes to categorizing goods and bads and how they affect our happiness. We always see and assess from what philosophers call an "epistemic standpoint."

As we said, we are not always free spontaneously to choose those standpoints. How we see may be the result of others' impositions, sometimes invisible—"hidden persuaders," whether through the work of advertising agencies or "social bots" corrupting an election. How we see or interpret situations can also be the result of systemic and profound forms of domination. So, a woman's crippling sense of shame as a rape victim may be someone else's opinion that she has internalized. The work of patriarchy and shaming runs deep. Similarly, a young altar boy's fear of a pedophilic priest's continued assaults may get muted by the priest's sacred robes and his avuncular role at the Sunday family table. The inner world can be a socialized construct. And it isn't always an enlightened place for freedom or peace. Yet it may be a place of retreat when external forces give few other options. The young boy finds safety in his mind, even if through psychological dissociation. Subordinated or in captivity, we push our will to the limit.

This is Epictetus's stance: a person enslaved and in bondage can still find inner freedom. It is what so inspired US Navy senior POW James Stockdale in his seven and a half years of imprisonment, two and a half years of which were in solitary confinement, in the "Hanoi Hilton" in North Vietnam. Epictetus's *Handbook* was his salvation. Stockdale and I met several times and talked about the torture he endured. He came to embody for me what it was to live as a Stoic in the most extreme conditions of deprivation.

Epictetus is politically disenfranchised. If there is any freedom, it has to come from within. That is his political reality, or at least, it is the formative conditions of his early life. His Stoicism is a response to it. The situation is different for other Stoics. Seneca becomes a public servant par excellence. He is politically enfranchised, powerful, and in the most elite inner circle as Nero's "minister." But he wasn't always in public favor. Recall his exile in Corsica for some eight years under Claudius. And under Nero, he knows well the cost of voluntary retreat. Retirement from the work of the commonwealth needs justification (public and private) and not just the sort that makes theoretical research its own kind of public action that serves the common good.

Seneca's concern about retreat, voiced in many of his writings, serves as guidance for our own times when public servants choose or are forced to retire because of evil or corrupt political leadership. In "On Leisure," Seneca aims to align his views with the orthodox Stoicism of Zeno: Whereas the Epicureans say, "the wise man will not engage in public affairs except in an emergency," Zeno says: "He will engage in public affairs unless something prevents him." The exemption rests on special circumstances, adds Seneca: "a state too corrupt to be helped" or "wholly dominated by evil." Nero is not far from the page here as Seneca eases himself out of public service. Forced suicide, on Nero's orders, will soon follow.

Seneca gives us a clear-eyed view of the systemic constraints that surround personal control and endurance. In this same essay he underscores the point: "the hindrance is not in the doer, but in the things to be done." We live in commonwealths, local and cosmopolitan. We work within the local commonwealths through the externals of power and office, until we can't. Assent to impression itself has limits in giving us freedom. We can push the limits out fairly far, but again, we are constrained by access to input, implicit bias, as well as our own intellectual curiosity and defiance. Mental control can hit barriers, even when we are not suffering dementia or neuropsychological disorders. Still, the Stoics have promising tools for greater empowerment. But that said, we need Stoic exhortation and discipline to push the boundaries outward, whether those boundaries are internal or external.

With assent to impressions as a starting point, let's turn to other specific Stoic techniques for self-control and how we can best implement them in our lives.

Physical Training and Mental Discipline

Recently, I found myself on a physical therapy table doing exercises for a rotator cuff tear, exacerbated by too much swimming. While doing my boring 30 × 3 shoulder abductions with a dumbbell, my physical therapist, Chris, asked me what I do for a living. "I'm a philosopher and I'm writing a book on Stoicism," I said. His face lit up. I now had his full attention. Chris is a well-built, athletic guy who trains hard and treats folks like me, as well as serious athletes. He tells me he's listened to Tim Ferriss's podcasts on Stoicism and has also read a Ryan Holiday book on Stoicism. He tried listening to Marcus Aurelius's *Meditations* on his commute to and from work. But it wasn't exactly a gripping yarn. "Too many disconnected snippets?" "Yup," he replied. "It jumped around too much." So he went back to podcasts on Stoicism. The philosophy really appealed to him. When I asked why, it became clear that it had to do with the idea of hard training and discipline. Building strength or regaining it in the face of injury is what he teaches and coaches. Transferring strength and stability exercises to a different arena made perfect sense to him. In my own case, he had told me that the natural "wear and tear" of a "mature" body plus repetitive overuse is what did my shoulders in. Psychologically, we face the grind of "wear and tear" daily. The mind, no less than the body, needs healthy exercises to mitigate the impact of injury and heal trauma when it occurs. Chris and I were on the same page.

Epictetus casts physical training as a model for overall mental discipline: "Whatever means are applied to the body by those who are exercising it, may also be valuable for training, if in some way they aim toward desire or aversion." He then warns that the point of a toned body or psychological toughness is not to build a fan base: "if their aim is mere display, these are traits of a person who has turned to externals, and is hunting after something other, and is seeking for spectators to exclaim, 'What a great person!'"

Training is for the purpose of discipline, not adulation. It helps build character, and is a sign of the effort and striving of aspiration.

Pre-rehearsal of Bads

One of the better-known Stoic exercises for finding calm is pre-rehearsing future evils or bads. Anticipate the traps that lay ahead. Don't be caught off guard. The exercise goes back to the early Greeks. Cicero approvingly quotes a fragment from Euripides:

> I learned this from a wise man: over time
> I pondered in my heart the miseries
> to come: a death untimely, or the sad
> escape of exile, or some other weight
> of ill, rehearsing, so that if by chance
> some one of them should happen, I'd not be
> unready, not torn suddenly with pain.

Euripides, he says, in turn, takes a lesson from the pre-Socratic Anaxagoras who, legend has it, said when his son died, "I knew my child was mortal." The Stoics turn the teaching into a pre-meditation exercise: Regularly rehearse potential future evils to mitigate the shock of accident and tragedy.

I don't think I have ever uttered Anaxagoras's remark in an undergraduate lecture on Stoic ethics without my students being horrified at the message. They roll their eyes in disbelief. It's cold and callous, they say. They can't believe I'm expecting them to take Stoicism seriously, if that's what it teaches. It's as if I told them then and there that their parents don't love them, or were willing to abandon them at any moment. It takes a lot of back-pedaling to make the Stoic message appealing. I typically do. And I begin with the fact that the Stoics, and especially Epictetus, went in for shock and awe. He clearly succeeded. Still, the gist of the message, I suggest, is quite humane: we shouldn't run from the fact of our mortality. But to stop running from that fact takes work. It takes daily pre-rehearsal and a willingness to actually think about potential losses. The Stoics claim that if we do, we can mute some of the "freshness" of a sudden loss. The Greek term here for "fresh" is telling. *Prosphatos* connotes not nearness in time, but "rawness," as in freshly slaughtered meat. We need advance exposure if we are to weaken the visceral, raw assault of close-up losses. The technique, presumably, involves more than just an incantation of words: "I always knew my child was mortal." "Dwelling in advance" may take immersion in imagination, but also some humor and love.

When my mother, Beatrice Sherman, was in her mid-nineties and in a nursing home, I often thought about how we would talk about death. She was healthy, but I knew the end would soon come and I knew her well—that she wanted to avoid talking about death at all costs. She wasn't a talker at the best of times. When I asked her about a book (she read three or four novels a week) I was lucky if I got out of her, "It was fine." That was her standard response: "Fine." Life was fine. She wasn't a complainer. But she was into denial of death. And so at some point, I decided we would have to make a joke of it. I would ask every so often as we talked about how much she liked the Hebrew Home and her caregivers and friends: "Remind me, Mom. We didn't sign up for the immortality plan, did we? Because if we did, it's going to be really expensive!" She would smile gently. She was very beautiful. And she chuckled a bit. Of course, she never said the words: "I always knew I was mortal." But she thought the idea. She couldn't talk about death. It just wasn't her style. But I think our little repeated pre-rehearsal, our joke about the immortality plan, made her last days easier for both of us. We shared our mortality, and we shared not dreading death, together.

My mother died just three days after we danced together, she in her wheelchair, and I swirling her around with other "couples" on the "dance floor" at the nursing home. She had been coughing a lot the week before, and we both knew that the end might be near. The antibiotics weren't working. The nurses were monitoring her closely. We spent the last day together, in her room, facing death together. Our little whimsical joke about the immortality plan was preparation, she for leaving this world and me for saying good-bye, and that it was going to be on my mom's terms: "fine."

Pre-rehearsal, as I've intimated, is a form of pre-exposure, a desensitization ahead of time. If events don't occur, then we take it as a gain. In the case of death, the question is only when.

There are contemporary, clinical parallels to the notion of pre-rehearsal. Some may be more familiar with exposure techniques that work on desensitization after the fact. Clinicians have for some time successfully used evidence-based prolonged exposure (PE) therapy, after the fact, to reduce post-traumatic stress disorder (PTSD). PE is a form of cognitive behavioral therapy (CBT, itself with roots in Stoicism) during which patients confront (*in vivo* or through imagination) situations or events that are reminders of traumatic situations, though now experienced in safe settings.

Through repeated approach, rather than avoidance, the fear response is deconditioned rather than reinforced. Take the case of military service members exposed to the constant threat of improvised explosive devices. Survival depends on quickly responding to those threats. But the fear response can become overreactive. Hypervigilance is adaptive in a war zone, but not always after war, at home when thunder claps are heard as gunfire, fresh bumps on a pavement read as newly planted bomb sites, a black plastic bag on a lawn a hiding place for an explosive. Re-exposure to stressors by talking about them, seeing them in virtual settings, and revisiting and processing memories in a relationship where there is trust and safety become a way of deconditioning both the avoidance response and hyper-reaction. The "neutral" garbage bag on a lawn or new bump on the neighborhood road over time loses its associated negative valence.

In more recent studies, researchers have begun to investigate pre-treatment exposure. "Attention bias" (or to cast the idea in Stoic terms, the patterns in our assent to impressions) is modulated by balancing focus between threat and neutral stimuli. The idea is to learn to shift attention, so that we develop perceptual and cognitive resources for focusing not just on threat, but on neutral situations. Research suggests that advance training of this sort in shifting focus between threat and unthreatening stimuli reduces anxious hypervigilance characteristic of PTSD. In a related research experiment, Israeli Defense Force combat soldiers in units likely to face potentially traumatic events were exposed to "attention bias modification training" sessions. Through computer programs, they were trained to attend to threat "in an attempt to enhance cognitive processing of potentially traumatic events." The idea is to make the response to stress cues adaptive and agile: elevate the response in acutely threatening situations in combat, but train it to be transient, so that it recedes in safe circumstances.

Again, we can put a Stoic gloss on this: train in advance to withhold inappropriate assent to impressions of threat by laying down alternative patterns of assent to impressions of calm and safety. Of course, Stoic standards of what is and isn't appropriate won't map onto what most of us commonly hold to be appropriate or adaptive. The devil is in the details of how we interpret the doctrine of indifferents and what will count as wise selection. But the general Stoic idea—of preventive exposure and training in what we focus on in our environment—is prescient.

The Stoics go on to suggest that pre-rehearsal may reduce the compounding effects of secondary distress—or as Cicero reports, the distress that we were caught off guard and "might have been able to prevent" what happened. Of course, "hindsight bias" can be magical thinking—a tendency, after the fact, to overestimate our ability to predict an outcome. "Should-have's" and "could-have's" can be grandiose ways of misattributing responsibility. Sometimes, they are ways of coping with grief or survivor guilt, as I learned in my work with military service members returning from deployments in Iraq and Afghanistan. We tend to take moral responsibility in order to make sense of what seems senseless. In the case of service members, many replaced flukish luck with failed moral agency. Moral injury, the extreme moral distress of real or apparent moral transgression, as agent, victim, or bystander, can result. Conscientiousness becomes overwrought and anguished. But moral conscientiousness needn't always be anxious. Many ways of being prepared, and being responsible for being prepared, are far from irrational or overwrought. They are what good people do to take care of themselves and others. This is in sync with Stoic notions of taking preparation seriously at a personal and societal level.

Still, Stoic pre-rehearsal, if it focuses on the glass half empty and not half full, can seem a recipe for inducing anxiety. Reducing future distress comes at the cost of increasing present distress. We ruminate about worst possible cases, imagine how we would react to bad news, become preoccupied with adversity and loss. We are in battle mode before there is a war to fight. But again, there are good and bad ways of being future-minded. Strategic thinking, risk analyses, long-term planning, and coordinated and collaborative efforts all are ways to mitigate disaster that help reduce the emotional overlay of individual debilitating fear or depression. They are not necessarily ways of being alarmists, but ways of being realistically prepared.

Anticipating a natural or medical disaster is a collective enterprise, managed by institutions. But anticipating profound personal loss is something else. And each of us has different resilience levels, to do with psychological, social, political, and historical factors and more.

Epictetus suggests that we can train for personal loss by gradually increasing the stakes. We move incrementally from rehearsing small potential disturbances to great ones: "In the case of everything that attracts you or has its uses or that you are fond of, keep in mind to tell yourself what it is like, starting with the most trivial things." He suggests we start with a jug: "If you are fond of a jug, say: 'I am fond of a jug.' Then, if it is broken, you will not be troubled." Again, the advice makes no sense if it's just a verbal

incantation—tacit or expressed. Let's try to fill it out. We give ourselves advance warning. I say to my husband, as I recently did: "I
really adore this Richard Batterham large fluted celadon crock. I'm
going to be really upset if either one of us breaks it." What's unsaid,
but both of us are now cued up to think, is: "let's be careful." And
that might lead to a conversation, again, half tacit, half spoken,
about whether it's the end of the world if it breaks: "It's meant
to be used." "Storing the bread in it now is a perfect use for it."
"We'll be really careful." "Why have it if we don't use it?" "And
if it breaks, well, it breaks." Maybe something like that is what
Epictetus is inviting us to rehearse. It's all too fast in his formula-
tion. But we're not at his lectures in real time, milling around with
other followers, analyzing and interpreting. We're doing it now,
some two thousand years later. We're trying to imagine rehearsing
loss at the same time as we think about recalibrating our values
about what really matters. We're trying to test how Stoic we are.

Epictetus then widens the sphere of practice. "If you go out to
bathe, picture what happens at the bathhouse—the people there
who splash you or jostle you or talk rudely or steal your things."
Remind yourself about what you might expect. The case, again,
hits close to home. I often think about going to the Y at the end of
the day for an outdoor swim, in winter and summer, and in winter,
a post-swim warm-up in the hot tub or sauna. But the locker room
is often crowded with screaming teens coming in from swim team
practice. Are they going to be there today? Is it a practice day? Did
I time my visit just right? If they're there, it's not what I want at
the end of a tough day. But now, if I'm listening to Epictetus, he's
telling me "if at the outset" I say to myself: "I want to bathe, but I
also want to keep my will in harmony with nature," that is, in sync

with how things turn out, then I'm less likely to "get angry about what is happening." It makes sense. I will have given myself an advance talking-to. I'm armed. If the swim team girls are giggling and gossiping at high volume, then it won't be what I wanted initially, but I may be better poised to adjust expectations.

Epictetus then graduates from triflings to what's most pressing in our lives. The now familiar anecdote gets embellished: "When you kiss your little child or your wife, say that you are kissing a human being. Then, if one of them dies, you will not be troubled."

Wait! This is a steep progression: from a broken jug to the loss of a loved one with an unruly throng at the bathhouse somewhere in between. Pre-rehearsal may give you a perspective on mortality, but to think that it averts grief suggests both the worst parts of Stoicism and psychologically unsound ways of dealing with loss.

Is there a way to humanize the view? The following may help, even if it doesn't soften the view. Stoic mental preparation involves working one's way up to tough tests that we might face and know we would if only we had fuller, divine-like knowledge of how things will unfold. Some of those future scenarios and counterfactual reactions to them (If this were to happen, then I would . . .) we might now find outright distasteful. Explains Epictetus: "Chrysippus was right to say: 'As long as the future is uncertain to me I always hold to those things which are better adapted to obtaining the things in accordance with nature; for god himself has made me disposed to select these." So, if I knew I was destined to be ill, "I'd have an impulse to be ill." And too, if my foot had a mind, it "would have an impulse to get muddy." That is, what are now "dispreferred indifferents" might in another context be preferred and appropriate to select. "Seeing that we do not know beforehand what is going to happen, it is appropriate to adhere to what is by nature more suited for selection." Of course, we don't know what it is "to adhere to what is by nature" in the absence of knowing nature's full secrets and how and when they will be disclosed to us. But what we *can* do is train to be adaptive and prepare ourselves for the worst, even if we hope for the best.

Pandemics are again a salient case. With guidance from expert epidemiological and policy teams, economists and medical researchers, take steps to prepare. Teach the public to imagine what seems unimaginable. And then prepare for the personal and emotional toll. Know the attitudes that travel with disaster—anxiety, dread, massive sorrow and grief, loneliness, dislocation, a sense of an empty future. And know the sources of comfort and support. There is no way we can be immune from psychological distress. Nor would we want to be. Moreover, any armor that claims to fully protect is a scam, a fool's errand. Still, there are Stoic lessons we can learn about possible ways of minimizing and managing distress, both on a personal and institutional level. And the app of pre-rehearsal is at its core: Try to make hardships that are distant and almost unthinkable real and proximate. And then imagine best responses in those hard cases—what is a path forward? That's a way to humanize the account and update it for our times.

Are there other Stoic techniques for mitigating emotional distress?

HEDGES AND RESERVATIONS

In addition to pre-rehearsal, the Stoics teach us to frame our plans and intentions in a way that mentally prepares us for the possibility that things might not work out as we'd like them to. They advise this technique: Tag on to your intentions, or as they say, impulses toward preferred indifferents, a tacit mental reservation: "if nothing happens to prevent it." We can think of the strategy as a way of hedging bets. Things may not work out. Always think of what you want as tentative.

Here's Seneca illustrating the mental technique: Say to yourself: "I will set sail *unless* (*nisi si*) something interferes." "I shall become praetor [a Roman magistrate] *unless* something thwarts it." "My business will be successful *unless* something interferes." Epictetus invokes a similar idea, reminding his listeners about effective ways to modulate attitudes toward indifferents: Given we are not sages, what is "up to us which it would be fine to desire," is not now present to you. "And use only impulse and aversion, but lightly and with reservation and in a relaxed way." Epictetus's points are compressed and in Stoic idiom. The gist is this: As non-sages, we don't yet have stable access to fine or noble desires directed at the only real good, virtue. Instead, what we have at our disposal are impulses (and aversions) directed at indifferents. In going "light" on those impulses, we avoid excess and strain, the ache of yearning and the anxiety of panicky avoidance. Mental reservation adds the thought like that of the cautious bather at the public bathhouse: It may be noisy there. Readjust your expectations. What you find may not be what you originally hoped for. A late first-century BCE Stoic, Arius Didymus, invokes a similar idea from the Old Stoa: "They also say nothing . . . contrary to his desire or impulse occurs in the case of the worthwhile man, because he does all such things with reservation and nothing adverse befalls him unforeseen."

But what exactly is the advice here? Should we always qualify impulses so they become fail-proof? Impulses, on this re-imaging, come with built-in cushions, a bit like car airbags that inflate upon impact in an accident. Formulated in the right way, impulses ensure psychological immunity that protects when you need it most. The idea seems a bit too good to be true, psychologically, if not logically.

Maybe a better way of thinking about reservation is on the financial trading model. Most of us are familiar with the tagline that's standard in market prospectuses: "past performance is no guarantee of future results." It's a warning not to assume an investment will do well in the future just because it did well in the past. Market climates change. We have to be adaptive. But equally, what did poorly in the past may just as easily be an opportunity in the future. Either way, we have to be agile, not market timers, but poised to re-balance on a regular basis to meet target asset allocations.

This is actually a useful way of thinking about key Stoic texts on mental reservation. No, the Stoics were not financial advisers. (If anything, their Cynic roots make them suspicious of money. Recall the Cynic motto from Diogenes: "Deface the coinage.") The point of the financial analogy is, rather, that information about the world and our best analyses of it are constantly changing. Impulses should change and be responsive to those updated ways of seeing the world. So to return to Seneca's example: I'll go on a boat ride. But I'll change my plans (and motive or impulse to carry it out) if I notice that a storm is setting in. I plan to campaign for election as a Roman magistrate. But I'll change my plans (and impulse to go forward) if my bid for election seems highly unlikely. And so on. In the sage's case, there is quick responsiveness to new information. This is a highly idealized case: The sage's impulses align with the present epistemic landscape. The sage doesn't assent to future (wished for) contingents. He keeps updating impulses in light of updated beliefs. In short, the sage doesn't get stuck on what's wished for or what was. Motive always tracks cognitive changes. And cognitive agility guarantees keeping up.

Seneca unpacks the idea behind mental reservation in this way. It captures the preceding idealized line of reasoning, but with a few critical additions: "This is why we say that nothing happens to a wise man contrary to his expectations—we release him not from the accidents but from the blunders of humankind. . . . We ought also to make ourselves adaptable, lest we become too fond of the plans we have formed. . . ." He accents the last point: "Both the inability to change and the inability to endure" are "foes to tranquility."

The first point to note is that the sage is protected not from "accidents" or misfortune, but from human error. And this is because a sage's knowledge keeps up with the facts—in the sense of what's objective and outside the knower. It's in this sense that things aren't "contrary to his expectations." It's not that the sage cushions all impulses against disappointment or failure. Rather, she changes impulses to keep up with what is now the case. We fallible beings are not so lucky: our knowledge isn't always one step ahead of accidents. But then Seneca brings the sage down a little to our human level. A sage may suffer by having to abandon plans and desires. So here we learn that the sage makes emotional investments that can actually lead to pain. But the suffering (*dolorem*) will be "much lighter," if success isn't promised (that is, if there is mental reservation), and there is a capacity to be adaptive. That is a tip for all of us, even we who are fallible and who invest with more passion than is often wise.

Overall, this is a remarkable set of lessons with implications for our times. If the fundamental point behind mental reservation is cognitive agility, facing facts squarely, trying to keep up with fluid informational landscapes, then the Stoic idea here is less about how to beat frustration than about how to change motivations in ways that align with new and reliably curated information. Beating frustration may be an indirect windfall, but the work in getting there is cognitive. Of course, as we said, the Stoics idealize the model. The sage is an exalted knower, indeed, an infallible one, who doesn't have to worry about assenting to misleading and attractive impressions or clinging too tightly to health or clean feet when the inevitability of disease or muddy feet is how nature is unfolding here and now and guiding what we should assent to. And he doesn't seem to have to worry either about all the unconscious ways we take in impressions without surveillance or will. But even so, the general idea of being responsive to a changing world, aided by exercises in pre-rehearsal, is a cautionary lesson for trying to find calm in unnerving times.

LIKE AN ARCHER

Another way the Stoics counsel us to adapt to the uncertainty of outcomes is through an analogy with archery. In shooting an arrow, the "objective" is to hit the target, but the "goal" or "end" "is to do all in one's power to shoot straight," "to do all one can to accomplish the task." So there are two values: an objective (about preferred outcomes) and an overall end or goal (about striving). In terms of living a good and morally decent life, "missing the mark" with respect to specific actions is compatible in the course of a life with achieving the overall end of excellence or virtue. Put otherwise, virtue is in the striving, in doing everything we can to live a good life; the accidents of bad luck may frustrate our objectives and preferred outcomes, but not the overall end of virtue or goodness. The two values—indifferents or preferences and virtue or goodness—are distinct.

Many would say, again, this is the harsh side of Stoicism. Shouldn't we be distressed by accidents and bad luck that frustrate the objectives of our good actions—to save lives as a healthcare worker, to keep innocents out of the cross-hairs of fire, to save a toddler in a playground accident? Even if tragic outcomes don't impugn our best judgment and fine efforts, don't they typically stress us and, if severe enough, shake our confidence that we did everything we could? And isn't that distress a good thing, a sign that we care and are invested in the world around us?

Consider the following case to test Stoic intuitions. In the fall of 2019 I gave a keynote speech on moral injury at the Psychotrauma Center in Amsterdam to a group of clinicians, senior first responders in fire, police, and the military, as well as humanitarian aid workers, among others.

Firefighter Aart van Oosten told us of a harrowing choice he had to make one Christmas Eve. He was having a holiday meal with his family when he received a call to lead a rescue operation in the close-knit, small Dutch town of Arnemuiden. The apartment above a Chinese restaurant was ablaze and four children of the restaurant owners were trapped inside. The parents stood outside the building in shock as they watched the flames balloon out the upper story windows. Three firefighters already on the scene had tried to rescue the children but the flames had overwhelmed their efforts. Conditions had only worsened. As Aart surveyed the scene, the question was no longer *how* to rescue the children but *if* they should be rescued. And his judgment with 30 years of experience behind him was that the mission was futile. The children couldn't be saved and the firefighters wouldn't survive the rescue attempt. With a heavy heart, he went to break the news to his colleagues and to a police officer who was with the parents.

When Aart arrived home that evening, his wife already knew of the aborted mission from having followed a news broadcast. She worried about his safety but also his career—they had lived through a previous incident of a lethal fire where the media had severely criticized the fire department for not being able to save lives. He assured her and his children that the causes of the deaths of the children were not his or anyone's fault. The firefighters could not have done more that evening.

The next couple of days were marked by psychological trauma aftercare for himself and his crew. He made sure that recovery of the bodies was carried out by the police who were doing the investigation and not by the firefighters who had been at the rescue scene.

Several days later, the police released a post-incident report determining that the children had succumbed to the flames before the firefighters arrived. That brought some solace. Still, the fire stays with Aart, because, as he explains, he made a conscious and deliberate choice to stop saving. Despite his years on the force, it was the first time that he had experienced an emergency of this magnitude. When he speaks to first responders, as he did to our group, he tells them that "it is almost impossible to fully mentally prepare" for this sort of emergency. "Everyone experiences a fire like this differently." And there should be "no shame or stigma in seeking psychological help."

I wept as I listened to Aart take us back to that night. I was spellbound by this fireman, admiring of his moral and professional leadership, his ability to make calm and circumspect judgments in an acute emergency, his psychological acumen, his protection of his people and concern for the family of the four children, his protection of his own family, and his clear-eyed sense of how a small town might judge him and yet his ability to separate accident, fortune, and reputation from doing his work well.

That is one Stoic lesson to reap from this case: Aart is a highly skilled, exemplary professional firefighter. And he leads his team with insight and professional intelligence. Not all actions and omissions in firefighting will yield the desired outcomes. It is a high-risk activity, and selecting wisely in this business means facing lethal fire and its consequences. Preparation trains, but it doesn't fully inure against disaster. That's a modified Stoic lesson. Aart's judgment to call off the rescue operation was validated by the after-incident report. And that gives some solace.

But the harder Stoic tonic to swallow is that even if the children had perished *after* the firefighters arrived, the wise selection in the circumstances, protecting the firefighters from a mission that would have cost them their lives, as well as the lives of the children, should also bring peace of mind. For the Stoics are committed to the view that virtue is a skill like being a good doctor: good doctoring isn't a guarantor that interventions will work. Will and intelligence, the best medical expertise and equipment, can only control so much. Medical workers live with the solace of doing their best. Good firefighters do as well. So, too, argue the Stoics, do good persons. Good professionals aren't always good persons. But many are. And aspiring to achieve the finest is common ground.

Healthcare workers on the frontlines know this implicitly, as does Daniela Lamas, a critical care doctor in Boston's Brigham and Women's Hospital. She is on the phone with the husband of a patient. It is the end of March 2020. Covid-19 is raging:

> I was not sure what to say.
>
> We were midway through one of the family update phone calls that have become our new reality in the visitor-free intensive-care unit when he paused. He had a question. . . .
>
> His wife had been on the ventilator a few days now and he understood that these machines might be in short supply. He just wanted to make sure: Were we planning to take her ventilator away?
>
> You don't know her, he went on. Yes, her cancer is advanced. But before this pneumonia she was taking conference calls from her hospital room. She's smart as a whip. Funny too. We have plans together, he told me. Places we want to see.
>
> It was then that I realized what my patient's husband was doing. He was trying to prove to me that his person was worth saving.
>
> . . . I hang up the phone and return to the buzz of the unit to check on my patient. Sepsis from her pneumonia, coupled with the immune compromise of chemotherapy,

threatens to overwhelm her. Though the ventilator is
helping to buy her time, she still might not make it.

But I know if she dies, I will be able to tell her husband that we did everything we could. I will be able to
tell myself that too.

This is sage counsel for a modern Stoic: goodness, and the
peace of mind that can come with it, is in doing our best, operating
at the highest levels of excellence with those similarly committed.
Excellence doesn't bring immunity from failure or suffering. It
doesn't bring immunity from moral distress. But it is a source of
psychological sustenance of a profound sort.

Dr. Anthony Fauci, age 79 at the time of an interview, is
asked how he would like to be remembered after the coronavirus pandemic is over: "You know, I just would hope that I'm
remembered for what I think I'm doing, is that I'm doing the very
best that I possibly can." Good doctoring is the model for what
the Stoics call the "art of living." And it is what most of us who
live honorably try to do—live well by doing the very best that we
possibly can.

Unknown artist, Boxer of Quirinal, 100–50 BCE, bronze, Palazzo Massimo alle Terme.

LESSON 4

———— ✦ ————

MANAGING
YOUR
EMOTIONS

"SCREAMS AND CLAPS AND HELL YESSES . . . SOMETIMES THEY CRY"

Publisher Andy Ward at Random House describes the emotional reactions in his office every Wednesday afternoon when the *New York Times* bestseller list shows up in inboxes. It's tense. "There's this moment of quiet as the attachment opens, and then you hear screams and claps and hell yesses echoing over the floor." It's "a beautiful thing," he says, "but not as beautiful as making that call to an author who has worked so hard to make her book a reality and telling her that she is an official NYT best seller. That moment never gets old; it's impossible to be jaded about it. Sometimes they get quiet, sometimes they cry, sometimes they yell OH MY GOD. All of the above are appropriate."

But are they appropriate for a Stoic? Ward's thrill, and that of his authors, hangs on success, external recognition, striving that paid off with tangible positive results. But is that delight, so tethered to externals, a permissible kind of Stoic joy? Conversely, what if an author were depressed that the book, to which she devoted so many years of hard work, was a flop, misunderstood, and poorly promoted by the publisher? Is being peeved, saddened, or angry appropriate for a Stoic? Or should a Stoic just take it all in stride, be calm, and carry on?

And what of grief at loss of life or livelihood? What about frontline hospital workers who feel the full emotional weight of work during a pandemic? They carry the grief of witnessing massive loss of life and the fear of infecting their families once their shift ends and they open the door at home. Many fear the loss of a paycheck should they themselves fall ill. Are these appropriate emotions for a Stoic?

If the Stoics forbid basic emotions such as desire, fear, pleasure, and distress, and all the many shades of emotions that fall under them, then what's left of the human face of emotional response? That's a way to begin to ask: Do the Stoics have emotional skin in the game? I answer that they do. But we need some background to make sense of their answer.

LAYERS OF EMOTION

The Stoics hold that there are three distinct layers of emotional experience. At the center are basic or ordinary emotions: desire and fear directed at goods and bads in the future; pleasure and distress directed at goods and bads in the past or present. These emotions and their subtypes make up the vast swath of emotional experience in our lives. Following Aristotle, the Stoics hold in an even more robust way that primary emotions are *cognitive*. They are beliefs or thoughts that are motivational: in the case of desire, that successful reception of my book is a good to be sought; in the case of fear, that the grizzly bear is dangerous and to be avoided; in the case of pleasure, that this wine has a lovely nose and is worth savoring; in the case of distress, that the death of my mother is a serious loss that brings pain. At a more granular level, beliefs are impressions that you assent to, ways of accepting how things seem. Assent is implicitly voluntary, and so, the Stoics hold, emotions are *voluntary* mental actions. They are up to us. Again, Seneca outlines the view in the case of anger. This key text makes explicit that emotions are things we do, not things we passively suffer:

> Anger is set in motion by an impression received of a wrong. But does it follow on the impression itself and break out without any involvement of the mind? Or is some assent by the mind required for it to be set in motion? Our view is that it undertakes nothing on its own, but only with the mind's approval. To receive an impression of wrong done to one, to lust for retribution, to put together two propositions that the damage ought not to have been done and that punishment ought to be inflicted, is not the work of a mere involuntary impulse. That would be a simple process. What we have here is a complex with several constituents—realization,

indignation, condemnation, retribution. These cannot occur without assent by the mind to whatever has struck it.

Anger does not happen to us. We choose it. The complex process mixes distress and desire—pain at being wronged, desire for retribution. Neither distress nor desire is a blind impulse; both are implicitly chosen motives consisting of two evaluations, of being unfairly wronged ("the damage ought not to have been done") and of what would count as an apt reaction ("that punishment ought to be inflicted"). An emotion is thus, as Cicero had earlier explicated Chrysippus's view of distress, a two-tiered evaluative judgment: that a bad has taken place and that it requires an appropriate or fit behavioral response.

This is a description, and an elaborate one. The broader Stoic prescription is simpler: basic or ordinary emotions, like anger, are fundamentally irrational. They are *perverted* cognitions, *false* evaluations about what is really good and bad. Insults and offenses, dangers and threats, love and grief attach to objects that are not genuine goods and bads. They are indifferents, in general, to be preferred or dispreferred, as we for the most part do, and should, by nature. But preference or "selection" is not the same as emotional investment. It is those sticky, ordinary emotional attitudes of wanting and holding, fearing and grieving, that can lead to perturbation and excess, and can derail control.

Chrysippus depicts the "excess of impulse" by a smart analogy with a runner—once in stride you can't easily stop. Seneca embellishes the metaphor: Being angry is like standing on the edge of a precipice. Once the descent begins, there is no going back. It's like a body "in free fall." It keeps going, without heeding reason. Still, there is a way of experiencing emotions without excess or loss of control. This happens when emotions are focused on genuine goods and bads, namely virtue and vice. The wise person, or sage, who is the ideal of Stoic morality has cultivated those "good" emotions.

This takes us to a second layer of emotional experience. Good emotions are the "healthy" analogs of ordinary emotions. They are emotions focused on virtue and the avoidance of vice. They evaluate the world correctly, the Stoics teach. They capture what is *really* good and bad. In this sense, they are moral emotions. Only a sage can perfectly cultivate these emotions. Our job is to aspire. While aspiration can be a setup for striving that can lead to no real progress, the Stoics are committed to the idea that disciplined moral training can lead to psychological transformation. Striving to cultivate good emotions, however imperfectly, is key.

The cultivated emotional analogs look like this: In place of clingy desire for external goods, the wise person will experience "rational desire" aimed at virtue and virtuous deeds. Granted, even a Stoic moral paragon will still prefer health over disease, love over loneliness. But her "selections," however much preferred, are wise and prudential based on an appreciation that what's being selected are indifferents: we might not get what we prefer. Similarly, instead of pleasure in external goods, a sage experiences "rational joy," or, as Seneca elaborates, "exhilaration" and "uplift of mind" in her good character and deeds and those of virtuous friends. So, for example, a sage will experience a thrill in giving or making sacrifices for the sake of what is fine or just. Presumably, too, even a sage will delight in good food and good friends, but in the way a truly good and virtuous person would, without any whiff of intemperance and with a deep sense of generosity free of annoyance or envy. In place of fear of death or loss of friends, a sage will have cultivated "rational caution," a kind of wariness of evil and moral compromise. A sage avoids the entanglements that come with people too fixed on ambition, or who put others at risk only for selfish gain. Death and loss of friends is, again, something a sage will "disprefer," but without anxious dread or distress.

Other sources echo the general view: "The wise person is companionable, tactful, encouraging, and in companionship is disposed to seek good will and friendship. . . . And they also say that cherishing, welcoming, and being friends belong only to the righteous." In short, these are the attitudes of mutual goodwill that make up the best sorts of friendship and moral and political fellowship.

So, despite the popular view of Stoicism as a philosophy that would strip us of most emotions, the ancient Stoics argue that the very best of us show rational exuberance and desire, and a cautious wariness, lest we be too easily led astray or deceived. We cherish friends and nurture warm and welcoming attitudes toward them. This is what it is to be righteous. Put bluntly, even sages have emotional skin in the game.

Still, we might wonder why there is no analog in the set of rational emotions for distress. Why isn't there a good or rational form of annoyance, frustration, shame, grief, pity, or sorrow?

The orthodox Stoic answer is that the only thing that would cause genuine emotional disquiet is the evil of your own wrong-doing or that of your close friends. And that's just not a possibility if you and your friends are among the perfectly righteous. But most of us aren't. And even if we were, if good persons can find joy in the virtue of friends of like character, then why shouldn't they be distressed when they lose those friends to death or illness? Or lose their own robust mental or physical capacities? What's the real worth of rational joy if it comes fully risk-free? Moreover, it is one thing to keep calm in unnerving times; it is another to not notice what is unnerving or to discount it as fake. The Stoics have an answer, and it takes us to the final layer of emotional experience, or more accurately, a sub-layer of pre-emotional experience.

The Stoics hold that we experience sub-threshold emotional arousals. Some are near autonomic responses, bodily responses to our environment, like "shivering when cold water is sprinkled on us," or our hand recoiling "at the touch" of slimy things, illustrates Seneca. Whereas ordinary emotional experience requires assent to impressions—that something seems attractive or not—these pre-emotional responses fall below the threshold of mental assent. We experience starts and startles, shivers and shakes, blushes and sweats, physical affective arousals that bypass volitional control. They happen to us without the mind approving. "They come unbidden and depart unbidden." Still, they have the impetus to start us on an emotional journey, and sometimes an emotional rollercoaster, if we fail to take control early on. Even the wisest person experiences these preliminary emotions without culpability. In her case, they are fleeting and short-lived. They are the body talking, we might say, not the mind: "If anyone thinks that pallor, falling tears, sexual excitement or deep sighing, a sudden glint in the eyes or something similar are indication of an emotion

. . . he is wrong; he fails to see that these are just bodily agitations," says Seneca. They may be involuntary, but necessary for our survival: "Thus it is that even the bravest man often turns pale as he puts on his armour, that the knees of even the fiercest soldier tremble a little as the signal is given for battle, that a great general's heart is in his mouth before the lines have charged against one another, that the most eloquent orator goes numb in his fingers as he prepares to speak." They are adaptive—a rapid registering of life and death signals, that the enemy approaches, that it's time to muster all one's strength, that the troops need to move immediately. In other cases, they give a seasoned orator an edge—an adrenaline kick to work at performance pitch even if it comes with stage fright.

In yet other cases, they betray us, as Philo suggests happened to Sarah when she laughed when told she would give birth as a centenarian. It was a nervous laugh, of sorts, and if sudden and quick, maybe just the emotional residue of a former life that slipped out before she could "prepare her mind" for a more controlled, serene joy. Still, the nervousness may be an important signal of fear: Could she really give birth in a safe way, even if God was behind it? Seneca's point, and Philo's maybe, is that pre-emotions, and their adaptive or signaling functions, do critical work even in exalted models of bravery and virtue. "The wise person conquers all adversity, but still feels them." And that is because that person still needs to track salient information through emotional stimuli— whether of an enemy advance, a miraculous birth, or an impending violent storm that may imperil ship and crew. That a skipper blanches white in a sudden typhoon, one Stoic commentator tells us, needn't impugn his virtue. The hardwired signaling may save the crew. How to regain composure is a next step, if there is to be one.

This sketch of the layering of emotional experience, from rapid-response bodily arousal to ordinary emotional responses to idealized moral emotions, gives some sense of the Stoic preoccupation with emotions and the sophistication of their response. On many dimensions, they are clairvoyant in their thinking about emotions. Leading neurobiologists distinguish between "low-road" and "high-road" neural pathways that process emotional stimuli differently. The leading emotion theory among both philosophers and psychologists is a cognitive theory in which emotions are evaluative beliefs, or appraisals. We may not yet rush to embrace Stoic prescriptions for treating emotions, but their descriptions about how emotions work are insightful and highly sophisticated.

ANGER

My father had a temper. Sometimes it would erupt from nowhere and be slow to abate. On one occasion, when I was about 10 or so, I remember him getting into some row with my mother, the contents about which I have absolutely no recollection. But what is imprinted, as if it were yesterday, was the rage with which he pulled the handset off the kitchen wall phone and flung the receiver. His snatch was so forceful that he detached the cord from the base (there were no cordless phones then). No one was hurt, but his next move was to grab his jacket, storm out the door, and slam it so we (and the whole neighborhood, it seemed) knew he was gone. We didn't see him for many hours. When he returned

(I stayed up late that night waiting for him), he had calmed down. But we all walked on eggshells the next week and watched carefully for any signs of a flare-up.

Anger is ugly. Seneca opens *On Anger* withholding none of his rhetorical skill:

> Eyes ablaze and glittering, a deep flush over all the face as blood boils up from the vitals, quivering lips, teeth pressed together, bristling hair standing on end, breath drawn in and hissing, the crackle of writhing limbs, groans and bellowing, speech broken off with the words barely uttered, hands struck together too often, feet stamping on the ground, the whole body in violent motion . . . the hideous horrifying face of swollen degradation—you would hardly know whether to call the vice hateful or ugly.

Seneca is feeding a Roman audience bent on violence. There's voyeurism here. But he's also warning about the excess and intensity of an emotion like anger. How it grabs hold and won't let go. And then ravages body and soul. "Surely anyone would wish to be restored to calm, once he realizes that anger begins with harm to himself, first of all."

The anger he describes is retributivist. Payback anger is written into the Greco-Roman psyche. It's the stuff of Homer, on display in the rage of a warrior. But even archaic warrior rage can go too far. When Achilles punishes a dead Hector for the death of his beloved Patroclus by dragging Hector's corpse facedown around Patroclus's tomb, the poet is no longer just describing anger. He's taking a clear moral stance: "that man without a shred of decency in his heart" outrages even "the senseless clay in all his fury."

Seneca argues that anger of this sort is a primitive defense, a bite-back mechanism that we should conquer: That is how "an animal, struggling against the noose, tightens it." "To bite back is the mark of a wretched little man; mice and ants, if you put your hand near them, they turn their jaws towards you; anything weak thinks itself hurt, if touched." There are infantile roots to this aggression, child psychoanalysts teach, as in Melanie Klein's vivid description of the "phantasied attacks" of "devouring and scooping out" the "bad" breast that withholds milk as a way of punishing the persecutor. Seneca's cautionary lesson is that the psychologically and morally weak bite back at the slightest provocation. Narcissistic injuries, status damages, a sense of being down-ranked or bested in competition all fuel the payback. The point resonates in the current political moment. Over and over again, we have seen President Donald Trump's vindictive payback in response to narcissistic injuries. The Stoic moral teaching is that the injuries are attached to diseased values. They are injuries we ought not to be suffering if we were valuing the right goods. They are morally flawed responses, in Trump's case, profoundly dangerous, flawed responses that imperil a democracy.

Still, if Seneca's lesson is a categorical outlawing of all anger, then he seems to be treading on thin ground. Most of us see important value in feeling and expressing moral indignation, resentment, and moral outcry, and we distinguish those feelings and responses from vengeance or payback. They are part of what motivates a fight for human dignity and rights. They are the passion that generates interest, commitment, perseverance, and adherence to a cause. And they are critical for signaling our commitment and for securing uptake by others as we solicit support and elicit responses. Most of us would argue that it is hard to imagine a sense of justice or goodwill fully stripped of these reactive attitudes and their emotional bite. Imagine a #MeToo Movement and its positive work on behalf of women and men without some moral anger propelling it. Or imagine the Black Lives Matter protests in this country in 2020 without public moral outcry at the brutal killing of George Floyd by police in Minneapolis, or of Breonna Taylor by police in Louisville. Or, in a tragically parallel moment more than a half century earlier, in 1955, John Lewis, then 15, witnessing the lynching of Emmett Till, just one year younger, by two white thugs and being motivated by that lynching to do what Lewis went on to call "good trouble." Could he have become the Civil Rights leader he soon would rise to become without feeling any animus that day or fear of the brutality of oppression?

The overarching question about the place of anger in political justice has been taken up masterfully by philosopher Martha Nussbaum recently. One key point is critical for understanding a plausible Stoicism: As moderns, we need to distinguish relative status, honor, and reputation from the intrinsic attributes at the core of human dignity that may be jeopardized by wrongful acts. The Stoic focus is on honor, rank, and reputation—goods that are ultimately externally dependent. Retaliatory strikes to "disses" to one's reputation or honor may downgrade a critic's relative standing, and so effect a reversal of status, but the rebalance is itself external. Injuring someone else's reputation relative to one's own doesn't itself improve the intrinsic quality of what one's own reputation may be built on—say, one's work or character or integrity.

Nussbaum gives the following case: "People in academic life who love to diss scholars who have criticized them and who believe that this does them some good, have to be focusing only on reputation and status, since it's obvious that injuring someone else's reputation does not make one's own *work* better than it was before, or correct whatever flaws the other person has found in it." The retaliation doesn't itself improve or restore the goodness of one's own work. It's magical thinking, a fantasy of restoration, she argues, to think it would. All the same, it's easy to think that flourishing or *eudaimonia* will hang on that kind of retaliatory rebalance if "status-focused concern" ("this is all about me and about my pride or rank") is how one fills out what's of ultimate concern in flourishing.

But note, this is precisely the force of the Stoic intervention. We mis-order our values if we peg them on what's outside our own doing, including external rankings.

Yet what about the intrinsic goods that from a modern perspective are the basis of a life worthy of human dignity—health and food security, economic security, bodily integrity, safety against violence, friendship, and the like? If the absence of these goods through individual or systemic injustices threatens dignity, then isn't that a legitimate cause for anger directed at the wrongdoers, especially if it is anger bent on correcting the injustice?

Again, in looking for illumination from the past, we have to be wary of not taking off our own glasses. The Stoics value these goods bound up with human dignity, but not in the way that modern social and political thinkers do. On the Stoic view, they are still preferred indifferents to be overall promoted in a good, flourishing life, but not themselves unconditionally good constituents of that life. They are the *material* out of which a good life is built, with wisdom governing the selections. "Selection," as we have said before, is not a typical emotional attitude, but a preference behavior meant to free us from the grip of emotional responses that can be sticky, futile, or impetuous. In the case of responding to injustice, a Stoic gloss on that preference behavior is that we ought to strive to make selections that aim at promoting dignity rationally and constructively. Specifically, our behavior ought to resist the fantasy of repairing a wounded ego by wounding someone else's. That kind of rebalancing act is irrational, though it doesn't seem irrational at all to say that sometimes rebalancing is required precisely because goods and positions are limited or are built on unjust structures that need to be redesigned more fairly. In such cases, anger might be an impetus for the restoration of justice, but still, not one pegged to a false narrative about how and why anger works.

Take the removal in April 2020 of Navy Captain Brett Crozier from command of the coronavirus-stricken aircraft carrier USS *Theodore Roosevelt* after the leak of an unclassified letter he emailed that detailed failures of senior leadership for help in moving his sick sailors (among a crew of nearly 5,000) off the infected ship. The letter was a last resource plea: "The spread of the disease is ongoing and accelerating." A carrier is a small city. I know from my own experience, having spent a few days on the USS *Eisenhower* in the mid-1990s. There is no room for social distancing or safe quarantine. Sailors sleep in tight berths stacked three-high, eat elbow-to-elbow, clamber up and down ladders all day, use heads with little space for privacy.

Once Crozier was removed, what followed was a remarkable show of payback against a crew that had cheered and saluted their skipper in solidarity as he walked down the gangplank and left his command. Then acting Secretary of the Navy Thomas Modly flew 8,000 miles to blast the sailors for their show of support and to condemn the character of the commander that sacrificed his career to protect them. In a profanity-laced speech delivered over the ship's PA system, Modly said Crozier "was either . . . too naive or too stupid to be a commander of a ship like this." The rationale for the message was that Crozier's public image needed to be downgraded in order to raise that of Modly and the Trump administration. The speech failed dismally—Modly soon resigned. Status had little to do with the real reason for the crew's support of the commander: that he showed good judgment and selflessness in an emergency at sea, even if he sidestepped the chain of command. They were saluting not his rank, but his character. Modly's payback couldn't touch that. Modly's anger is exactly the kind of which the Stoics disapprove.

Still, the question remains as to whether Seneca leaves room for anger that can be harnessed for good without either ravaging its possessor or fixing on futile fantasies of restitution that downgrade a victim. Seneca casts himself in dialogue with Aristotle, whom he rightly says "stands up for anger" as "the spur to virtue." Its "removal would leave the mind unarmed, sluggish and useless for any serious endeavor." Aristotle, he says, "gives it a function," "summons it as though it had uses and supplied us with enthusiasm, to battle, to public action, to anything that needs doing with a certain fervour." Aristotle's real position is that we can cultivate "smart" anger so that it is directed at the right objects at the right time in the right way. This is what it is to "hit the mean." But on Seneca's view, smart anger is illusory. There is an inevitable slippery slope: A "spur" becomes fervor, and fervor becomes rage. Full abstention, on the model of sobriety, "sober and wineless days," is the only way to contain the disease.

Despite Seneca's insistence that all anger is dangerous pathology, is there room within the Stoic taxonomy for anger that isn't a pathogen? Pre-emotions may give us the space. Anger in its early, sub-threshold moments might be the fuel for more developed constructive protest and reparation. The idea would be something like this. Take the case of systemic sexism: A woman, Betty, repeatedly experiences catcalls on the street, sexual innuendos in professional meetings, professors attributing her remarks to a fellow male student and then endorsing and repeating them as his. In a new job, where she is the only woman in her academic department, "old boy" sexual jokes are part of the routine banter. Betty's experiences are varied, but what she endures is deeply engrained misogyny. On various occasions, she experiences some distress, a bodily and mental twitch—call it proto "worry, annoyance, mental pain, vexation." She may let it slide, and things may improve in the department culture without her direct intervention. The #MeToo movement educates.

What if the experiences or memories persist, and are more severe and disabling? And the time is right to acknowledge, to assent to the impressions, as the Stoics might put it, that these are deep wrongs endured. The acknowledgment may, at some point, even have to be public, very public. This is the case of Dr. Christine Blasey Ford. She felt a civic duty to disclose what Brett Kavanaugh, the then Supreme Court nominee, had done to her as a 15-year-old girl while he was very inebriated at a high school party. At the time of the sexual assault, she feared he was going to inadvertently kill her by suffocating her as he was pinning her down. What she remembers vividly about the assault was his uproarious laughter. She told the Senate how she still hears that sound and responds with traumatic fear. As a psychology researcher, she explained that the threat experienced that day was imprinted in the hippocampus—the brain's rapid fear warning system (like Stoic pre-emotions) that helps keep us alive but also primes us for post-traumatic stress.

Blasey Ford did not want to testify before the Senate. She did not want to relive the trauma and endure the political whiplash and potential death threats. "These are the ills I was trying to avoid." But "now I feel my civic responsibility is outweighing my anguish and my terror about retaliation." After the defense circulated the claim that she named the wrong man in the sexual assault, she was asked directly, "with what degree of certainty do you believe Brett Kavanaugh assaulted you?" She answered: "100%." The hearing has been highly politicized and for some falls on partisan lines. But for many, myself included, her testimony was credible: her conduct, her composure, her grace and courage under intense questioning, her clear reluctance to have to be there to testify, convinced me that she had not come with a retributive interest in downgrading Kavanaugh or rebalancing status. What motivated her was a moral imperative, a civic duty to share her story about the character of a man nominated to the highest court. Brett Kavanaugh's testimony gave a glimpse of a contrast case—"belligerent and aggressive," his voice loud, his face contorting at times, defensive bite-backs at various moments, the sort of depiction that brings to mind Seneca's warnings about anger's ugliness.

In Blasey Ford's case, we can imagine early and residual feelings of fear and anger that at some point, privately, and then very publicly, animate duty and a public cause. In speaking up, she also educated a public while empowering other women to break the silence, all at great personal cost.

On a generous reading of Stoicism, anger itself, and not just pre-anger, might be the impetus for principled and constructive action. For recall, ordinary emotions, such as anger, are two-tiered: there is the evaluative judgment of being unfairly wronged and the evaluative judgment of what would count as a fit response. Seneca holds, as many ancients do, that the conventional norm is to respond with retribution. But how we act is based on a voluntary evaluative judgment. Culture and history have heavy hands. But the Stoic claim is that emotion is a choice, as is, especially so, how we behave.

The point here is that the Stoics give us transitional space for harnessing the impulse of pre-anger and anger in non-retributivist ways. One last illustration makes this vivid. Consider the Netflix four-part mini-series *Unorthodox* about a young Jewish woman, Esty, fleeing her husband and Hasidic Satmar roots in Williamsburg, Brooklyn, to start a new life in Berlin. The series is an adaptation of a memoir by Deborah Feldman, who herself was raised in the Satmar community. What one sees in the early episodes is suppressed anger, frustration, a confused sense of not fitting into the world of arranged marriages and baby-making, yet not knowing any other world. The distress is cognitively hazy because horizons are so limited and subordination ubiquitous. Anger is a simmering, steady agitation, expressed in a tight face, a pursed lip, a blank stare, that doesn't have easy words or concepts. What we see and read is perturbance in the body. But then there is flight. Literally. An airline ticket that takes Esty from JFK Airport to Berlin's Tegel Airport. Generalized anger at not fitting in is impetus for flight. And impetus to seek something else. A chance Americano coffee leads to an open conservatory door and a world of music closed to her in her Hasidic community. There, women are forbidden to play an instrument or sing. It is a violation of modesty. It shames a husband.

Every step of Esty's new life is an exploratory moment in how to navigate an uncharted world. But something fuels it. And it is the constriction, the hollowed out, "contracted" feeling that the old world has robbed her of her autonomy. She never gives the words "injustice," "wronging," or "persecution" to what she has suffered. She says she hasn't lived up to what God has asked of her. But it is the anger of failure and at falling short of standards that are to her oppressive that propels her to explore a new life of dignity. Consciously or unconsciously, she is making decisions about how to respond to anger appropriately. And that response is nothing short of choosing how to live a good life.

GRIEF

Grief, according to the Stoics, is another form of distress. Since it focuses on losses largely outside our full control, it is an emotion that needs to be managed. It signals that we are hostage to fortune. Loved persons and things, homes and homelands, cultural heritages and religious sites, all are indifferents to be preferred and wisely selected. But their loss ought not totally destroy us.

The notion of managing grief in a way that might silence it strikes us as preposterous, especially in the wake of a raging pandemic that has blanketed us in massive and unfathomable loss. We don't *choose* to say good-bye to loved ones without being able to hold a hand or kiss a brow or sit in a hospital room together to chant a final prayer or lullaby. We have been *forced* to as a medical necessity. The need to grieve, in ways we think proper, is profound.

But just how radical are Stoic consolations on loss? If grief is to be outlawed, then indifferents do seem, after all, really matters of indifference. Preference is denuded of positive feeling, whether love of your family or joy and pride in your work. Conversely, dispreference is robbed of the pain that comes with loss. We go toward or avoid with detached selections. We select wisely, but at the cost of our humanity.

Cicero and Seneca challenge the orthodox picture. Cicero's challenge is profoundly personal. Having lost his daughter Tullia in childbirth in the late winter of 45 BCE, he retreats to his country estate in the Tusculan hills outside Rome and immerses himself in consolation literature and writes his own consolations as self-help: "For my mind was swollen, and I was trying out every remedy I could." Between mid-July and mid-August, he has penned most of the *Tusculan Disputations*, which includes an analysis of Stoic views of grief and an endorsement of a mild form of Stoic therapy. It is important to remember that Cicero is not himself a Stoic. He self-identifies as a Skeptic. Still, he is a careful Hellenistic reader and transmitter of texts, attracted to some Stoic ideas and critical of others. He is eclectic in his philosophy and in his therapeutic method: "Some hold that the comforter has one responsibility: to teach the sufferer that what happened is not an evil at all. This is the view of Cleanthes. . . . Chrysippus, for his part, holds that the key to consolation is to get rid of the person's belief that mourning is something he ought to do, something just and appropriate."

"Different methods work for different individuals," Cicero adds, and the timing of the intervention is as important as the method of intervention. Still, he has little good to say for the method of Cleanthes, the second head of the Stoa. Orthodox Stoicism undermines the very point of consolation: "I pass over the method of Cleanthes, since that is directed at the wise person, who does not need consoling. For if you manage to persuade the bereaved person that nothing is bad but shameful conduct, then you have taken away not his grief, but his unwisdom. And this is not the right moment for such a lesson." In short, the sage has lost his ignorance and, with it, the attachment that breeds grief. But for us mortals, like Cicero, offering a sage's lesson at the moment of bereavement is, at the very least, bad timing.

Is there a Stoic intervention that has more promise? Cicero contends, "the most dependable method as regards the validity of its reason is that of Chrysippus," the third head of the school. It's a method that doesn't deny profound loss, but works rather on changing how we respond to it. That is, it's focused on the second evaluative judgment, what one takes to be apt behavior. But even this is a hard sell for someone, like Cicero, in the throes of loss: "It's a big task to persuade a person that he is grieving by his own judgment and because he thinks he ought to do so."

Seneca takes on just this task. His consolations, in keeping with the Roman literary art form, begin by acknowledging the loss and anguish. They then move on to explore ways to restore calm and decorum: "I am sorry your friend Flaccus has passed away, but I want you not to grieve excessively." He makes clear what he means: "Not grieve at all. That I will not venture to ask of you. . . . Such firmness of mind belongs only to the person who has risen high above misfortune." Perhaps that's a sage. But even a sage will feel some distress: "And even he will feel a twinge at something like this, but only a twinge. As for us, we may be forgiven our tears, if there are not too many, and if we do regain control." The twinge is again a pre-emotion, an emotional scar from the past that the sage can feel without culpability.

In another letter, we are told that the wise person's tears flow more generously, "they well up of their own accord" "at the news of an untimely death," or "when we are holding the body that is soon to pass directly from our embrace into the flames." The tears "are squeezed out of us by a necessity of nature." There's no assent here. It's the body's natural response "when struck by grief's blow." Tears, tremors, breath seizing up are all involuntary responses to the shock of loss, whether we are moral exemplars or not. Emotional calm comes later. And even then, calm leaves room for tears:

> These [preliminary] tears are shed . . . involuntarily. There are others, though, to which we give egress when we revisit the memory of those we have lost and find an element of sweetness in our sorrow—when we think of their pleasant conversation, their cheerful company, their devoted service. At that time, the eyes release their tears, just as in joy. These we indulge; the others conquer us. So you need not hold back your tears because another person is standing near, or sitting at your side; nor should

you make yourself cry because of them: neither tears nor the lack of tears is ever as shameful as when tears are feigned. Let them come of their own accord.

So, the foe is forced tears, not public tears, as we might have thought, or tears brought on by memory or reflection. What's objectionable is nursing the tears, encouraging them to flow beyond what's in accord with norms of nature or decorum. The problem is excess and theatrics.

Some of this sounds reasonable, and gentler counsel than we typically think of as coming from a Stoic. Seneca is a complex figure, some would say hypocritical, and to be sure, inconsistent at the best of times. There is no shortage of tough love in his consolations: "The one you loved passed away: find someone to love. Replacing the friend is better than crying." Friends are fungible; people and not just income are disposable. That's hardly a Stoicism we want to embrace.

But Seneca is never one to hide his own vulnerability: "I am writing these things to you—I, who wept for my beloved Annaeus Serenus so unrestrainedly. . . . I understand, now, that the main reason I felt such grief was that I had never thought it possible that his death should precede my own. I kept in mind only that he was younger than I, much younger. As if birth order determined our fate!" The repetitive thought—"but he was so much younger"—keeps the grief alive. Processing *this* loss, that even youth was not armor enough, offers some calm. He desperately wants calm, as we all do, but also the friendships, like that with Serenus, that sustain us. And so he is a Stoic in the game with us.

He is a psychotherapist who treats patients but also treats himself. His times are calamitous: exiles, forced suicides, Rome burning while Nero fiddles (or, at least, performs on his lyre), Lyon burning, endless wars, political upheaval, unchecked disease. What his friends are going through, he's going through. The angst is everywhere. It is easy to hear him talking to us. It was that kind of glory he thought was worthy—that his letters live on. At the moment, letters from a therapist living in anxious times, with consolations for calm, are all too relevant.

A modern therapist's creed is not to share your own grief or neuroses with your patients. You absorb theirs, and if you are a psychoanalyst, make interpretations, without burdening the patient with your own treatment or personal history. But if you are living in a pandemic with deaths mounting every day, what patients are feeling is just what you are feeling—grief, fear of an unknown future, isolation and forced retreat from a face-to-face social world. Freud recommended "abstinence," the therapist's "blank screen" so that the patient could see her own conflicts and emotions in the transference, and not the therapist's. But when everyone is suffering together, it's harder for the boundaries not to slip.

Seneca is a *moral* counselor. He is not just a listener, but a talker. He admits, he is often talking to himself in his letters. "I am sick myself." "The man who lives here is not a doctor but a patient." The doctor, too, needs healing. The preferred treatment is philosophical—about the nature of loss and how one responds to it. But the core point is that his consolations are never blanket banishments of grief. They are about coping with grief, not about eliminating it.

Grief that honors loss is only possible with attachment. Yet attachment to persons is perhaps the surest mark of our vulnerability. It is also key to our resilience. If Stoic resilience is rooted in hard endurance and grit, then what are the social bonds that glue that grit? That is the topic of the next lesson.

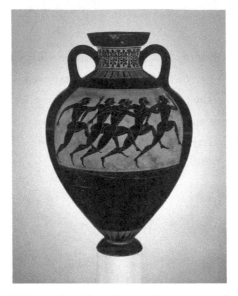

Unknown Euphiletos Painter, *Terracotta Panathenaic prize amphora*, circa 530 BCE, terracotta.

Metropolitan Museum of Art.

Giambologna, *Hercules and Centaur Nessus*, 1599, marble.

Loggia della Signoria in Florence.

———✦———

STOIC GRIT AND RESILIENCE

DANCING: A SINGLE FLOCK

She lived with a Dad who preached the Lord's words. "Butter and honey shall he eat." "That he may know how to refuse evil, and choose good." The next morning, the fridge was purged of milk and cheese. Butter was evil. Honey was good. And barrels of it now lined the basement. School was also evil. It carried the taint of Government doctrine. Not going to school meant all the girls thought she couldn't read. And they wouldn't talk to her.

Her dad was violent. He raged and he punished and he forbade conventional medicine, because it, too, was contaminated with the wrong beliefs.

Somehow, she survived it all. She had grit and gumption. And a subversive grandmother, her father's mother, ready to pack her up and take her to a safe place where she could go to school: "Won't Dad just make you bring me back?" "Your dad can't make me do a damned thing." Grandma and she were allies. At times, she and her mom were allies. She took her to dance classes; it was their secret.

Dance meant another kind of alliance. An alignment. Bodies talking to each other, mirroring and miming, knowing others because you are doing what they're doing. You connect, become connected. You become a single corps, a *corps de ballet*, even if you have no idea what that means. "Learning to dance felt like learning to belong. I could memorize the movements and, in doing so, step into their minds, lunging when they lunged, reaching my arms upwards in time with theirs. Sometimes when I glanced at the mirror and saw the tangle of our twirling forms, I couldn't immediately discern myself in the crowd. . . . We moved together, a single flock." Even if a goose, she was now a swan.

The story is Tara Westover's in her piercing memoir, *Educated*. She gets "educated" in spite of her father. Whatever resources help build her resilience, and they are many, high on the list, crystallized in dance, is coming to feel connected.

This is a key factor in Stoic grit. It's not the one most modern Stoics focus on. Usually, it's tough self-reliance. "If you want anything good, get it from yourself," Epictetus says in one of his quotable one-liners. The idea of rugged individualism rooted in Greco-Roman tradition is for many precisely the appeal of Stoicism. Autonomy and independence. Self-discipline. A can-do attitude.

But Marcus's imagery, we know, cuts a very different picture: Without each other, we are severed body parts, fragmented and disconnected. We can't function well or at all.

The sense of being at home in the world through social connection with others is a deep and pervasive Stoic theme. Stoicism, whether ancient or modern, sees social supports and not just inner strength as critical to how we surmount rather than succumb to adversity.

RESILIENCE

Resilience comes from the Latin *resilere*, to bounce back or rebound. In material science, it is the ability of a substance to absorb energy when it is deformed and then release the energy. When you squeeze a squishy rubber ball, and then let go, it recovers its shape. Resiliency is elasticity. In contemporary psychological writing, resilience has come to mean an ability to cope and find strategies for adapting despite adversity. Resilience is no longer thought of as invulnerability, but rather as adaptability. It involves flexibility and the capacity for growth and recovery in the face of hardship and challenge.

Adaptation to adversity is key to Stoicism's strong appeal. As we have seen, some Stoic techniques for meeting the challenge of adversity seem credible, such as focusing on skill and its effective use and not exclusively on outcomes. Similarly, "mental reservation," interpreted as a way of adjusting expectations to keep up with shifting information, seems sensible. These techniques, as well as anticipating adverse events so you're not caught totally by surprise, don't offer full immunity. They're protective factors that reduce risk. They don't eliminate it. The overarching Stoic promise is that it is not the stress events, acute or chronic, that build our resilience. It is how we give those events meaning. It is our attitudes and evaluations. Stoic anxiety-reducing methods have at their core the idea that we can learn to shift attention to what we can control.

But skill building of this sort is a cooperative endeavor, not a solitary one. The ancient Stoa, after all, is a school for cultivating the resources for personal growth through a teaching relationship and the fellowship of disciples. Ongoing friendships, face-to-face or through letter writing and consolations, are central to the Roman Stoic model of how you model and build strong character.

Adaptability, as understood these days, also has a critical social element, such as being open to the support of others and actively reaching out to them through supportive networks. Strong bonds with empathetic caregivers are predictive elements of resilience in children. Across the life span, positive family interactions and thick and strong community bonds are vital resources in fostering the resilience that allows us to face life's challenges. We recreate community in virtual platforms when we can't meet face to face.

Hotlines, trauma centers, suicide prevention numbers, substance abuse groups, survivor networks all speak to the need for access to social support. Of course, a willingness to open up to others requires a level of trust in them and the structures of which they are a part. Do they have your interests foremost in mind? Are they fronts for profit? Are they based on sham ideologies? Are providers adequately trained? Are there too many layers of bureaucracy before you can reach help, and so on?

Reaching out to others for emotional support requires, in addition, a level of self-trust about what you're feeling and that you have the words or other media to express it. Trust and empathy point inward as well as outward.

But the notion of social and empathic support in facing fears and reducing anxiety doesn't sound particularly Stoic. Is it? How social is Stoic resilience?

Intertwined

We can begin again with Marcus Aurelius and his battlefield meditations. In Lesson 2 we saw how Marcus paints a vibrant picture of our social interdependence. He builds social support from the ground up. Mind and reason are universally shared. The sharing is concrete. It shows up in coordinated behaviors, synchronies and alignments, mutual benefactions that are near unconscious and don't beg for notice: "a horse runs, a hound tracks, bees make honey, and a man does good, but doesn't know that he has done it and passes on to a second act, like a vine to bear once more its grapes in due season." Goodness begets goodness without grandstanding. We do good deeds as part of what it is to live in a community: "Reasonable beings, constituted for one fellowship of cooperation, are in their separate bodies analogous to the several members of the body in individual organisms. The idea in this will come home to you more if you say to yourself: 'I am a member of the system made of reasonable beings.'" We are in it together, a unified whole, that survives on cooperative endeavor.

Reason, *logos*, is the cement of the universe on the Stoic view. In some form or other, it is also the stuff of our psyches, including our emotions. To share in reason is to be connected to others through language, argument, emotional expression, and motor resonances, like those felt in battlefield cadres or *corps de ballet* sharing the dance floor. Marcus regularly invokes this tangible image of reason binding us together in synchronous movement. We are in "mutually intertwined movements," "working together" consciously and unconsciously. Even sleepers, he says, are fellow-workers in cooperative enterprise. The idea of mutual endeavor and coordination runs wide and deep. And strength and endurance rely on it.

Marcus's remarks are about social connection. But still, they seem to paint a picture of emotionless social distance, with reason doing its connecting and emotions playing little or no role. Reason brings us together, but without much zing or zest.

However, in his other reflections, Marcus's attitude is not in the least detached. Thoughts about friends, their deeds and example, inspire joy and are a spur for his own character growth. He prods himself to concretely visualize these exemplars when he needs a morale boost: "Whenever you desire to cheer yourself, think upon those who live with you; the energy of one, for instance, the modesty of another, the generosity of a third. . . . For nothing is so cheering as the images of the virtues displayed in the characters of those who live with you" and especially, he adds, when they are brought to mind as a group. "So keep them ready to hand." They are part of his personal *Encheiridion*, or handbook. His character sketch of his adoptive father Antonius suggests a relationship he can draw on for investing trust and hope in himself in moments of self-doubt or moral wavering: I should be "a disciple of Antonius . . . his evenness of temper in all situations, his piety, the serenity of his expression, his sweetness, his disdain of glory."

These brief portraits are consistent with the famous opening remarks in the *Meditations* in which Marcus lists individuals in his life to whom he is indebted for valued character traits. The catalog is long and the traits concern manners and morals: "from my grandfather . . . a fine character and even temper"; "from my mother, piety and generosity"; from Diognetus, Marcus's painting tutor, avoiding idle sport and impostors; from his mentor Rusticus, to not strut at home in ceremonial garb or waste precious time on superficial thinkers or "those who talk around a subject" without having any real expertise; from Alexander the grammarian, verbal precision matched with tolerance for those who fall short, whether because of an occasional howler or too "exotic" a phrase or "harsh expression." He taught that the right reply was not by "carping," but by modeling the correct phrase. That's the sort of positive, "happy reminder" that builds a trust exchange. It's an example of the subtle work of goodwill that goes into building and maintaining strong social bonds.

Marcus's catalog of debts reads a bit like the acknowledgment pages of a book like this one. We recognize those whose contributions have helped shape our intellectual and personal development. But Marcus isn't offering public thanks or acknowledgment. Remember, he's writing "to himself," an emperor in the lull of battle, invoking beloved friends and family as supports. The relationships are present, in the tent, so to speak, and formative. Building resilience is an ongoing project, even for an emperor preparing for the next day's battle. The resources reach beyond self.

BEING AT HOME IN THE WORLD, CONNECTED

Social connection assumes another shape in Stoic thought. And that is through the notion of "being at home" in the world. The Greek Stoics coin a technical term, *oikeiōsis*, variously translated as "affiliation," "familiarization," "appropriation," or "endearment." Its most general sense is that of belonging, hence, being at home with oneself in the world. In the case of animals, *oikeiōsis* has to do with self-preservation, being adaptive in one's environment. In the case of humans, the Stoics are keen to tell a developmental story about what is "dear" to us as naturally good and what is alien to us as naturally bad (that is, the externals or indifferents). As physical beings we aim for self-preservation. As beings with reason, we are committed to its development in a virtuous life regulated by reason. This natural affinity with reason connects us with others. As Marcus fills out the picture, the normative push of nature is for us to live in a commonwealth with fellow rational and reasonable beings. Reason is the common good that binds us and that helps build that social world.

The idea that we are social beings by nature has its roots in Aristotle. Aristotle holds that we even owe the existence of our cities not to social contracts, but to the workings of nature and its growth in partnerships from families up to politically organized cities. The Stoics aim to deepen and widen the developmental picture. We begin with a primary impulse for physical survival. As we mature, we come to recognize that our true nature (and sense of self and natural constitution) has to do with our reason and its perfection. Reason draws us to others and grounds cooperative behavior and the duties, or "fitting actions," that are due all human beings. The developmental story is complex. But this distills the main themes.

What is key here is that even with the shift to reason as the primary focus, it is not *my* reason, but *shared* reason. Being at home in the world is sharing in that most fundamental way. We may start with a sense of self as primarily to do with *my* self-preservation. But over time, the valuations change—including understanding universal reason. It's like making a new good friend, Cicero tells us, through a mutual friend's introduction: "one comes to value that person more highly than one does the person who made the introduction." So it is with perfected reason. When we reach the developmental stage of reason coming into its own, we are finally at home in a world: we order values correctly and are sustained by others who share a similar system of values—one also regulated by the norms of reason.

Once again, the idea has roots in Aristotle. Aristotle argues that genuine self-love is expressed not in possessing external goods, but in developing the excellence of reason. That doesn't entail, he insists, that self-love is a narcissistic attachment to that reason. When you identify with the authority of reason, you are identifying with how it functions best: "in virtuous activity that strains every nerve to do the finest deeds" in pursuit of the "common good." The Stoics then widen the common good from the *polis* to the *cosmos*: "The wise person realizes that nothing is more his own than what is allotted not to him alone but to the whole human race." Coming into your own is sharing in humanity.

Still, there is an abstractness to this way of being at home in the world. Common pursuit through common reason seems lofty talk, without little insight into the concrete and emotional bonds that connect us to each other.

But one way that the Stoics ground reason in the earthly is by making emotions and emotional attachments expressions of reason. More to the point, reason or cognition just is the stuff of emotions. Emotions, as we saw in the previous lesson, are *umphy* or highly motivational and "charged" beliefs. Even the cleaned-up "good" emotions of the sage zig and zag with uplift and sometimes deflation. They are robust, filled with the expansions and contractions, pushes and pulls, highs and lows, characteristic of all emotional experience. Bodily umphs motivate even the wise. The most divine-like mortals scaffold the social structures of resilience and human connection through emotions.

For practicing Stoics like Seneca, not yet wise but committed to moral progress, sharing in reason is equally an emotionally laden experience, exemplified in supportive friendships, including epistolary relationships. In the *Letters on Ethics*, we have a record. We read of Seneca's excitement in sending off a letter and his eagerness in receiving a response, his consolations in grief, his disclosures of his own suffering, his reports of the trivia of the day, and his earnest aspirations to constancy and wisdom. We get a sense of solidarity and empathy meant to sustain each side in hard times.

Seneca writes these letters in the last few years of his life, in political retirement, with mortality and the enmity of Nero on his mind. Anxiety and the search for calm swirl on the pages. There is a retreat away from externals to the inner life. But it is done with a friend. "When I devote myself to friends, I do not even then withdraw from myself."

Paragons from history are part of the support system. We needn't restrict our friends to the living, insists Seneca. Inspiration comes from the giants of the past—Socrates demonstrating his steadfastness to his philosophical principles in his death, Cato's cleaving to the path of virtue in the face of political ambition, Scipio and Cincinnatus in exemplary military leadership. The demigod Hercules cuts a more complicated figure, as we shall soon see. For although exceptional, his glory-seeking makes for a toxic and unstable mix, however arduous his struggles.

Seneca tells us that the sage rises only as often as the phoenix, every 500 years or so. For critics, a sage so rare is too daunting a model to be emulated. But a sage who shows emotions and who also can be clothed in concrete, historical detail is a way to make what's godly earthly. And that is a part of the Stoic strategy for resilience—we are to visualize exemplary models, including divine ones, who can teach us how to face adversity.

This is just what Seneca's contemporary Philo does in his Hellenistic commentary on the *Old Testament*. Once again, imagine the moment when Sarah nervously laughed to herself in learning that she would give birth to a child. How does surprise, and frankly fear and disbelief, at being able to conceive at such an old age move from trepidation to joy? Sarah, as Stoic matriarch, demonstrates how it's possible to loosen the grip of emotions that make her "stagger and shake" and come to feel steadier ones that bring inner calm and joy. There are no pointers here about technique. What we get is an example of hope: how anxiety about a most improbable and dangerous birth can gradually shift to trust in a higher authority and equanimity. That is the Stoic Bible lesson.

Connections with real or allegorical figures from the past, and friendships in the present, are social elements in building Stoic grit. Seneca's letters are addressed to his younger friend, Gaius Lucilius Iunior. The letters are undisguised moral counsel, but they do their work through rapport building. There are no known return letters from Lucilius. This is a literary art form. Still, Lucilius's presence is on the page in questions and answers, news about him from mutual friends, a relationship built through the imagined to and fro of anticipated and received letters. "Every time a letter comes . . . I am with you." Seneca has his eye on posterity here—merited praise that he has "been the cause of good" of others. If glory lives on through these letters, it's in part in the record of how the Stoics teach through a relationship, and continue to do so.

A VIRTUAL RELATIONSHIP

"I swell—I exult—I shake off my years and feel again the heat of youth, each time I learn from your letters and from your actions how far you have surpassed even yourself." This is Seneca, the coach, teaching through an idealized virtual relationship: "We get joy from those we love even in their absence." We are to imagine a gifted moral tutor focused on the character development of her young students and taking enormous joy in the teaching. "Their presence, their conversation has in it a kind of living pleasure." This is especially so "when you not only see the one you want, but see that one as you want him to be." All this may seem a bit Pygmalion to us, a moral mentor molding a student as he wishes him to be, with little room for choice or inner freedom on the mentee's part. It sounds un-Stoic, an imposition from without.

To be sure, goodness is the explicitly taught goal. That's what a Stoic coach wants of his students, and reasonably so. But that obviously leaves a lot of room for how goodness comes to be developed and expressed.

The idea is elaborated upon by an earlier Stoic, Panaetius, preserved by Cicero. We have four different roles or *personae* in life. One is our shared rational nature, a persona common to all in virtue of our humanity; a second is our distinctive individual temperaments or constitution; a third is who we are by "chance or circumstance"; and a fourth, who we are in terms of what "we assume for ourselves" as we become adults, making choices about "who and what we wish to be, and what kind of life we want." The picture is hazy about how we can make meaningful choices about our lives if chance and circumstance radically undercut our freedom. We may not be able to. But when we can, the core idea here is that goodness comes in many flavors. We make choices about what counts as a flourishing life, with our personalities, talents, and natural gifts often guiding those choices. Some of us become by avocation what we are by temperament. Litigators may be litigious; stand-up comics funny; nurses caring, and so on. We have to know our natures in order to choose the right roles in life. "We are actors in a play," Epictetus tells us. It's a stock theme in Stoicism. Cicero fleshes out the idea: we make wise dramaturgical choices when we pick the right parts, and here he means career choices "most suited" to our constitutions and temperaments. You shouldn't feel pressure, he insists, to "copy someone else's nature and ignore your own." If we are lucky, we get the right teachers to help guide our choices, especially in late adolescence, when we most need outside counsel.

Seneca's accent note often falls on the teacher side of the relationship. Hope in others and aspirations on their behalf begets its own joy. The relationships sustain us as teachers and parents, worthy friends and partners. In other writings, Seneca details the emotional exchange that makes giving gifts and showing gratitude more than just a thin crust of good manners. In the teaching case, here in the *Letters*, giving is reciprocated in the teacher's own growth and pleasure. Even when we hope in others on credit— that they will pull out of a slump or right themselves after consorting with evil, we still are in a certain way educating ourselves. We reinforce the lessons, Seneca writes to his junior, even when death nears, as it now is for Seneca. We model. Good teachers are in the mix with their students. They have been there, or at least can show some empathy for what it must be like. They are still learning and growing. The empathic connection is crucial in effective teaching.

Consider a recent political case. In February 2019, Michael Cohen was called before the House of Representatives Oversight and Reform Committee investigating President Donald J. Trump and his inner circle for tax fraud and campaign violations. Cohen was Trump's personal lawyer and "fixer" for a decade or more. He was brought before Congress to testify, shortly after he had been convicted in federal court on tax fraud and lying charges.

The Chairman of the House Oversight and Reform Committee at the time was Elijah Cummings, a senior Congressman from Baltimore. Cummings is an African American, the son of a sharecropper. He speaks with preacher cadence and passion. In a televised hearing, he is reaching out to Cohen, who famously said he would take a bullet for his boss, but now insists that he is giving truthful testimony.

"You made a lot of mistakes, Mr. Cohen, and you have admitted that. And you come saying I have made my mistakes, but now I want to change my life." Cummings draws on his own past career as a lawyer who represented a lot of lawyers, he says, who got into trouble. "And you know if we . . . as a nation did not give people an opportunity after they've made mistakes to change their lives, many people would not do very well." So here we have a lesson about the possibility of rehabilitation from a criminal defense lawyer. He has seen how people can go on after a criminal conviction. He's seen people turn around their lives. He's signaling the possibility of post-traumatic growth, even after a transgression of this magnitude.

He then acknowledges the seeming unfairness of it all: that Cohen got caught, but others in the Trump administration who may have done equal or worse are going scot-free. See it as an opportunity for growth, he again says, a moment to choose, as Cicero would say, a new path forward. "I tell my children when bad things happen, 'Do not ask the question why did it happen *to* me. Ask the question why did it happen *for* me.'" He doesn't know why this is Cohen's destiny, but if it is, he says he hopes it may play a role in making him better and making our democracy better. Again, it's a Stoic moment: "Life is indifferent; the way we use it is not," says Epictetus. Don't become careless about what falls to you as your lot. Cummings's moral tone here is religious and impersonal: you are the sacrificial offer for others, and though others are, no doubt, as guilty as you are, you are the temple offering. There is something coldly utilitarian here: a person is a fungible placeholder for bringing about the good, even if that individual is culpable and deserving of punishment. Still, in this play, he is the scapegoat for all.

But then Cumming's tone switches. The moral point of view becomes deeply personal, an eye-to-eye morality, with a parent talking to another parent. And here is where empathy enters in stunning form:

"Let me tell you the picture that really pained me. Really pained me. You were leaving the courthouse. And I guess it's your daughter who had braces on. Man that hurt me. As a father of two daughters it hurt me. And I can *imagine* how it must feel for you." Cohen, his head hanging low, dark rings under his red eyes, starts to cry. And then Cummings expresses his gratitude, compassionate concern, and aspirational hope. "I want to first of all thank you. I know this is hard. I know you face a lot. I know you are worried about your family."

He builds another bridge. This time he connects with Cohen and his future in prison. This is a Black man teaching a white man about incarceration, and the price of going to the cops and being an informer, in essence, what Cohen did in his trial and now in this hearing:

"I know it's painful going to prison. I know it's painful being called a 'rat.' Let me explain. I come from Baltimore. I live in the inner city of Baltimore. And when you call somebody a rat, that's one of the worst things you can call them. Because that means when they go to prison, they're a snitch. That's one of the worst things you can call someone. And so, the President called you a 'rat.' We are better than that. We really are."

This is a remarkable civic lesson with Stoic teachings about moral progress, choice, and resilience racing through it. What's germane for us now is that empathy is the vehicle of this moral lesson. Cummings is emotionally connecting with this fallen man: I feel your shame, and I understand the remorse you must feel in acknowledging your moral degradation so publicly. I see what it must feel like to bare your soul to your children. I know what it's like to be in prison and be called a "rat." But I have hope that you and that we as a nation are capable of investing in worthier ends and of striving toward them: "We are better than this," says Cummings in repeated chant. We are in it together, now and for the future: "Our children are the messages for a future we will never see." Prophetically, Cummings dies a few months later.

But is this a Stoic *mode* of counsel? Can a Stoic preach moral probity in a way that builds bridges by exposing the teacher's own palpable pain?

To be sure, the style and register of an African American legislator are very far from a Roman orator's, even if the rhetoric of both can take on a sermonizing tone in the public arena. Still, hardship and anguish *are* the very conditions that create a practical Stoic ethic. Epictetus teaches a new kind of freedom knowing what political enslavement is. Seneca struggles with abstention with the taste of wine still fresh on his lips. He tries to give up wealth while enjoying palatial opulence. He is the doctor and the patient. Marcus tames his home parade while reveling in the full public splendor of imperial pomp. He minimizes power and glory, but he is, after all, an emperor conquering an empire. Stoicism is born from the wide gap between what we aspire to and where we find ourselves. Few teachers inspire without sharing their own struggles. The Stoics are no different. Stoicism appeals because of the shared need on all sides for calm and composure, humility and ego-taming, even if you are an emperor, or in Seneca's case, a minister in the court of an emperor.

STOIC EMPATHY

Empathy is a core element in building the social bonds that undergird resilience. How to build that kind of social capital when individuals and groups are so far-flung becomes a pressing challenge for the Stoics. The lesser known second-century Roman Stoic philosopher Hierocles takes up the challenge through a metaphor of shrinking the distance between a series of concentric circles. The centermost circle is you—your mind and body and what's essential for survival. Next is your immediate family, then your extended family, and after that, more distant relatives, followed by neighbors, then tribal connections, on outward to fellow citizens and eventually all of humanity. We connect with the outermost circles by drawing them closer to the center through exercises in imagination and respect: "We keep zealously transferring those from the enclosing circles into the enclosed ones. . . . It's incumbent on us to respect people from the third circle as if they were from the second," and so on. It takes zealous exertions to move beyond tribe and recognize others as parts of your community.

Hierocles mimics a contrivance from Plato's *Republic* to try to contract the distance between the circles. If we call everyone of a certain age group "cousins" or "brothers," "uncles and aunts," "fathers and mothers," we might simulate closer kinships. Aristotle never thought Plato's ploy would work. Calling all women in a cohort group "my mother" or all boys in a cohort "my son" would just make for diluted relationships all around.

I had a Taiwanese American student who agreed. After reading this passage from Hierocles in a seminar, she told the class that when she went to visit Taiwan from her home in the States, her mother insisted that she refer to all her distant relations and friends there as brothers and sisters or aunts and uncles precisely to simulate a sense of a close-knit family. She found it extremely awkward, even when she accepted that she was an outsider to local culture and that cultural differences and distance had made a sense of strong family ties strained. On her view, family building required more than just enforced nomenclature and address.

Hierocles is not trying to create family as much as meet the challenges of a Stoic global community. How do we take on the interests of others we don't live with or know? How do we come to feel like we benefit when they benefit or that our welfare is wider than narrow self-interest? How do we make respect concrete? Hierocles claims it takes a zealous effort, and sustained psychological work to make what's foreign less alien.

Later eighteenth-century Enlightenment thinkers sharpen this Stoic idea. Empathy, writes Hume (although he uses the word "sympathy" for what we today mean by empathy) is a vicarious arousal. It's as if we are attached by a cord: when someone tugs at one end, the other feels the pull. We catch the other's sensation, as if by contagion. "We have no extensive concern for society but from sympathy." Hume's contemporary and fellow Scotsman Adam Smith develops a more cognitive view of empathy: we trade "places in fancy," imagining what another's life is like. We don't just put ourselves in their shoes, but try to *become* them in their shoes. The imaginative transport is robust. We "beat time" with the emotions of others though "we have no immediate experience of what other men feel . . . it is by the imagination only that we can form any conception of what are his sensations. . . . By the imagination we place ourselves in his situation, conceive ourselves enduring all the same torments, we enter as it were into his body, and become in some measure the same person with him."

For these thinkers, the challenge for morality is to contract the world without making it a projection of self. To do this, we need empathy and imagination, but also checks on our self-interest and bias. And so, the notion of an impartial judge or observer becomes critical in the Enlightenment construction of a moral perspective.

The Stoics haven't arrived at this point yet. Hierocles pictures bringing distant others into one's orbit. We are at home in the world when we make the world a less foreign place. But sharing a world and its resources requires a home base that's bigger than the self. The American founding fathers, many of whom were readers of the Stoics, shared the Enlightenment concern: how to construct a society that preserves a sense of collective belonging without making membership local and tribal.

HERCULES AND A FATHER'S PLEA FOR A DIFFERENT KIND OF STRENGTH

We've been sketching Stoic notions of affiliation and empathy key to individual resilience. We are at home in the world when we have a sense of belonging and connection, even to the most distant others. A social self, on the Stoic view, is a global self, however challenging it is to care about, and to be cared for by those outside one's own local circle. Distance and difference are barriers. But so too is the myth of indomitable strength. Stoic resilience can often seem Herculean. The image conjured up is of strength that vanquishes all foes and fears, impossible labors met with mental toughness and physical stamina. Hercules is a hero who risks danger after danger and is still safe. He is invincible. He is a person of action who doesn't admit fear as part of his image. For some, that is a picture of Stoic fortitude.

But Hercules is a tragic figure. At least he is in Seneca's play *Hercules Rages*. Seneca portrays the tragedy as, in large part, to do with Hercules's addiction to superhero action, nursed by a madness sent by Juno. She's jealous of Hercules, the most glorified of Jupiter's illegitimate sons. Having forced 12 labors upon him, she has one final act of wild revenge. This will test Hercules in unparalleled ways. Resilience in this play, Seneca cautions, will come from a source of strength very different from what we associate with Hercules's power.

The setting is this: Hercules is poised to come up from the underworld, having finished the last of his 12 labors, the capture of Hades's guard dog Cerberus. He is eager to see his father, Amphitryon, and wife Megara and children, all suffering under the tyrant Lycus who killed Creon, Megara's father, and captured his kingdom during Hercules's absence.

Juno rages at the anticipated reunion. "Stamp out his great ambition!" "No more monsters." This time, "let him fight himself." "Capture Hercules' mind." Pervert his wish, turn his impetuous courage against himself.

Hercules then pierces the barrier to this world. He's puffed up with all his works and their glory. "If I had wished to rule the underworld, I could have . . . I scorned death and returned." His hands are now idle and itch for more action. He is drunk on action. "More labours for me. Father, wife, I must wait to hold you in my arms." He has Lycus to vanquish and then worship at the altar to re-sanctify the city and its new rule under his reign. The family has to wait. Reconnecting with them through hugs and caresses, visceral contact, is put on hold. He has tasks to finish. His father offers to help with the sanctification. "No, I want to do it myself."

The plans keep growing. The adrenaline mounts. He has returned, but his family is still waiting for him to come home.

And then he's crazed. The self-destruction begins. The family that waited is now his prey. Juno has ensured that Hercules knows no calm. She captured his mind. First, he kills his toddler with Megara watching on. Then he bashes his wife's head.

Amphitryon begs to be the next victim so he can't see more. But Hercules has gone numb. Juno is just lifting the curse. He's quieted down now. Hercules sleeps, unaware of the disaster—until he awakens and sees "hordes of ghosts." Still, he has no idea that he is the slayer.

His father is the bearer of the ghoulish news. He is gentle, soulful, a father who needs to hold his son, touch him and embrace him, at the moment of a tragedy that's near impossible to comprehend. "The grief is yours. The guilt your stepmother's. Bad luck is not your fault."

Amphityron enacts the role in this play of the benevolent Stoic therapist: "Who has ever called an accident a crime?" But if the accidents are bad enough, protests Hercules, they are major crimes. But his father stands stalwart in his benevolence. He won't judge. Bad luck and accident, a vengeful god sending the Furies, is not our doing. "Forgive yourself for just this one bad act." Show compassion and empathy toward yourself. I am here for you to mirror mine.

When Amphitryon's pleas seem to fall on deaf ears, Hercules's companion and close friend, Theseus, intervenes as empathic peer counselor. His ploy is to make good on Hercules's indomitable pluck. Turn it to the right end. Restrain anger and use your famed courage to fight suicidal rage and the ignominy of being potentially cast as a parricide without the excuse of insanity. "Your father's prayers ought to work, but let me also try to move you with my tears." "Burst through your troubles, with your usual energy." "Use your heroic courage" to not stay angry at yourself. Now is the time to muster your spirit to face a different kind of danger—moral and psychic trauma not just of losing your beloveds, but of unwittingly killing them.

This is a remarkable play in which Seneca lays bare the social bonds that must undergird even Herculean courage. Physical strength is insufficient. Self-reliance is inadequate. Hercules's courage has to come from mercy that he can't show himself. Others must model it for him. He must lean on them in order to learn how.

And so, Hercules's last labor is the hardest for him: accepting trust and love and reciprocating it. The mutual bond will be his strength. Amphitryon begs him not to take his own life: "I beg you, do not leave me lonely in old age. . . . You are the one support of this ruined house, the one light for my pain." "Grant me the joy of seeing you and touching you. I beg you." A relationship, father and son, an embrace, touch, the reciprocation of love and care, are foundational for the courage necessary for both of them to go on. It is a courage foreign to Hercules now and earlier, when he first burst through Hades and saw Megara. And yet there is no other at this point.

This is theater. Seneca is not writing a letter to himself, or picturing a friend receiving it. This is not a consolation on loss. Theater, performed or not, allows the mythic to become real. And here, what is real are the tragic flaws of an over-sized person in the grip of glory who has to face the worst kind of agony—the mental and physical anguish of seeing his family murdered and the conviction that he has committed the crime even while not being culpable.

A colleague who is a therapist told me of a case that in an eerie way brought to mind this play—or, at least the trauma of an un-witting accident. In this real case, it is an omission that felt as hei-nous as any criminal commission. She had been treating for some time an emergency responder. He had a complicated psycholog-ical history with misfortune and accident riddling his past. But one event wracked him. He was called to the scene of a fire as part of a police team. It fell to him to look for three children trapped in the burning apartment. He found two and rescued them. But he couldn't find the third child. He searched all over her bedroom, and found no sign of her. The room was thick with plumes of black smoke. It was impossible to see. He relied on sound and touch. "I felt for her in the bed but did not find her."

He later learned that the child who burned to death had crept under the bed. "Why did I not feel for her under the bed? I have been trained to think clearly under pressure. How stupid can one be?" "Did I save her?" "No. I left her." "It doesn't matter if a judge says it wasn't my fault." "I failed in matters of life and death." He can't forget. The traumatic memory comes back in flashbacks. He holds himself morally accountable for her death. If treatment is about coming to feel less guilty, about finding some self-mercy, he's sure he's not deserving. "It may be correct that I feel so guilty." But guilt threatens to swamp him.

Like other first responders, he views himself as part of a tough warrior caste. Showing emotions is weak. It's not what's valued in his work. His work is about action and quick response and not failing. Sifting through the emotional residue of an accident is not part of the job profile. But he can't go on without it.

This is a human-sized tragic portrait, yet in the mold of Seneca's Hercules. Heroic labors and rescue deceive us about our strength. None of us is self-sufficient. We need others in good times and bad times. We need others to help us understand our fears and failures. We need others to show us the compassion we can't show ourselves. We need others as we fight fires ripping through homes and ancient redwood forests. We need others to soothe us as houses, and lives, and jobs, and nature are lost.

This is a most urgent lesson now. Millions of emergency responders must come to terms with what they could and couldn't do on the frontlines, whether in the face of fire or disease. They have lived with torrents of fear and anxiety. They have felt helpless. In the case of those working in medical frontlines, they have worried about what would happen if they paused to get treatment. They have seen cities and hospitals once under control come under siege again. Some have kept distant from their immediate families out of fear of accidentally killing them by spreading the disease.

They worry about leaving a job that is too dangerous, but is the source of rent and food and health insurance.

To have a chance of making it through these desperate times requires material and economic resources but also strong emotional supports, virtual and face to face. Building Stoic grit is not just a matter of inner toughness. It wasn't in ancient times. And it isn't now.

Stockdale emerging from his plane one week
before he was shot down.

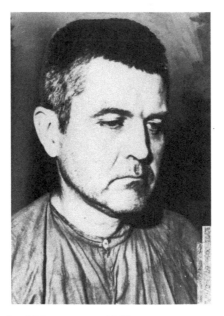

Stockdale as prisoner, 1966.

——— ✶ ———

HEALING THROUGH SELF-COMPASSION

Stoic Warriors

STOCKDALE AND THE STOIC CULTURE OF THE MILITARY

Just three weeks after 9/11, I flew to San Diego to interview Admiral James Stockdale. I was a bit anxious about flying. We had dropped off our daughter two weeks earlier at Dulles for her studies abroad in France. The airport was a ghost city. But Stockdale and I had planned this interview months ago. I was going forward with it. I had met him a few times before at Navy speaking events. In fact, I had given the Stockdale lecture at the University of San Diego in his honor. I knew of his legendary status within the military, and especially at the US Naval Academy. He had left a deep Stoic imprint there. Stoicism lived and breathed through Stockdale. What I didn't know until that morning at his home in Coronado was that, years after retirement, he was still channeling Epictetus. He still had most of the *Encheiridion* memorized. It remained a source of his resilience.

Shot down over North Vietnam on September 9, 1965, James Bond Stockdale, then a senior Navy pilot, muttered prescient words to himself as he parachuted into enemy hands, "Five years down there, at least. I'm leaving behind the world of technology and entering the world of Epictetus." A Stanford philosophy professor and dean, Philip Rhinelander, had given Stockdale the *Encheiridion* as a small gift upon starting his mid-career Master's degree there. Stockdale was skeptical about the gift, he confessed to me: "What would a Martini-drinking, golf-playing, naval aviator like myself do with a book like that?" And yet the nights were long on the USS *Ticonderoga* and then the USS *Oriskany* in the Pacific. Epictetus's slim handbook became his wardroom companion. He committed it to memory. He summoned up its teachings the moment he ejected from his A-4 Skyhawk.

When he hit the ground, a street gang pummeled him. That beating and more that would follow left his left leg badly broken, and he walked with a limp for the rest of his life. When we met, he still couldn't bend the leg. And so, we sat at the dining room table with room for his leg to jut out straight. That was part of his connection with Epictetus. He, too, had a lame leg, either congenitally or from beatings in enslavement. I mentioned the uncanny coincidence and he shot back Epictetus at me, in a kind of James

Cagney voice that was Stockdale's own, "Lameness is an impediment to the leg, not to the will; and say this to yourself with regard to everything that happens. For you will find such things to be an impediment to something else, but not truly to yourself."

Epictetus taught that you can rule yourself, even as an enslaved person. Stockdale internalized that lesson during his seven and a half years as the senior prisoner of war in the North Vietnam Hoa Lo prison (or "Hanoi Hilton," as it was dubbed by the POWs), four years of which he spent in solitary confinement, and two years in leg irons. One fellow POW whose cell was two doors down from Stockdale's was John McCain, who would go on to become a senator from Arizona.

As the highest ranking officer, Stockdale took charge of the internal chain of command of POWs. "Taking the ropes" became the euphemism for the sustained and methodical torture they all were to endure. Confession was the end goal for the torturer. Punishment for the crimes of being the treacherous enemy was six or eight more weeks of isolation. Stockdale's orders to his fellow prisoners was Epictetan: "My mind set was: 'We here under the gun are the experts, we are masters of our fate.'" He wasn't going to issue "guilt-inducing hollow edicts," or reiterate government policy of giving name, rank, serial number, and date of birth, that had no chance of standing up in the torture room. The message would be clear and would be the backbone of resistance and collective survival. The principal order had to be an easy-to-remember acronym. He settled on: "BACK US. Don't Bow in public; stay off the Air; admit no Crimes; never Kiss them good-bye. The US was the United States, but really it meant, he stressed, 'unity over self.' It's always 'we,' not 'alone.'" They were still a cadre fighting a war, this one a war of wills, and he was the leader of the expatriate colony.

In all this, Epictetus guided him. Harm was not a broken back or leg but the guilt and shame of betrayal of the self and group. Harm was underestimating self-mastery and authority. Harm was mistaking the taste of a cigarette or a night out of leg irons for real autonomy. Harm was forgetting the power of wily reason in resisting the torturer's will.

These core Stoic thoughts, "attitude-shaping remarks," he called them, were survival tools in prison. They were still with him close to 40 years later. "Here's Epictetus on how to stay off the hook." He then rattled off Epictetus: "A man's master is he who is able to confer or remove whatever that man seeks or shuns. Whoever then would be free, let him wish nothing, let him decline nothing, which depends on others; else he must necessarily be a slave."

The enslaved Roman Stoic from Phrygia was a lifeline. But so too was his wife Sybil. They communicated in letters through secret codes and invisible ink, the stuff of espionage novels. And it was Sybil, a fierce advocate for the POWs, who organized the families and brought international attention to the torture of POWs by the North Vietnamese and the ongoing violation of Geneva Accords. Her dining room table in Coronado became the hub of tireless activity for many of the POW wives for whom the Pentagon's "keep quiet" policy was no longer acceptable. She made repeated trips to Washington, cutting through red tape to advocate on behalf of the prisoners. The release of nearly 600 POWs finally came in 1973.

It was at that same dining room table that Jim and I were now talking. Sybil was in the kitchen and overheard some of the conversation. At one point, Jim said that there was a silver lining in all those years of being a POW tortured and in leg irons: He had come to understand the true freedom that Epictetus taught. He'd do it again for that. Sybil would have none of it. She dashed back into the dining room and took her seat at the table. If Stoicism was a religion, she'd get her religion in a different way!

They were each in their own way and together indomitable forces. They supported each other in deprivation, and in illness. Jim succumbed to Alzheimer's disease and died in 2004 at the age of 81. Sybil died of Parkinson's disease, some 10 years later, at the age of 90.

Stockdale bequeathed Epictetus to the Navy, and indeed to the military, of the post-Vietnam era. But Epictetus and Marcus Aurelius were already long part of the military ethos. Stoicism teaches how to adapt to cruel deprivation, how to find freedom in duress, how to tutor love so what we value is integrity and not glitter. Throw "a bit of glory" between the closest of friends, warns Epictetus, even father and son, and they may wish for each other's death. This could be a lesson for fighters. Unit members fighting side by side for the same cause can put each other at risk to rack up medals and ribbons. "Ribbon chasing" in the military is glory chasing. Epictetus warns service members to spurn false glory and aspire toward real virtue. Core values of the military and the service branches, like those of the Navy—"honor, courage, and commitment"—mean little if the words just point to career boosters—stars and grades and conspicuous glory flashed on metals that shine on a uniform.

I taught at the Naval Academy in the mid-1990s in the wake of a massive cheating scandal. I was the inaugural ethics chair, brought on board to "rehabilitate" 133 midshipmen who had cheated on an electrical engineering exam. I ending up staying on for several years to teach ethics and integrate ethics into the curriculum. I taught what I had long taught in my classes at Yale and Georgetown—texts drawn from Bentham and Mill, Kant and Aristotle, just war theorists, with case studies sandwiched in between. The sequence was thematic, not chronological, and we came to the Stoics fairly late in the term. But when we got there, our ship had finally arrived! I had led the 1,000 youngsters (sophomores) and junior and senior officers that were my section leaders to *their* philosophy. Epictetus spoke to them in a way no other philosopher could. The students already had their own version of a stoic mantra from the moment they became plebes. It was: "suck it up and truck on." That was what you needed to survive in the military. Now "Stoicism" with a capital "S"—Epictetus channeled through Stockdale, with lessons in virtue and tough discipline—filled out the credo.

A TENSION IN THE MILITARY: STOICISM AND MORAL INJURY

Greco-Roman Stoicism is a natural fit for the military. Yet it's in tension with what many experts now acknowledge as a pervasive psychological fact of war and after war. And that is moral injury. The leading research and clinical mental health professionals working on war-related moral injury define it as "a syndrome of shame, self-handicapping, anger, and demoralization that occurs when deeply held beliefs and expectations about moral and ethical conduct are transgressed." Transgressions can arise from the point of view of the agent (as perpetrator), from the behavior of others (as victim), or by being close-up witnesses, say as immersed war journalist or photographer. Consider *Toronto Star* photo-journalist Paul Watson who was in Somalia in 1993 and took the Pulitzer Prize–winning photograph of Staff Sgt. William David Cleveland—a bloodied corpse, bound, and dragged through the streets of Mogadishu by the Somali rebels. As Watson aimed his camera, what he heard Cleveland whisper was: "If you do this, I'll own you forever." The photo ended up being instrumental in the pullout of American forces from Somalia under President Clinton. But the guilt of having taken the photo tormented Watson for decades. It was as if Watson's camera shot was one of the shots that killed Cleveland.

Moral injury is a trauma response to a severe moral conflict or challenge. It's related to post-traumatic stress (PTS) with overlapping symptoms, yet distinct from it in that moral threat, and not overwhelming life threat, is the trigger. The potentially injurious experiences have to do with breaches of morality, not breaches of safety. The emotions that manifest moral injury can burrow deep, like guilt, shame, resentment, and a sense of betraying and being betrayed. They are part of a broader palette of emotions that philosophers call "reactive attitudes." They are testaments to the fact that we hold ourselves and others to account.

Service members wield the most lethal of weapons in high-stakes situations. Those who are conscientious wrestle with what they do and what they leave undone and what they leave behind. While moral injury may be especially traumatic in the military, it also exists in civilian life, even when lethal weapons aren't wielded.

There are lessons to be learned for everyone in how Stoicism handles moral injury.

AN ACCIDENTAL KILLING

Layne McDowell was meant for a cockpit. He had wanted to fly since junior high, and the Naval Academy, unlike the Air Force, took a gamble on a guy that had just had a knee injury. He graduated in 1995 with a 3.84 GPA and soon discovered he also had the physiology to fly. He was a G-monster, able to withstand 9-G's over time in the "spin and puke" centrifuge. He could physically endure and had made peace with willful self-defensive killing of enemy combatants in what he took to be "just war" ways. But one event early in his career unhinged his sense of moral calm. It was a midday strike on a radio-relay site in northern Kosovo in May 1999. Intelligence imagery was grainy. In order not to alert Serbian forces, he had to go south of the target and make a quick turn back. Aircrews now had less time to locate and verify the target. Serbian Air Defense opened up fire and that took McDowell's attention away from the targeting screen.

"I felt good about the release. Then clouds obscured the target until about 13 seconds to impact. At that time I began having doubts about the target. It didn't look right, but in those 13 seconds, I didn't say anything, and we took out what we were targeting with 2 GBU [guided bomb unit]-12's."

Dread started to mount. Back on the carrier, McDowell looked at the strike footage on a big screen. The bomb had struck not the target but a carport next to a house. McDowell saw signs of civilian occupation, and unmistakably, four bikes, two of which were child-sized.

There were never any legal proceedings or Navy follow-up to determine if and who and how many civilians and children may have been killed in the strike. But he carried the moral burden in a repetitive intrusive dream in which he did his own after-incident investigation. The dream replayed again before he deployed to Iraq in 2005. The building he bombed was somehow still standing but there was thick dust everywhere, insulation and wires dangling, boards littered all over the ground. The smoke was thick and it was hard to make out who, at all, was in the structure. He aches to turn back the clock, to be given time to steer the bomb to an empty field. But he can't. In the structure, he definitely saw a small boy huddled in the corner, coated in dust, severely injured but still breathing. He knew the face. It was McDowell's own son, Landon. "He lifted the boy to his chest, tightly for a hug, cupping his hand behind the child's little head, to hold it. The back of his skull was gone."

The case I have retold, drawn from American journalist C. J. Chivers's *The Fighters*, is not one of collateral killing of noncombatants, but of accidental killing. Unlike some collateral killings that may be justified as necessary militarily or excused as part of eliminating a serious threat, accidents like these, all too numerous in war, are never justified as necessary or eliminative killings. There is no military good to be achieved: killing the noncombatant is not part of a proportionality calculation.

Still, the accidents may be legally or morally excusable—due to poor intelligence, sudden blinding by enemy air fire, unpredictable shifts in flight patterns or cloud cover. This is the fog of war that McDowell faced. And yet innocents were horribly wronged. As the aviator who dropped the ordnance, McDowell carries the moral burden. In his accounting, he had a little over 10 seconds to readjust the targeting. Doubt crept in during those seconds. Why didn't he listen to the doubt? His punishment comes in the recurrent nightmare, in his wishing to turn back the clock and steer the bomb differently, in growing lukewarm over time about flight missions, in his yearning to know who was killed so he and the Navy can make atonement through compensation.

This is a stunning example of military moral injury. In this case, a fighter can't exculpate himself, even if the doctrine of war can.

We could say this is just the grandiosity of moral perfection at work, especially of warfighters who are raised on zero-tolerance for screwing up, whether in keeping a rifle clean or in hitting a target with expensive precision munitions. Many hold themselves "strictly liable," even when they ought not. I know from my decades of teaching military men and women that some can be rigid in their moral codes, sticking to a black-and-white sense of right and wrong in a world of war where there is too much gray.

But shunting all or most military moral injury to psychological overreach misses the greater moral landscape. Even if we can't always count on sensitivities to accurately track what we morally should and shouldn't do, still, for those of us who aren't morally callous, the panoply of emotions experienced with moral injury—guilt, shame, moral indignation, resentment, betrayal, a yearning to atone—speak to our moral aspirations. Moral anxiety is inseparable from the desire to be good and to do better, even in the most cramped circumstances and in the face of horrible tragic luck. If those who go to war didn't feel anguish at the detritus of war, whether incurred by act or omission, suffered or witnessed, we'd wonder about their humanity.

But can a modern military Stoicism rooted in ancient teachings find room for moral injury? Can a Stoic, bent on the calm that comes with discipline and virtue, leave space for the anxiety of perceived or real failure, or anger at those who make sport of war and take innocent civilians as their prey? Can civilians also learn how to forgive themselves for making mistakes or for accidents which have more to do with bad luck than with failures of moral responsibility?

These aren't rhetorical questions. I pose them as an educator teaching civilians and military who serve and will serve, here and abroad. Some will serve not as public servants, but in private capacities, in their workplace and communities, and in their homes. The answer to these questions has ramifications for all: When we teach Stoic texts, are we reaping the right lessons? Can we construct a healthy modern Stoicism, grounded in ancient wisdom, that recognizes moral injury and the possibility for post-traumatic growth?

BACK TO STOIC EMOTIONS AND THE "MORAL PROGRESSOR"

The Stoics don't talk about moral injury, per se, but they do talk about moral distress. And they teach that such distress has no place in the personality profile of the ideal moral person. For with Socrates, they hold that the only real harm is to become unjust, and that is not a possibility for the truly virtuous person. A truly good person, teaches Socrates in the *Apology,* cannot be harmed in life or death.

The Stoics fill out the paradoxical picture. Bad fortune, loss of loved ones, and physical or mental injury, even being wronged by others, don't affect our happiness or genuine well-being. We don't wish these things to happen, but all too often, they lie beyond our control. Our own moral wrongdoing, by contrast, is within our control. Or at least, the Stoics have us focus on pure cases where our hands aren't forced. They draw a bright line rule for a sage's behavior: A sage can do no wrong by definition. And so, there is no room for moral anguish or angst.

But what if you are not a sage? After all, a sage rises only as often as the phoenix, about every 500 years. It's an ideal, and maybe one impossible to apply in our non-ideal, imperfect world. What if you are, like Seneca says he always is, just a moral progressor, aspiring to become better but subject to error, misevaluations of what is really worthy, caught in struggles with those in power who compromise moral autonomy and self-rule? For many of us (though maybe not all in our contemporary political scene), the compromises may not rise to the level of imperial court intrigue, with execution, poisoning, banishment, imprisonment, and enforced suicide looming in the background or foreground. But the basic condition of not being sin-free and yet aspiring to become better is, in part, what has appealed to readers of Seneca throughout the ages, in the Hellenistic world and the Judeo-Christian period that followed. And it also is part of the implicit appeal of Stoicism for the military. For their culture is one not just of unbridled can-do-ism, but of constraint and chains of authority that squeeze autonomy and force choices that leave moral detritus in their wake.

Where do we find this thread of moral aspiration in Stoic writings? We first have to go back to Plato. For a famous teller of Stoic texts recalls this scene.

THE TEARS OF ALCIBIADES

At the conclusion of Plato's *Symposium*, a banquet in honor of the god Eros, Alcibiades, the morally flawed and disastrous military leader who betrayed Athens to the Spartans, bursts into the drinking party and addresses his love encomium directly to Socrates, his beloved moral tutor. Socrates, he confesses, is the only one who can really hold up a mirror to his errant ways and bring on the tears of shame. The anguish is, at times, excruciating, especially in Socrates's presence. For at those moments, says Alcibiades, "He always traps me, you see, and he makes me admit that my political career is a waste of time, while all that matters is just what I most neglect: my personal shortcomings which cry out for the closest attention." "Socrates is the only man in the world," he says, baring his soul, "who has made me feel shame." "Ah—," he says knowing his audience, "you didn't think I had it in me, did you? Yes, he makes me feel ashamed."

Alcibiades is a tormented soul. He's not a typical weak-willed or "akratic" person, as Aristotle understood the term—someone who knows clearly what he should do but doesn't do it. Alcibiades doesn't have firm moral principles that get trumped on occasion, through temptation or self-deception or the like. He's far more ambivalent. He occasionally dips his toes into the waters of virtue, especially when Socrates is looking on and casting judgment.

But, as he confesses, he hasn't really dedicated himself to the hard work of building new habits and weaning himself from old ones. Glory and fame still hold sway for him. He needs external prods and sanctions to keep him on course. In those moments, with Socrates *in vivo* or vividly in mind, he feels the deep shame of his "old ways" and of having too often caved into desires "to please the crowd." And that is a spur to do better.

The "tears of Alcibiades" becomes a challenge for Stoic thought: How can we understand moral distress as a part of moral improvement? Cicero poses the challenge. Not himself a Stoic but a Roman redactor, an editor and preserver of the texts, often attracted to Stoic ways, Cicero insists in the *Tusculan Disputations* that Cleanthes, the second of the three Greek patriarchs of the Stoic school, doesn't take the problem seriously enough: "It seems to me that Cleanthes does not take sufficiently into account the possibility that a person might be distressed over the very thing which Cleanthes himself counts as the worst of evils." And then Cicero reminds his readers of the *Symposium* passage: "For we are told that Socrates once persuaded Alcibiades he was unworthy to be called human, and was no better than a manual laborer despite his noble birth. Alcibiades then became very upset, begging Socrates with tears to take away his shameful character and give him a virtuous one." Cicero presses the Stoics to make sense of Alcibiades's tears: "What are we to say about this, Cleanthes? Surely you would not claim that the circumstances which occasioned Alcibiades' distress was not really a bad thing?"

Cicero hammers home the point later in the same essay: "Suppose a person is upset about his own lack of virtue—his lack of courage, say, or of responsibility or integrity. The cause of his anxiety is indeed an evil!" It is an "impulse toward virtue itself," he says. Cicero admits that it can be an "all too vigorous impulse" that can lay us low. His therapeutic counsel is not to dismiss the cause of distress, but to control the outer expression. We should try to manage the tears and inconsolable depression. If the core cause and object of distress is our own wrongdoing, then we should seize the moment as an occasion for moral aspiration. It is a first step and impulse toward moral growth and repair.

Let's return to our aviator case in Kosovo. Maybe there is some degree of culpability in this horrible accident. Whether or not there is, Lane McDowell holds himself responsible. So, too, do so many service members that I have interviewed and written about over the years, who come home from war when their battle buddies do not. They hold themselves morally responsible—for being on leave the day when improvised explosive device (IED) blasts ripped through the Army vehicle of a best friend, for having squatted rather than stood on the roof the second the insurgents took aim, for having given permission to a squad mate to get out of the Humvee to relieve himself in a spot that ended up being booby-trapped with mines. Survivors' guilt, accident guilt, holding yourself morally responsible for events in which you may not even be causally responsible is how service members carry the burden of care for each other. The guilt may be fitting of good character and care. You don't just feel grief; you feel you could have done something differently. Agency steps in to fill the horrible void. But all the same, the self-blame is too harsh and unfair. The right therapy in these cases involves redrawing the lines around agency and accountability. It's a case where letting go is understanding the limits of control.

Self-compassion may have to come through others. That was a lesson Seneca urged in *Hercules Rages*, as we saw in the previous lesson. It is a critical lesson for many who serve.

Take checkpoint incidents in Iraq. A car with two military-aged men and a child fails to stop at the first round in a series of checkpoints close to a large, heavily populated US military installation and arsenal. The car pushes through two additional checkpoints that come in quick succession without showing any signs of slowing down or heeding a sentry's warnings at each point. The man in the front passenger seat reaches for something under the seat as the car progresses through the checkpoints. As the passenger lifts his head and straightens his torso, he seems to be cradling an explosive device familiar from recent incidents. The sentry shoots just after the third checkpoint, killing everyone in the car, and seconds before what, in fact, turns out to be a bomb detonates. As the Army sentry considered his options, he was aware that his shots might kill the child, but also aware that in giving multiple warnings to the driver and in restraining fire until the third checkpoint, he was taking considerable risk onto himself in order to minimize the risk to the child and maybe other innocents in the car while still securing the base.

This is a hypothetical case, but not unlike those I have been told. Even if the child is being used as an involuntary shield, the soldier still feels horrific guilt at doing what he regards as unimaginable—killing an innocent child. And yet, according to the obligations of war, his action is unavoidable. His own self-sacrifice, as a way of avoiding the killing, would only lead to the death of many more soldiers on the base and abort the staffing and materiel for future missions.

Again, the soldier's guilt seems fitting and yet harsh. This is the cruel reality of much moral injury in war. The reflexive reactive attitudes, of shame, guilt, moral distress, and a sense of a shattered moral self that can come with killing, especially of young innocents caught in war zones, are attitudes we expect soldiers to feel. It is a way they hold themselves accountable in the face of conscientiously wielding lethal weapons. It is not just grief that they ought to feel for the loss of life in war. They rightly and fittingly view themselves as responsible agents. And for many, the line between just and unjust killing is thin and constantly shifting.

But even so, the self-blame can be harsh, too punitive and unremitting. And one way of seeing that is by taking up an interpersonal perspective. A soldier likely wouldn't reproach another in a comparable checkpoint incident. He'd excuse him, or refrain from blame, appreciating what was an unavoidable and constrained action in the circumstances. And similarly, another might be a benevolent counselor to him, helping him see what he can't himself see or feel. Again, that's just the image Seneca depicts at the conclusion of *Hercules Rages*, as Amphitryon refrains from blaming his son, Hercules, for the forced murders of his family and so, too, Hercules's close companion: "Use your heroic courage" to not stay angry at yourself, begged Theseus.

But we don't easily give ourselves the same "pass" that we urge on others or others urge on us. It seems right, in the checkpoint incident, for the soldier to see what he did as morally unthinkable. Indeed, we want soldiers to keep something of the conscience of their civilian souls in the very act of soldiering. But we also want to help them find ways to lessen and relieve fitting guilt, so the burden they bear is fairer. And again, this is where Seneca teaches that the point of view of others should enter. Even if we sometimes motivate morality by self-reproach, by shame and distress, we need others to correct our self-regarding attitudes when they are over-wrought or far too punishing. The benevolence and goodwill of others, their forgiveness and at times mercy, are what's needed to nurture our own self-empathy so critical for resilience.

SENECA'S PLEA FOR MERCY

The idea of having erred and finding a way forward as moral as-pirant is nowhere more evident than in Seneca's essay *On Mercy*, addressed to Nero. In writing it, Seneca says he holds up "a mirror" for Nero to better see his ways. But the mirror is one Seneca holds up to himself, as well. As public spokesperson for the court, Seneca is also expressing the hope of the greater public that the tyrant will somehow show restraint, especially in the wake of having just mur-dered his half-brother Britannicus (at age 14) to thwart his claim to the throne. The essay's shadow twin is Seneca's play, the *Trojan Women*. In the essay, we see the promise of mercy. In the play, we see the wasteland of an after-war world bereft of it.

Mercy, in the essay, is cast as the humane virtue in a world of human frailty. It is not pardon, "the remission of a deserved pun-ishment," but "leniency in exacting punishment." It is "stopping short of what might have been deservedly imposed." It is a staying of the hand, restraint and calming of vengeful anger, an acknowl-edgment that most accusers are not themselves free of all blame: "We have all sinned—some in serious, some in trivial things; some from deliberate intention, some by chance impulse, or because we were led away by the wickedness of others; some of us have not stood strongly enough by good resolutions." Even if we become perfectly virtuous, we would have arrived there by some moral erring along the way. There is no sinless path in moral progress.

Mercy makes good on the gentler side of Stoicism, lost on critics, protests Seneca, who see only Stoicism's sturdy austerity. The Stoic moral tutor, like the good farmer (or vintner, as Seneca was in his country estates), is ready to adjust soil in need of nutrients, prop up a tree growing crooked, or prune the branches of another so those dwarfed by its shadow are now open to the light. Moral tutelage, by analogy, is a matter of tender cultivation and willingness to show lenience, even if, by a stricter reading of rules and norms, harsh punishment might be rightfully imposed.

Such is Andromache's plea to Ulysses in the concluding scenes of Seneca's *Trojan Women*. The Greeks, despite their victory, find themselves once again stuck without the right winds to set sail. And following a familiar script, Calchas, the Greek priest, recommends Hector and Andromache's young baby son, Astyanax, be sacrificed and, too, that Polyxena, the young daughter of Priam and Hecuba, be slaughtered as a war bride on Achilles's tomb by his proxy, his son Pyrrhus. The children must bear the crimes of their forefathers. The ghost of Achilles kills his young bride and a baby boy is thwarted from becoming a warrior who can reignite another cycle of the Trojan war.

The future Trojan warrior boy must face his fate. But his mother, Andromache, is in a mortal battle with Ulysses to protect her innocent child. She has hidden him in her husband Hector's tomb, a place safe from enemy destruction. She begs Ulysses for mercy, for kindness, for herself as a hostage of war and as a mother whose child is her only comfort. The boy is no threat, she pleads, too young and without any power or backing to rearm a city. The boy may be a royal, but he is as good as a slave now: just put a yoke on his "royal neck."

To kill him is a crime of war, protests Andromache, and the atrocity will be pinned not on the gods but on you, Ulysses. But a Greek warrior, set on vengeance, cannot stay the impulse. Anger, as Seneca once again teaches, can't be stopped, once set in motion: "I wish I could be merciful. I cannot," answers Ulysses. The transmission of war, across generations, will go on, in violation of war's permissions. Once the appetite for warrior anger is whet, it knows no bounds. Innocent children, killed by mistake or vengeance, are war's pawns. Ulysses, the wily warrior, cunning strategist, cannot find a strategy for showing mercy, once the warrior mode grabs hold.

What we next see is the stunning consequence of the rage: a little boy forced to step off the steep embankment that was once the site of his grandfather Priam's watchtower. The boy's body shatters with the impact of the plunge. His corpse is mangled, his skull cracks open, brains spurt out, a little boy pulverized as if by a high impact bomb. Pleas of leniency, entreaties to restrain a victor's revenge, reminders that these children are victims, not contributors to war, the impotency of a ghost warrior groom—all reminders that though the aggression of the war is over, none of this stays the hand of ruthless rage.

This is a strange play, we might think, for a moralist of calm. Or maybe not, for it's a cautionary tale about excessive punishment and the difficulty of staying the impulse of raging revenge in war. But it is also about leniency in the face of overzealous punishment, whether directed at an external enemy or the enemy within. We hope Ulysses might hear the plea for mercy, for the sake of a mother and a child. But also, for the sake of himself and his troops. For maybe he will come to feel guilt, and his soldiers, too, for what they have done to an innocent. Maybe the guilt will wrack them for years to come and be the next feared Trojan War, but this one an inner war, that is fought over and over and over.

Mercy is, of course, far more elusive than anger. It requires discipline: first you have to vanquish anger. So there is space to heal. Guilt is self-anger. Self-mercy may be its therapy.

A PLEA FOR SELF-MERCY

Let's return to the naval aviator Layne McDowell. There were no formal investigations of the incident over Kosovo. It is not clear whether by following fuller procedures, McDowell could have averted the accident. What we know is that McDowell, above all else, is his own judge and revisits the scene in flashbacks. He probably also revisits the scenes in his mind as he checks for accuracy in Chivers's typed-up account of his quotes and then, later, his story, as Chivers narrates it, when he turns to reading the book.

What McDowell pictures is strikingly like what Seneca pictures in Astyanax's demise—a young boy's body shattered, the back of his head missing, an innocent made all too vulnerable in war. What we hope for on behalf of this navy pilot is some mitigation of the self-punishment, some leniency and self-empathy that allow for a way to move beyond the rage of distress without losing the moral meaning that comes from the anguish. What we hope for is self-mercy. We want him to be able to loosen the rage of his felt guilt by imagining if he would blame others as harshly as he blames himself. His feelings may be apt, but relentlessly harsh. As I have said, there is often asymmetry in how we hold self and others to account, especially, in the case of military moral injury: self-blame may be far harsher than blame for those who cover your back. But that opens a path for healing: We need to show ourselves the compassion we would show others in similar circumstances—or, show ourselves what we imagine that they show us. The benevolence of the benevolent spectator, at times, needs to become part of the moral self.

There is a political lesson here, too. We who don't go to war need to start taking greater responsibility for the wars to which we send others to fight on our behalf. We need to carry the moral burden by doing a better job of knowing which causes of war are just and worth our nation's most precious resources.

Seneca is a complex spokesperson for calm. What sometimes parades as conscience is the rumbling of the unconscious and its conflicts. He yearns for simplicity and tranquility at the same time he is attracted to the messy world of high-stakes power and hierarchy. Modern-day warriors (and many in frontline and emergency relief work) also live in complicated moral worlds—committed to excellence but working in institutions that vastly limit their individual control, exposed to situations that constantly test their best judgment and capacity for steady restraint. Exposure to moral injury is no surprise in those environments. But the Senecan lesson I have been urging is that this very injury may open the way for moral growth and the calm of repair. To read Stoicism as forswearing the possibility of "good" moral distress is to miss Seneca's more profound lessons for modern resilience.

Unknown artist, Marcus Aurelius, circa 175, bronze.

Capitoline Museums, Rome, Italy.

LESSON 7

———— ⭐ ————

LIFEHACKS

From Dye to Textiles

Legend has it that Zeno from Citium was a dye merchant, ship-wrecked with a cargo of purple dye on the Aegean Sea, when he safe harbored in Athens. He wandered into a bookshop, stumbled upon Xenophon's account of Socrates, and immediately sought out teachers like him in the marketplace. It wasn't long before he gathered his own disciples there on a colonnaded porch with panel paintings (the *Stoa Poikilē*), and developed a following that took its name from their meetingplace—the Stoics. Fast forward some two millennia. Another merchant drifts away from the textile market, stumbles upon the writings of Epictetus, Marcus Aurelius, and Seneca, and gathers disciples on a virtual porch through daily email blasts and a website that reaches hundreds of thousands of people. The Stoic marketer is Ryan Holiday, former director of marketing for American Apparel and author of many best-selling books for finding calm, but also a primer on public relations, *Growth Hacker Marketing*.

Through Holiday and others, the idea of Stoicism as a "life-hack" has gone viral, with entrepreneurs and billionaires, personal trainers and coaches, programmers and educators all turning to Stoicism for lifehacks for resetting values and quieting stress.

But what exactly is a lifehack? My husband, Marshall Presser, has been in the computer industry longer than most. As a tech author, he knew what a "hack" was, and a "hacker," and "hacking into a system," but not a "lifehack." And so, he pulled a signed book off his shelf, tucked in next to the many big data manuals: *The New Hacker's Dictionary*, a 1991 revised edition. We started there:

> Hack: 1. n. Originally, a quick job that produces what's needed, but not well.

In short, it's a way of jury-rigging something inelegant but effective for solving a problem. The next definition struck a more positive note:

> 2. n. An incredibly good, and perhaps very time consuming, piece of work that produces exactly what is needed.

But there was no "lifehack" in 1991.

The term seems to have been coined at a 2004 O'Reilly Emerging Technology Conference in San Diego by a technology journalist, Danny O'Brien, who used the term to describe the shortcuts productive IT professionals use to get their work done. By 2005 the term spread in the tech and blogging community and was runner-up by the American Dialect Society for "most useful word of the year" behind "podcast." By 2011 "lifehack" was added to the august *Oxford Dictionaries Online*. A "lifehack" is a shortcut for handling life's challenges.

So, is Stoicism a lifehack? Maybe, in the sense that the ancient Stoics offer strategies for managing the emotional stress and strain of life. The Roman Stoics simplify the practices for public consumption. It's no surprise that angel investor and bestseller author of the *4-Hour Workweek* book and podcast, Tim Ferriss, turns to Stoicism for "simple but powerful exercises" for overcoming anxiety and paralysis. He has championed Holiday's book *The Obstacle Is the Way* as a must-read for lifehackers.

In his 2017 TED talk with over 7 million views, Ferriss recasts the Stoic technique of pre-rehearsing evils as a way of dealing with hard choices that involve, as he puts it, what we "most fear doing, asking, saying." He dubs the technique "fear-setting," and it's meant to replace the usual "goal-setting" of business plans and strategies. The method is concrete and the stuff of a Silicon Valley whiteboard brainstorming session. But it's aimed at self-health, not organizational health. He instructs viewers to divide a sheet of paper into three columns. In the first column, from 1 to 10, name and write down a list of fears in full detail, visualizing worst-case scenarios. In the second column next to each fear, write down what you can do to prevent the bad outcomes, again in full detail. In the third column, write down what damage repair would look like if you just can't prevent the bad outcomes. In a nutshell, know the enemy you might be fighting, do your best to prevent the worst, and if prevention doesn't work, focus on fixes.

The Greek Stoics, as we said in Lesson 3, dub that proactive strategy as "dwelling in advance." Vividly imagine future evils, as if now present. They formulate a lifehack prototype: "stamp out an image, as it were, within yourself of what is going to happen, and . . . habituate yourself to it little by little as to something that has already happened." If prevention doesn't work, move on to treatment—learn to separate and accept what you can control from what you can't. Epictetus opens the *Encheiridion* with that dichotomy of control: "Some things are up to us and some are not up to us . . . If it is one of those things that is not up to us be ready to say, 'You are nothing in relation to me.' "

In Ferriss's case, the preoccupying fear was the downside of taking a break from his manic work schedule to go to London for a month to unwind and extricate himself from a bottleneck in the business. His top fear, as he began to break it down, was that if he went to London, he'd just get depressed in the rainy, cold weather and so the plan of going there for a positive, healthy retreat would be pointless. His second fear was that he would miss a letter from the IRS and so get audited or raided. He'd have more business worries than when he left. In the "prevent" column, next to the first fear about the gloomy weather, he jotted down that he could take a portable blue light lamp with him and use it for 15 minutes every morning to stave off a depressive episode. The second fear was easily managed by a forwarding address so the IRS could send paperwork directly to his accountant. But then there was the third column: "Repair." What if the worst-case scenarios unfolded? What would he do? Ferris is not short on cash. If he gets depressed in London, then he can always fly to Spain for some bright sun. That's what the Brits do. And in the case of the IRS letter getting lost, he could hire a good lawyer who has experience in this kind of case and could repair the damage.

Ferriss's net worth is estimated, by some, at $100 million. His problems are of the mighty and the elite. "*Some* problems," many of us would snicker. They're problems of his making, from his massive success, that he's now profiting from. His target audience are mid-level white-collar workers stuck in cubicles for countless hours in deeply unsatisfying jobs. They don't have his money or means.

Still, Ferriss's interest in Stoicism may not just be entrepreneurial. In his 2017 TED talk, he shares that he suffers from bipolar depression, and that he was suicidal in his senior year at Princeton. Managing the symptoms seems to be in the background when he mentions several times in the talk turning off the high-speed chatter of his "monkey-mind," or dealing with the threat of depressive episodes. His emotional highs and lows may be more extreme than those many of us experience. But he is convincing, in part, because he knows emotions and their turbulence. He knows the cost of not managing frustration and threat, and the paralysis that can set in if they are left unattended. The teachable lesson is not that Stoicism is an empirically based treatment for bipolar disorder. If Ferris misleads in that way, then he's a dangerous salesman and a quack. But I don't think he's naïve about psychiatric illness and its serious medical treatment. The more charitable read is that he has found Stoicism a useful philosophy of empowerment. And he knows how to sell it.

LIFEHACKS: WHOSE GOOD?

Ancient Stoicism appeals to many precisely because of its promise of self-mastery and inner freedom. Epictetus's writings and life are emblematic of the point. He was an enslaved person under Epaphroditus, an administrator in the court of Nero. If there is freedom, Epictetus taught, it has to be inner. Tyrannical emperors, banishment, and forced suicides turn people inward. Roman imperial history is filled with accusations of conspiracy and the cost of opposing power. These are lessons now to heed. But inner retreat then, and inner retreat now, can be ways of avoiding threat and not just managing it. Lifehacks can be selfish in that they disregard the external problems in the world that need fixing. They become about me, so that selfless courage disappears.

This can't be the full promise of ancient virtue. From Socrates onward, virtue was never just about me and my temperance, but about others and my generous and just treatment of them. Plato's just soul required the mirror of a just city. Aristotle frames ethics within the larger context of social and political discourse. Courage, he insists, has to do with standing one's ground against fears "for the sake of what is fine." And what is most fine, he says, is not just the goodness of a person, but the collective good. "Though it is worth while to attain the end merely for one person, it is finer and more godlike to attain it for a *polis*, a city-state." The Stoics expand the *polis* to the cosmos. They have an early vision of a global community and the affiliations and obligations that bind it. The ideal of moral goodness, then and now, is about how we share our humanity and the promise of common reason. Virtue can't just be about finding tranquility through retreat.

All this has profound application now as our nation wakes up from its own retreat of sorts from the legacy of enslavement. A pandemic and the brutal killing of George Floyd by Minneapolis police have been catalysts for social unrest. The two are linked in that a new virus has laid bare how it disproportionately kills those who have for decades suffered from an old virus of racism.

Philip Ozuah, chief executive of Montefiore Health System in the Bronx, New York, knows those links and his own battle with each. In a moving opinion piece, he writes that in March, April, and May of 2020 the coronavirus killed over 2,000 patients in his hospital center and over 20 members of the staff, despite best efforts to save them. No sooner did the pandemic caseload drop than he had to come to grips with another fearful crisis, "the lethal effects of racism, the pain of which," as a black man, he writes, "is all too familiar to me." And so, he watched with anguish the video of Amy Cooper, a white woman, calling 911 in Central Park telling the dispatcher three times, "an African American is threatening my life," a false accusation. The black male, with binoculars slung around his neck, was Christian Cooper, unrelated to Amy Cooper, and an avid 57-year-old birder who politely was asking Cooper to leash her dog, as required by park rules. That was the provocation. The incident occurred just a few hours before George Floyd was killed.

Ozuah knew how the park incident could be marshalled to advantage. And what could come next. In his own case, too familiar to those of color, how you could be walking in a white neighborhood, running for a bus, and the police could ask you to put your arms up, "turn around, walk backward," get on your knees, interlace fingers behind your head, and get frisked, "before any questions were asked."

Cory Booker, the longest tenured current black senator in the Senate, lives with similar fears. "I'm still very conscious when I'm not dressed like a senator, and even when I am, that I still could be one misunderstanding away from a very bad incident." He feels near shame, he says, and profound regret, that 30 years after Rodney King's brutal beating by Los Angeles police, he has to have the same conversations with his young mentees about learning to fear police for their own safety that adults had with him in his teenage years. He has to teach them the same "coping mechanisms."

Epictetus insists that "it's not what happens to you, but how you react to it that matters." But coping mechanisms can't be a permanent or viable fix for oppression. If modern Stoicism aims to dismantle disabling fear, then it has to address fears at many levels—like those of Ozuah and Booker, that are responses to collective fears about threatened loss of status and power, and those of cultures, embraced by white and black police officers alike, that support a troubling and vicious warrior model of lethality.

Modern Stoic self-mastery can play a role in reform. As a life-hack, Stoicism offers proactive techniques for taking stock of near-blind habits and impulsive reactions. These include how we see and the near-automatic emotional arousals triggered by what we see. Implicit and explicit bias fuels perceptions of threat and impulsive responses to it. The Stoics famously teach that we can learn to put space between our impressions, even the "impulsive impressions" (*hormetikai phantasiai*) and our assent to them, especially when those impressions distort or are part of a tapestry of wrongheaded values.

Racial profiling and all forms of implicit bias are ways of assenting to impressions without inserting space between the impression and the assent. Facial recognition systems are a high-tech form of racial profiling. They rely on mug shots and criminal databases that are seldom "scrubbed" of innocent people. Some tests struggle to distinguish among darker-skinned faces. They are a virtual way of assenting to impressions that easily distort.

In *On Anger*, Seneca argues that "habituation and constant attention may lessen" near-automatic responses. He is well aware that automaticity can be life-saving. We are wired for fast track emotions, for quick responses to life threat, for a good reason. They are "fortuitous mental impulses," Seneca writes with near clairvoyance: "Thus is that even the bravest man often turns pale as he puts on his armour, that the knees of even the fiercest soldier tremble a little as the signal is given for battle." These are what we now know as the flight or fight responses of the autonomic nervous system that allow fast response to perceived dangers. Seneca writes that those involuntary movements may need to be monitored and consciously attended so there is space for more "deliberate decision."

Seneca is a precursor to psychologist and decision theorist Daniel Kahneman. Kahneman posits that we have two systems in the brain, one that operates automatically with little or no voluntary control, and a second that is more effortful and associated with choice and greater analysis. We navigate life "thinking fast and slow," as he famously puts it. We need to mobilize attention when cognitive errors and biases, products of thinking fast, put us at risk of being manipulated by irrational fears.

Honorable police and service members fight on the frontlines of violence. They have to react fast under threat. But those same quick responses are sometimes defensive bulwarks against just conduct, whether in the battlespace of war or on the streets of a city. In the use of lethal weapons, they can be ways of assenting to impressions too impulsively, without the courage of restraint.

MARATHON OR SPRINT

In another day and age, at the beginning of the last century, Freud viewed avoiding fears, including not talking about them, as a form of denial. Denial is a pervasive feature of defense mechanisms that keep at bay disturbing events, feelings, or thoughts. We engage in all sorts of defenses, like projecting our insecurities onto others in order to protect ourselves from inner conflict, or magical thinking, where we deny reality so we can miraculously triumph over what might be too unpleasant to face. The tropes are well-worn. We may succeed in warding off some anxieties, only to have them talk through our bodies in the form of symptoms we'd prefer to chalk up to purely physical ailments.

Freudian-inspired psychoanalytic psychotherapy is a marathon, not a sprint. It's not a hacker's shortcut. It's an investment in process, and time and money, that could take you back to early childhood and parents, but also to the dynamics now in this room with this therapist as a screen for seeing how you are perceived and how you see yourself perceived. You watch yourself in a safe clinical space without all the tension of family dynamics. You develop an "observing ego." The prototype is Socratic: "Know thyself." And it requires talking. It's the "talking cure," as Anna O., or Bertha Pappenheim, the famous patient of Freud, dubbed it early on in Vienna.

Lifehacking through modern Stoic coaching is a different model. It's a behavioral therapy of sorts in that its primary focus is not discourse, but action and concrete steps to change entrenched habits. Still, it starts with talk—name your fears, jot down meditations, as Marcus did at night on the battlefield. It's an early form of cognitive behavioral therapy. Stoic coaching aims to accelerate change in a way unimaginable in the multi-year, four times a week, 50-minute hour plan of psychoanalytic psychotherapy.

Still, modern Stoic counsel shares with traditional psychotherapy the goal of self-exploration. Ferriss's turn to Stoicism, like that of many who are attracted to it, comes at a critical juncture in a personal journey. Many are after personal growth or self-transformation in the wake of a painful breakup or work-life crisis. They want to find meaning after being in a place that's no longer fulfilling. "Divorce shocks you," said Jeff Loesch, a 57-year-old senior technology consultant and infrastructure architect who went through a painful divorce (after 19 years of marriage), four years before he lost his job of 17 years when his company was acquired in a corporate takeover. A business networking event led him to a life coach, and then his own life coach training and certification. A few years later, he stumbled on ancient and modern Stoic thought through Holiday's *The Daily Stoic* meditations, and moved on to other online Stoic sites and podcasts, like Simon Drew's *The Practical Stoic*, where I met him when I was interviewed as a special guest and he was a listener.

Simon Drew himself turned to hosting the podcast almost full-time after he quit his job running a gym on the Sunshine Coast of Australia. It was Ferriss's podcasts that originally gave him an interest in Stoicism and led him to his current path. Never much of a reader, now, in his late twenties, he has read many of the major Roman Stoic texts, and has even dabbled in Diogenes Laertius's colorful, and at times, gossip column–like biographies of ancient lives. His home studio is stacked high with ancient texts as backdrop behind his retro-vintage radio mic. Some who follow

Drew's podcasts are drawn to his style of coaching through explicit Stoic texts. Drew was raised religiously as a Mormon, and he is at home with the idea of turning to the teachings of a text and quoting them by heart. He brings on his podcast scholars as well as practitioners. What appeals to many of the followers is the overall notion of ancient Stoicism as offering highly practical and yet time-worn insight into finding calm through virtue.

But stress is not always to do with me or what I can fix through self-quest. Stress comes from relationships and the implicit and explicit valence in our interactions. It comes from living in functional and dysfunctional families. In the business world, it comes from poorly run organizations and processes, from promising too much to clients with tools that are outmoded or not enough headcount to carry out the work. For some in the military, it comes from deepening conflicts of conscience and career. In a nation divided by color and class and technology, it comes from systemic injustice and economic inequities. Stress is caused by lack of physical security, health security, food security, and more. Stress is caused by fear of police and by entrenched municipal systems of police force unresponsive to reform from within or without. Mental stress is not just about threats of my own making. If Stoicism is to offer credible lessons for modern resilience, then it can't teach that we leave the line of what is within our control where we find it. We often have to move the line, so that the way things are, is not the way things must be.

But moving the lines is not easy, and it can lead to painful discussions about protection and risk, as in this conversation aired on NPR between a son and mother, days after the killing of George Floyd. Shawn Richardson is 17 and a runner. For Shawn, running track feels like freedom. "Winning. Running. Everything. I mean I love everything about it." But with school closed due to Covid-19, track has been canceled. And running now means doing it solo in the streets of Minneapolis without the protection of his white friends, that he just took for granted. He wasn't really that different from them—a runner who loves running. But Shawn now can't hide from the dangers. Nor can his mother, Minnesota State Representative Ruth Richardson. They live 15 miles from where George Floyd was killed. Shawn tries to cope. He tries to reassure his mother, "If I can't run in the neighborhood, I can run on a track or something, you know?" "It's not the end of the world." But his mother sees it differently: "It *is* the end of the world. Because if you can't run in our neighborhood, if you can't walk out into the world and just be seen as a 17-year-old boy who loves to run, there's something deeply wrong with that."

This is a conversation about freedom. It is not one that Epictetus would be having with his young disciples. But it is one that we as teachers are having with our students. I've had my own hard conversations about freedom with a first-year student at Georgetown who only six months earlier learned that he was a descendant of one of 272 enslaved persons who were sold by Georgetown's Jesuits in 1838 to keep the university afloat. It changed how he saw his life, how he now came to understand why he was raised Catholic. His freedom felt new. And he felt vulnerable. He came to see me a lot in office hours. He just wanted to talk—about how to study, about how much coffee to drink to stay awake and focused, about how much he liked certain readings, about how to balance a job and a heavy course load. We read Ta-Nehisi Coates in class. We watched parts of the documentary *I Am Not Your Negro*, based on

James Baldwin's unfinished autobiographical manuscript. But he never talked about his own past in class. He kept his newly discovered family history close to him. He was still figuring it out. And I respected that. That semester, in a class of about 25, I had four students of color, three African-Americans and one American student raised and schooled in Southeast Asia. That student of color wrote about his own sense of being excluded from a dominant narrative of race and struggle for freedom. Ta-Nehisi Coates's story and James Baldwin's were not his. His oppression was different. He was a remarkable student, but lonely in America.

For moderns, like my students, psychological freedom can't be pried apart from freedom afforded through dignity and respect and a sense of inclusion. The idea is ancient, however absent in history and practice. Cicero lays the foundation of dignitary respect, grounded in our shared common reason: "Thus we must exercise respectfulness towards humans, towards the best of them and also towards the rest. . . . The duty which is derived from this . . . leads to agreeing with and preserving nature." It is "suited to bonding humans together." It falls on modern Stoic coaches and disciples to do their part in constructing a society founded on that promise of respect and dignity for all.

THE GLOBAL CONNECTION

Jack Dorsey, cofounder of Square and Twitter, is another Silicon Valley entrepreneur drawn to Stoicism. What especially appeals to him is the idea of building toughness through deprivation. In

Dorsey's case, unlike that of a young military recruit or POW, he gets to pick and choose his deprivations. He opts for ice baths at 5 a.m., walking five miles each way to and from work without a coat even when it's cold, and eating a single meal a day. There are shades of Diogenes the Cynic here, and Socrates, Stoic inspirational icons, both of whom famously did away with outer garments, ate little, and gave the air of being impervious to the cold. In Dorsey's remake of the ancients, you do uncomfortable things to build neuropathways that make you more resilient. "Nothing has given me more mental confidence than being able to go straight from room temperature into the cold." To which one reporter quipped, "Try Toronto in the winter, sir."

But there is a more substantive recasting of a Stoic theme. And that has to do with global connection. Twitter's mission is about instant dissemination of information—"in ways that improve—and do not detract from—a free and global conversation." There is no shortage of good reasons to be extremely cynical about how shrinking discourse to 140 or even 280 characters can improve global conversation. Lax self-policing on Twitter and other social media platforms contributes to misinformation and incendiary bombast. Over the years the platforms have widened the so-called Overton Window, a term named after Joseph Overton for the range of political ideas the public is willing to accept. Discourse once deemed unsafe or too fringe is now more mainstream. Within that expanded range, social bots and trolls spread half-truths, hyper-globalized discourse mixes within siloed spaces. Megaphones create noise in ways that readers of traditional media often find uncomfortable and dangerous. Twitter and other social media kickstarted the Arab Spring but also gave birth to a battlefield that helped to tear apart the movement. Twitter is a tool, and like any tool, as the ancients taught, it can be used for good or ill.

Still, if visualizing fears and bads in vivid detail is a Stoic technique for confronting what's unsettling, then Twitter, these days, has functioned as a lifehack for a collective reckoning with racism. The current changed conversation about race owes much to the graphic viral video of Floyd's murder by police, with Officer Chauvin's knee pressed to Floyd's neck for nearly nine minutes. Three days after Floyd's murder, nearly 8.8 million tweets contained the #BlackLivesMatter hashtag. Similarly, the racial confrontation in Central Park was captured on camera by Christian Cooper, whose sister later posted the clip to Twitter. It has been viewed more than 40 million times. Twitter, Instagram, and Facebook all give us ways of seeing bads more directly, many of which we may not anticipate ourselves suffering, but that we may be complicit in helping to create. If we are undisturbed by these images, then freedom from emotional distress may come too easily.

There is a final point about Dorsey's commitments and their intersection with Stoic themes. Dorsey has emerged as one of the most generous billionaires, donating about one-third of his assets to a combination of coronavirus relief efforts, universal basic income, and support for girls' health and education. When asked why he gives, again he cites global connection: "I live by the principle of everything is connected, so if someone is in pain, I'm in pain, ultimately over time." Whatever other factors go into his gifting, Dorsey has spurned the usual Silicon Valley mantra of "earn now, figure out the giving later." He is also transparent about his giving, disclosing each gift in real time on a public Google spreadsheet.

Giving quickly and publicly may be a way of avoiding all the "asks" of those chasing your money. But it also is a way of leading by example.

Seneca in *On Favors* (*De Beneficiis*) has much to say about the subtle nuances of wise benefaction—when to give openly, and when to give in secret. There are gifts, he says, that "contribute nothing to preferment or prestige, but simply help against infirmity, poverty, or degradation." He rails against gifts that are simply for the public record or by benefactors who make you feel "frayed and crushed by continual reminders of service rendered. . . ." Pointless gifts, like giving "books to a country bumpkin or hunting nets to a scholar or man of letters" or "winter clothes at midsummer," undermine the purpose of giving. So, too, do gifts given out of greed for gratitude or approbation. Tweeting your gifts in real time is certainly a kind of applause drawing. But it is also a nudge to others to stop sitting on their fortunes.

Gift giving in ancient times was viewed as central to social cohesion: it, "more than anything else, holds society together," says Seneca. This is of a piece with the more basic Stoic point that our natures are social and that our self-sufficiency is relational; we rely on each other for goodwill, concretely, in material and emotional conveyances. Cicero anticipates the point with a rhetorical question: "Scan the contents of your mind." Would you prefer an Epicurean life of the calm of continual pleasure, or a life where you endure pain but do good for all of humanity? Beneficence and gratitude are the weave of social fabric. Modern philosophers, most famously Peter Strawson, recast the point: The expression of goodwill and gratitude are ways we hold each other to account as members of a shared community. Benefits don't themselves express goodwill. We look for the "manifestation of attitude it-self" in those benefits.

Philanthropy is no replacement for social justice, however wide we take the community. Twitter's aim is to widen the boundaries, at least of conversation. It, along with other social platforms, needs to be more aggressive in monitoring that conversation against dangerous falsehoods and lies. But the core idea of *logos* or conversation connecting a world is a modern twist on an ancient Cynic and Stoic idea.

A LIFEHACK FOR BEATING DEATH

Silicon Valley has played with another lifehack that is stranger to square with Stoicism. And that is beating death. The Stoics famously meditate on facing death through rehearsal of the fact of our mortality. Their mantras are not about defying death but facing it with equanimity. That is the point of their urging repeated practice of *memento mori*: "keeping death in mind." Of all the fears, this is one we especially need to conquer: "The person who fears death, will never do anything worthy of one who is alive," as Seneca says.

In the *Letters*, Seneca faces his own age and declining health. He has difficulty breathing. He has suffered from asthma since his childhood. And now there are more gasping fits. It feels like suffocation. The doctors say it's a physical rehearsing for death. He's been preparing for it philosophically all his life. That again is an idea portrayed by Socrates: "Philosophy is practice for dying and death," Socrates famously says in Plato's *Phaedo.* Seneca casts the philosophical training this way: "Wouldn't you say a person was quite stupid if he thought that a lamp was worse off after it was extinguished than before it was lighted. We too are extinguished; we too are lighted. Betweentimes is something that we feel; on either side is complete lack of concern." This is an argument for symmetry on either side of life made familiar in the first century BCE by the Epicurean writer Lucretius.

In practical terms, says Seneca, facing death means seizing the day now. "Present time is very brief." It is easy for the "engrossed" to get distracted. "Do you want to know how they do not "live long"? ". . . old men beg in their prayers for the addition of a few more years; they pretend they are younger than they are. . . ." But "the wise person will not hesitate to go to meet death with steady step."

If death, on the Stoic view, is to be accepted as an indifferent, even if a dispreferred one, then how do the lifehackers justify enlisting the Stoics as allies?

This is a place where some moderns see the Stoics as giving a nod to push out the boundaries of control. Here, fear is not the obstacle, but lack of time. And it is just the sort of thing the love of the hack might fix.

Take biohacker Geoffrey Woo, an influential figure in San Francisco, whose company, HVMN (Health Via Modern Nutrition), is a human enhancement company, making "nootropics," compounds for improving memory, cognition, stamina, and more. His tech company also instituted an intermittent weekly fast day for staff. When pushed, in a Vox interview, about the end goal of biohacking, he embraced immortality: "Yeah. I'd like to live forever." "Why," pressed the interviewer. "Why not?" "It's a very cultural notion that we're expected to perish." "I don't think it's techno-optimism. I think it's human desire." Aristotle might urge some sanity here. We need to distinguish mere "wish," he says, from desires connected with choice and action. "Choice cannot relate to impossibles," he insists, even though "there may be a wish even for impossibles, such as for immortality." "Wish," Aristotle continues, "may relate to things that in no way can be brought about by one's own efforts."

But that's precisely the biohacker's challenge—to redefine what's possible, including human immortality.

Woo may not himself be an avowed Stoic devotee, but many of his followers are, especially the fasting billionaires who want high performance and years added on by controlling caloric intake. There may be growing science here about diet and fasting. But the modeling of this on Stoic control oversteps the Stoic vision of self-mastery. Stoic athletic discipline of mind and body includes wise selection of the externals that affect our life chances. We are taught to select in ways that accord with nature, however inscrutable nature's laws. But one thing that bounds our human nature, even if we share reason with the gods, is that we, unlike them, are finite mortals. Any idea that wise and prudent living can eliminate death is decidedly un-Stoic.

Still, we might think that the Stoics open themselves to just this kind of misappropriation. After all, their techniques are about protecting against vulnerability. Yes, but, as we have seen, they frame protection in terms of adaptability, not bulletproof invincibility. So, Seneca reminds us, "We ought also to make ourselves adaptable (*faciles*) lest we become too fond of the plans we have formed." The danger is rigidity about end goals, including what some Stoic biohackers fashion themselves as doing, becoming bulletproof against death.

Indeed, it's hard to avoid seeing the aspiration to immortality as something other than glory chasing or hubris. Even if the hack to beat death is driven by an engineer's curiosity and tech-based faith that the sky is the limit, there is still the wish to be around long enough to see the fruits of one's technical innovations. And that, again, is more about ego and success than virtuous striving.

There is a final Stoic lesson about biohacking to beat death. The Stoics famously faced death in ways that were both visceral and dramatic. Chosen and forced suicides were a part of Roman life. Rubens's famous portrait of Seneca, with bulging veins, suggests that facing death by suicide was neither solitary nor necessarily serene. As with Socrates's death in the *Phaedo*, which Seneca re-enacted, friends were present, there was conversation, and in Seneca's case, the trust that his last words would be remembered. But there was also in the Stoic canon the idea that again derives from Socrates, that there can be a "rational departure" from life, a way of reading reason in nature that justifies suicide.

For the Stoics, suicide belongs to a special class of what is fitting or appropriate actions (*ta kathēkonta*). The proper reasons for rational departure are detailed and lengthy, especially given that our normal duty is to preserve life and our natural constitution. Diogenes Laertius tells us: "The wise person will make a rational exit from life, either on behalf of his country or for the sake of his friends, or if he suffers intolerable pain or mutilation or incurable disease." Those last conditions are the negative external goods (the so-called dispreferred indifferents). And since life itself only has real value as the material means for virtuous action, if we can't act virtuously because lack of material means precludes meaningful choices, then suicide might be justified. Immanuel Kant offers a case with Stoic overtones. He tells of a person bitten by a mad dog. The man believes with good reason that he now suffers from an incurable disease, hydrophobia, a symptom of rabies in humans, that will leave him demented. In a suicide note, as Kant relates the case, the man said "he killed himself lest he harm others as well in his madness." The example is telling. For although Kant, in general, holds that suicide is contrary to duty, here he argues that bodily disease can rob you of the means to act morally. And when it does, suicide may be justified. That is Stoic.

What's germane for us in all this is that the Stoics were acutely aware that life could be cut short by illness or autocratic decree. Their philosophy of viewing life as the material condition for virtuous action offered them a way to justify rational exit. They never viewed the body as itself a material to be made resilient against all affronts. That's a modern notion of control it would be hard for a Stoic to think was Stoic.

STOICISM AND TOXIC MASCULINITY

Another appropriation of ancient Stoicism and, more generally, the Classics is by hyper-masculinists who spread their views on digital sites like Reddit, which hosts the misogynist Red Pill community. This is one of a number of alt-right misogynist platforms, sometimes referred to as the "manosphere." The appropriation has been well researched recently by Donna Zuckerberg. For some, the appeal can be summed up in the monumental statue of Marcus Aurelius, a dead white warrior emperor, astride a horse, personifying notions of manly courage and vigor. Zuckerberg rightly laments that many who celebrate the rise of Stoicism as a self-help philosophy "neglect to engage with the popularity of Stoicism in antifeminist internet communities."

Hateful ideologies have long appealed to the ancients for intellectual legitimacy. As classicist Curtis Dozier points out, the white supremacist website Stormfront.org features images of the Parthenon as a backdrop to its slogan "Every month is White History Month." "The implicit argument," says Dozier, "is that since white people built these structures, the white race is superior to other races." His own website *Pharos* (pages.vassar.edu/pharos/) documents many similar ways the Classical past has been appropriated in support of oppressive politics against race and gender.

The misogynist appropriation of Stoicism is especially suspect since the Stoics held that virtue has no gender. As Zeno understood it, an ideal moral community of sages included women in that utopian society. Since the Stoics also held that there are no degrees of perfect wisdom—you either are or are not a sage—women and men are equally sages and equal models for the ideal of full virtue. Moreover, if reason, for the Stoics, is a common feature of all humans, then that also has implications for the education of girls and boys. For even if there are gender differences, so long as reason is shared and at the core of human good, then the cultivation of human good through educating reason ought to be open to all.

Musonius Rufus appeals to this in his advocacy of teaching women as well as men. It is worth quoting the passage in full:

> When someone asked him whether women too should
> do philosophy, this is how he began to argue that they

should. He said: Women have received from the gods
the same rational faculty [*logon*] as men, the faculty that
we use to communicate with one another and to reason
about each thing, whether it is a good thing or not, and
whether it is noble or shameful. Similarly, the female has
the same faculties of sense perception as the male: sight,
hearing, smelling, and the rest. . . . Furthermore, a desire
for ethical excellence and a natural orientation toward it
belong not only to men, but also to women. For women,
no less than men are pleased by noble and just actions,
and reject the opposite.

In short, in the best sort of moral world, women are moral models
no less than men. They may not be astride a horse as a monument
of Stoicism and Roman rule, but by "desire" and "natural orientation," they are fully at home in the world of reason. Education
ought to reflect that, argues Musonius.

More can be said here. The feminist picture is incomplete by
modern standards. But the key point is that feminism has a place
in the ancient world, whether in Plato's *Republic*, Book 5, in the
radical proposal that women are to be included in the guardian
class of the just city, or in the Stoic reconstruction of that ideal
society and its education program.

The broader lesson in this chapter is that invocation of the Stoics
takes many forms. Some of the texts can be abstruse and filled with
newly minted philosophical terms. Others are deceptively simple:
The Stoics give us their own short cuts. Finding effective shortcuts
is, of course, the point of hacking. The Stoics are tech allies because

they often give their own hacks, or at least prototypes of them. They offer pithy quotes that can populate the internet and form the stuff of self-help. Stoicism fits the needs of modern hackers in a way that Aristotelian or Platonic philosophy just doesn't.

But Stoicism is not just about self-help or self-enhancement. It is about moral progress and envisioning ways of enlarging the bonds of community through affiliation and obligation. "Let us cultivate humanity," Seneca says at the conclusion of *On Anger*. One way he argues we can do it is by managing emotions and impulsive impressions that distort. Sometimes we need to learn to pause before we react. In the midst of a groundbreaking national conversation about Black Lives Matter, that is a powerful Stoic lifehack.

SAY THEIR NAMES

Tim Ferriss's fear-setting hack instructs us to face fears concretely. Say the fears. Write them down. Visualize them. That modern Stoic notion of rehearsing fears resonates with me now. Say their names: George Floyd, Ahmaud Arbery, Breonna Taylor, Tony McDade, Trayvon Martin, Freddie Gray, Eric Garner, Ayana Stanley Jones, Michael Brown, Sandra Bland, Tamir Rice, Martin Luther King Jr., Medgar Evans, Malcom X, Emmett Till. The list goes on. For those of us living with white privilege, saying their names is not just memorialization, but fear-setting. It is facing our vulnerability and what we take, and sometimes choose to take, as threats. The Stoics would have us stress the "choose to take." What they teach is that we have more control than we tend to think in changing habits of perception and emotion. Even when arousals are near automatic, we may still need to control what comes next, including assessing whether threats are real, and whether we abuse our power or authority in our reactions. That is a kind of facing fears. It is a kind of courage.

Lucas Vorsterman after Peter Paul Rubens, *Seneca*, 1838, engraving.

Dhyani Buddha Vairocana sculpture from the Borobudur.

LESSON 8

───────── ✦ ─────────

THE ART OF
STOIC LIVING

MEDITATION: WEST
MEETS EAST

Following a Pythagorean custom, Seneca tells us his bedtime meditation is to "interrogate" himself. He combs every crevice for faults and vices, concealing nothing from himself. He is his own "secret examiner," reporting on his character. As a soporific, the nightly exercise may strike modern meditators as odd. If the Stoics teach that wisdom is the path to serenity, and meditating on virtue and vice is at the heart of that wisdom, then how is working full tilt on your character late at night a way to find calm? As a bedtime ritual, will it put you to sleep or keep you awake with brooding? Carl Reiner had a quick answer when Steve Martin called him late one night to discuss the next day's film shooting: Martin asked,

"Am I interrupting you?" Reiner said, "No, I'm just lying here going through a litany of my failures."

The Stoics weren't comedic self-deprecators. They might be more fun to read, if they were. But they *were* self-deprecators: "Bring an accusation against yourself, as stringently as you can," instructs Seneca in the *Letters* to Lucilius. "Then conduct the investigation. Take the role of the accuser first, then the judge, and let that of the advocate come last. Be harsh with yourself at times."

The Greek Stoics had a special term for this introspective examination of the mind: *prosokhē*. It's a way of focusing attention and training vigilance. Epictetus, with usual hyperbole, urges that there is no part of your life "to which attention does not extend." Just a little bit of laxity can lead to a more serious "habit of not paying attention." And before long, you're on the path to moral lassitude: "Is it possible to be altogether faultless? No, that is impracticable." But "we shall have cause to be satisfied if, by never relaxing attention, we shall escape at least a few faults." Contrary to current psychological findings, effort and cognitive focus, on the Stoic view, aren't resources that get depleted. Mental energy is renewable, and concern about how one's doing doesn't weaken self-control or performance by distraction with anxious thoughts. Mental effort only strengthens it.

Marcus follows Epictetus's urging with his own nighttime meditations during the Germanic campaigns. Written to himself and imploring honest moral self-scrutiny, they would become the famed *Meditations*.

Seneca urges a similar heightened vigilance in his nighttime summoning of the mind "to give account of itself." "When the light has been taken away and my wife has fallen silent, aware as she is of my habit," reports Seneca, "I scan the day and retrace all my deeds and words." The day has the usual irritants. With minor adjustments, the irritants could easily be ours. Seneca gives us a sample of his bedtime self-interrogation:

1. You were a bit too direct in what you said to your friend or family member. "You were franker than you should have been in admonishing him. You did not help him, you just annoyed him."

2. You were at a dinner party. The conversation loosened with drink. You overheard a joke "at your expense which struck home." It aimed to sting you and it did. Remind yourself that next time you'll be more careful about the company you keep. (We might think Seneca would remind himself to be less sensitive to slights rather to pledge to avoid certain people. But here is an example of Stoic behavioral and not just cognitive modification: we should try to withhold assent to initial impressions and arousals that may disturb. But we should also try to avoid situations that arouse those responses.)

3. You saw a friend lose her temper when she was refused entrance by a doorman at the home of a prominent lawyer or citizen. "You yourself, on her behalf, lost your temper." Seneca reproves himself. Instead, "Stand back and laugh." ("Roll with the punches," I can hear my own father saying to his earnest daughter.)

4. You were at a banquet and your host seated you at a table in the rear of the room far from the guest of honor, and other persons of note. You're angry with the host, and envious of the guest who's seated where you think you should be. You chide yourself now: "You lunatic," Seneca scoffs. "What

difference does it make" where you're seated? Does your honor or shame, he chides, really depend on where you sit your bottom?

5. Someone has criticized your work and your talent. "Is this to be a rule?" If so, says Seneca, then those you've criticized, the great orators who preceded you—Hortensius, Cicero, and others—"would be your enemy for mocking" their speech writing. Thicken your skin, Seneca tells himself in so many words. Imagine if you were running for office: "You really must put up with the way people vote."

6. And then there are the insults from cocky students or factious litigators. Remember what happened to Diogenes, the Stoic philosopher from Babylon. At the very moment he was lecturing on anger a cheeky student spat on him. He bore it gently and wisely. "No," said Diogenes, "I am not angry. But I am not sure that I should not be." And Cato, says Seneca, had an even wittier repartee when he was pleading a case and one Lentulus, apparently angered by the proceedings, worked up a hefty mass of spittle that landed right on Cato's forehead. Cato kept his calm, and tossed back his own salvo: "I will swear to anyone, Lentulus, that people are wrong to say that you cannot use your mouth." The one-upmanship here doesn't seem to offend Seneca as a not-too-nice downgrade to upgrade your own standing: A sly, intellectual putdown is okay if it keeps a lid on angrier behavior. It deflects a critic and now gives Seneca, ever the rhetorician, an anecdote to entertain his own audience.

Meditations, private or shared, and entertaining or not, are meant to bring calm to the meditator: "Think of the sleep that follows the self-examination! How calm, deep and unimpeded it must be," Seneca assures us. Nighttime meditations followed by pre-meditations the next morning prepare you for the traps that may lay ahead. Again, following a Pythagorean teacher, Seneca says he learned to practice another exercise: when he started to get angry, he would look at his distorted face in a mirror. What "oozed out" was only a "tiny fraction" of anger's "true ugliness." "What if it were revealed naked?" That's what meditative exercises try to lay bare: the true state of the soul.

Honest self-reflection may in the long run earn us peace of mind, but, again, it's not what many of us think of as the stillness of "meditation" or the equable serenity that follows.

If we are practicing a form of Eastern meditation, we are trying to quiet the chattering mind, not arouse it. Ancient Stoic meditation is obviously a different species. It's discursive; it's self-judging; it's disciplined and aspirational; it sets the bar high for striving and insists on markers for evaluating progress. Whether day or night, the method requires talk, even if silent talk. The practice is intensely cognitive. It requires the work of a busy mind.

The Stoics don't offer "hard" empirical evidence for their methods. They are empiricists in the sense that Aristotle was in doing ethics: they survey the phenomena around them and the practices and beliefs, as Aristotle puts it, of "the many and the wise." What the Stoics see is that "the many" try to get joy from "short-lived enticements," from the highs of "election campaigns and crowds of supporters," from "applause and acclamation," from a display of erudition that feeds on accolades and prizes. But all that, urges Seneca, "costs you great anxiety (*sollicitudine*) both to get and to retain." Anxiety is not from *moral* effort but from *misplaced* effort.

Effort better spent is the road to wisdom and to the serenity and "steadiness of joy" that is the sign of wisdom. "This joy has only one source": "a consciousness (*conscientia*) of one's virtue," that is, the "conscientiousness" and "attention" to the habits of the mind that rigorous moral self-examination is meant to afford. Attention is a means. The end goal is certainty in establishing virtue as the only genuine good in life. The Stoics weren't so much interested in how strongly convinced or dogmatic you are in what we believe about your virtue as they were in whether you could rationally and consistently maintain your beliefs in the face of tough tests: *Would* the beliefs you espouse about temperance hold up if you *were* challenged by the enticements of real temptation or ease? That "consistent, virtuous, error-free view of the world" is what constitutes wisdom. It's the achievement of the Stoic sage. And the Stoic sage is rare.

The Stoic sage is a kind of "ethical and epistemic super-being," as philosopher Tad Brennan puts it aptly. Serene joy is an equally rarefied moral emotion, in that upper layer of cultivated rational and "good" emotions reserved, as we saw in Lesson 4, for perfect virtue. Still, the Stoic sage functions as an aspirational touchstone, a model, however remote, of what it might be like to experience calm when we reliably invest in something more meaningful than material riches or a Twitter fanbase. The sage gives us a glimpse at a life free from turbulence. Seneca's metaphor for that moral paradise is equally lofty—a "superlunary heaven," a firmament high above the stars, free from clouds and storms. Idealized moral theory never easily applies to real world conditions, especially if it demands something non-human from humans, namely infallibility. The Stoics are aware of their push to the heavens:

self-examination, Epictetus concedes, may help us "escape at least a few faults." We go for progress.

In all this, the Stoics inherit Socratic wisdom: "The unexamined life is not worth living." John Stuart Mill, the nineteenth-century British utilitarian, would go on to refine a theory of higher pleasures on the basis of it: "Better to be Socrates dissatisfied than a fool satisfied." Higher pleasures derive from activities that exercise our higher capacities. Self-scrutiny is among those activities.

I'm thinking about my own habits now. Some nights my self-reflection does take on a Senecan tone. I need to unpack a day, especially if I am upset by a conversation that I might have had with a family member or close friend. Was I too direct? Should I have bitten my tongue? Did I project my own needs rather than listen? Did my anxiety spill out? I need to talk matters through with myself, maybe meditate through journaling. If I am going through a particularly rough patch, then I seek outside counsel and work on issues. Psychoanalytic and psychodynamic talk therapy, cognitive and behavioral therapy (the latter, in its origins directly influenced by Stoicism) all have been in the mix. In a safe place, with a trusted therapist, I work through how I see things, what I said and did and showed in response, how I could have responded better, listened better, understood another better, forged a better relationship. Sometimes it's the dynamics of a present relationship that are at the center, other times, the near and distant past creeps in. All that is fair game. The therapy can be short-term or long-term, depending on what's being churned up and the external challenges. Is the process calming? Often, yes. For many, myself included, insight and self-observation can be extremely helpful in working through what causes anxiety and depression, or disappointment and anger. Reframing situations can open up space for more adaptive emotions and behavioral patterns. Obviously, these are not the only kinds of therapeutic interventions. Medication for depression or anxiety, such as SSRIs (selective serotonin reuptake inhibitors), have their place. But in their focus on talk, many psychotherapeutic methods owe something to the ancients, and especially the Stoics. Stoic meditation, through talk, is, as they said, a therapy (*therapeia*) of the passions.

But, again, this isn't what many of us have in mind when we say we meditate. We are typically engaging in some form of Eastern meditation—Buddhist, Hindu, Vedic, Taoist, mindfulness, and so on. Calm comes from letting go, not from searching into every crevice for hidden defects. It comes not from rumination, but from finding a space to silence the chatter.

And so, here's another practice. And one I do every morning, and some afternoons, for 20 minutes. It's Vedic meditation, from which transcendental meditation derives. Seated in a comfortable easy chair, with eyes closed, I gently focus on my mantra. As my mind begins to drift into list making and the business of the day, I "favor" the mantra, as a teacher put it, using it as a vehicle to focus my mind on something other than the chattering talk. At some point, I'm just "in the zone." I can't really tell you where I am, but I lose track of time, my head falls to my chest a bit, and I feel remarkably relaxed. I don't set a timer, but check a clock. By now, a few years into the practice, I have a fairly good sense of when 20 minutes is up. I then take about two minutes to ease my way out of the meditation, with my eyes closed. The result: I feel like I have been washed over with a calm that's remarkably restorative.

An afternoon meditation is sometimes even more peaceful: the whirl and spin of a busy day stops for a while. And I get recharged. There is some supporting medical and neurobiological science. And I dip into it on occasion. But what I go on, by and large, is my own self-report. I feel better for meditating. And as a result, like daily exercise, eating healthy, and lifting weights, it's become part of my habit.

Do we have to choose between meditation practices of the East and West? I see little reason why, other than the fact that life is short and that as with any use of our time, we should make wise choices on the basis of the best information, and in this case, what seems effective for living well.

Consider, for example, Shammi Sheth, a young medical doctor with the National Health Service, in practice outside London, with a special interest in elderly care. He came to Stoicism in the wake of a personal crisis. One book and podcast led to another, then journaling, and soon a dive into Stoic texts. "On the face of it, Stoicism sounds inherently quite dull," he confessed, but all the same, it was the "start of the bug." "I just adored the simplicity and the practical side of it."

His spiritual journey, like that of many, draws on an eclectic blend of sources. Born and raised in England in the Jainist faith—an ancient Indian religion with close ties to Buddhism—he never was really religious, though his parents were. But he's studied Buddhism, attended a 10-day silent retreat, and came to experience, he tells me, "the real magic in the silence behind the chattering mind." "It was powerful. Purgative. I felt unburdened." "I wasn't trying to guide myself. I was trying to empty the noise." Stoicism offers something different that appeals to his more analytic side and resonates with philosophical studies that were part of his medical degree at University College, London. While as a doctor he's focused on results and medically proven interventions, as a student of Stoicism he has come to accept that there is a lot that's outside his control. Many of the patients he helps aren't the ones that return for visits to the office. Those who come back are often the ones who aren't improving or whose needs aren't otherwise being met. For some, the problems aren't just about physical health, but have more to do with social and emotional challenges. Stoicism has opened a window for him to see patients in a more holistic way, and to appreciate that doctoring is often about being "an empathetic coach," helping patients to build better life habits. Good doctoring is the model for what the Stoics call "the art of living." By that they mean the goal in life is to do the very best we possibly can, even though, like the skill of the best doctor, it doesn't guarantee the preferred outcome, long life, and enduring health.

Personal journeys, like Shammi's, mix Stoicism and Eastern practices. Some modern Stoics are keen to underscore the points of convergence. Take Tibetan Buddhism and Stoicism. Both focus on freedom from cravings and anxious attachments, spiritual journeys, and mentors who proffer inspirational wisdom. Both view benevolence as an important part of enlightenment. Both view enlightenment as waking up from the stupor of false values. Both teach that we are limited by what we choose as our models and what we focus on as possible. One modern Buddhist theorist pictures layers of realms we live in or imagine: "If some parts of California and Australia spring to mind as the realm of the gods, you can see the demigod realm being acted out every day perhaps in the intrigue and rivalry of Wall Street, or in the seething corridors of Washington and Whitehall. And the hungry ghost realms? They exist wherever people, though immensely rich, are never satisfied, craving to take over this company or that one, or endlessly playing out their greed in court cases." This is from Sogyal Rinpoche's *The Tibetan Book of Living and Dying*. But we could imagine a modern Stoic painting a similar image. Not surprisingly, philosophical teachings that look at human craving, hypocrisy, and ambition have content overlap.

But the foundations of the two philosophical schools couldn't be more different. The Stoics don't posit as fundamental, in the way Buddhists do, the notion that all things in this world are ephemeral or that wisdom requires a robust detachment from self, a "personal selflessness" or "emptiness" that liberates you from the busy-ness of words and discourse and quiets a mind for insight into a deeper reality. The Stoics invest heavily in the self and its reason. Therapy of the emotions is engagement of reason. Cicero says, "row the oars of dialectic," if you are to transform the soul. The Stoics follow that lead. You meditate by argument and by engagement with rival philosophical schools—whether Skeptics, Epicureans, Platonists, Aristotelians, or others. You coin new terms and concepts to be able to carve the world at new joints. Neologisms are not just an exercise in theory. They are aimed at practice and self-transformation. Change, for the Stoics, is at the granular level—noticing what you notice and what you ignore, what impressions you assent to. That act of assenting is forming beliefs and emotions. Stoic meditation is effortful attention that engages reason and keeps a mind busy.

"RELEARN HOW TO PROPERLY LIVE":
IN THE CLASSROOM

"To relearn how to properly live" is how Dobbie Herrion describes Stoic teaching. He's a higher education leader in Missouri, who happened upon Stoicism a few years ago through a philosophy podcast. It was nothing short of a spiritual awakening. It put him at "a crossroads," he says in all earnestness, "hovering between this way of life and that." It humbled him and quieted a temper too easy sparked. "I fell in love with Stoicism. I study it. I read it every day." He quoted me lines from Epictetus, Seneca, Musonius Rufus, and others. He now has a mission to train character through Stoicism. "To not use Stoicism, especially in this time of transition, would be almost unjust."

Dobbie is African American and lives just a few blocks from Ferguson, where Michael Brown, an 18-year-old unarmed Black man, was fatally shot by a police officer in August 2014. The killing sparked the Black Lives Matter movement. We spoke just a few days after the killing of George Floyd in Minneapolis. Ferguson exploded again. Like his neighbors who were part of massive protests, then and now, Dobbie, too, urgently wants "justice and change." But the frontlines for him are not on the streets, but in the classroom. He has teamed up with another practicing Stoic, Bob Cymber, a middle school and high school English teacher, also based in St. Louis. Together they've cofounded Behavior Mods, an ethics and behavioral curricular supplement for K–12. "I grew up as a Christian," Bob told me. He majored in philosophy as an undergraduate. The honesty of Marcus's self-meditations "really spoke to me," and especially, the plea to "be strict with yourself and lenient with others."

Together, they are piloting their program in the St. Louis neighborhoods near where they teach. In one scenario with young elementary school children, they place a bowl full of candy on a desk behind a curtain. Students line up, and are invited, one by one, to help themselves to the sweets. They have to decide "unobserved what's the appropriate amount to take," said Bob. The scenario may bring to mind psychologist Walter Mischel's famous "Marshmallow Test" exposing a four-year-old to a cruel dilemma: a choice between a small reward (one mini marshmallow) that is sitting in front of her, along with a bell that the child could ring at any time to call in the experimenter, or a larger reward (two mini marshmallows) that will be offered to her if she can wait 15 minutes. The experimenters watched through a one-way mirror to see how a child either resisted temptation without any toys or books to distract her, or rang the bell, ate the reward, or maybe showed signs of distress while waiting. Mischel's test is about willpower and allocation of attention away from a tempting reward. In follow-up studies, Mischel discovered that the longer a child could wait, the better she would fare later in life, academically or professionally, and more generally, in terms of being healthier and happier. Self-regulation early on is a powerful predictor over the life course. Bob and Dobbie are not experimental psychologists designing a study about thought and deferred gratification. They're interested in character training. Bob sees the simulation as teaching temperance. Dobbie sees it as teaching equity.

A student has taken more than her fair share. "Well, how do you react to it?" asks Dobbie. "One student gets mad." Another one says, "I'm gonna...yadda yadda yadda." Maybe another starts picking on a student who was at the front of the line. "They're real life situations. Real reactions. We create a moment of pause to let the students see how they are reacting to the situations," Dobbie says. "So, when they leave the school setting, and they go home and their neighbor steals their bike or their mom doesn't get them the shoes they want, they have practiced a different type of behavioral response." They'll feel the "onset of anger," explains Dobbie. But "what we don't want to do is let the anger take them down a path that (1) they've been used to going down and that (2) is uncontrollable once they've gone astray."

Seneca's teaching in *On Anger* is background here: "The first mental agitation induced by the impression of wrong done is no more anger than is the impression itself. The impulse that follows, which not only registers but confirms the impression, is what counts as anger." Seneca, as we saw in Lesson 4, has a view of ordinary emotions, like anger, as chosen actions: Anger is "a movement generated by decision" that "can be eliminated by decision." What these Stoic-inspired teachers are trying to teach is control at that pivotal first moment of decision—the "assent to an evaluative impression." It's that assent to an impression of having been cheated in the case of these young kids, that gets the impulse of anger going.

Of course, fast reactions to impressions often serve us well. These are the mental operations of what psychologist Daniel Kahneman calls System 1—the "automatic system." They enable us to "detect hostility in a voice," "make a disgust face when shown a horrible picture," and "orient to the source of a sudden sound." Seneca describes similar sorts of automatic arousals—recoiling "at the touch" of slimy things or showing "a sudden glint in the eyes" at the sight of an unexpected threat—as examples of pre-emotional responses that don't impugn even a sage's behavior.

But as Kahneman argues, while some quick responses are fine unchecked, others that distort or bias need to be monitored by what he calls System 2, "the more effortful system." We operate routinely with both systems: "When System 1 runs into difficulty, it calls on System 2 to support more detailed and specific processing."

In essence, Bob and Dobbie are trying to open up space for System 2's more effortful monitoring. They're teaching young children how to pause so they recognize charged impressions that can lead to impulsive emotional behavior, like a greedy grab or thirst for payback, and how to find room to explore alternative ways of seeing, feeling, and reacting.

EXEMPLARS AND HEROES

Model the behavior of exemplars. "If you need a model, take Socrates." "Would you like a second model? Take the younger Cato," Seneca writes to Lucilius. "Learn what to do from someone who is already doing it."

The Roman Stoics teach by argument, but also by example. And the examples abound, despite the privileging of Socrates and Cato as the preeminent figures who stood up to fortune's assaults. Cicero boasts that while the Greeks had just a "modest list" of exemplars of courage and temperance, the Romans far outstrip the Greeks in their exemplars. Exemplary material is inexhaustible, he crows, in history and in the present. A later Roman rhetorician, Quintilian, amplifies the boast. The Greeks may have had precepts, but the Romans "produce more striking examples of moral performance."

The tradition of moralizing through examples is central to Roman moral experience. Seneca relies on it regularly in his letters, consolations, and plays. He turns to history for raw material, but also to daily life to set an example and a model for moral guidance. Examples becomes patterns for imitation and emulation. They are more direct than precepts or dialectical arguments. They cut to the chase: "Formal discourse will not do as much for you," he writes to Lucilius, "but direct contact, speaking in person, sharing a meal. You must come and see me . . . learning by precepts is the long way around. . . The quick and effective way is to learn by example." He then lists how Cleanthes was "molded" by Zeno, how Plato and Aristotle "derived more from Socrates' conduct than from his words," how Epicurus influenced his disciples not so much by formal instruction as by companionship and community. In the case of a living example and mentorship, there is the added benefit of mutual growth: "If wisdom were given to me with this proviso, that I should keep it shut up in myself and never express it to anyone else," he confides to Lucilius, "I should refuse it: no good is enjoyable to possess without a companion."

Stoic mentors show you what's possible to endure—as in Stockdale's remarkable "courage under fire" as a POW in Vietnam for more than seven years. Lucilius is encouraged to focus on examples of the mighty who have fallen, a Pompey or a Caligula, in order to grasp that losses afflict even the most powerful. You face your own future by contemplating the fate of others: "if it can happen at all it can happen today." Examples to follow and avoid, moral deterrents as well as moral guides, decayed and privileged examples, and those that have been forgotten or too long hidden are all part of how we learn by example.

In an unwitting way, when I was the ethics chair at the US Naval Academy, I helped keep alive the story of a man of remarkable moral courage whom the Army had once tried to forget. It was the spring of 1998, 30 years after the My Lai Massacre in which a group of US Army soldiers tortured and killed some five hundred unarmed Vietnamese civilians, many women and children and Buddhist priests. Hugh Thompson was the 25-year-old Army helicopter pilot who, with his 18-year-old door gunner, Lawrence Colburn, and his 22-year-old crew chief, Glen Andreotta, landed his helicopter that day and stopped the massacre, likely preventing the massive slaughter of hundreds more. I invited Thompson to speak at the Naval Academy. I knew something of his story, but I also knew that initially the Army had tried to cover up the massacre and that some in Congress at the time had urged him to be punished. What was his crime? When he landed his helicopter, he gave his crew the order: If the GIs try to stop me, "open up on 'em and kill them." "It was time to stop the madness," he said to himself, even if he risked court-martial. Leaving the helicopter with just a sidearm, he put himself between Lieutenant William Calley and Captain Ernest Medina, and the civilians they were marching out of a bunker into a ditch already teeming with bodies. Calley and Medina did not open fire.

I taught with many Navy and Marine retired senior officers who had served in Vietnam. We were committed to teaching midshipmen about the massacre and about the example of an officer who put his career on the line to stop an atrocity.

The lecture was an academy-wide event, but also open to the public. I somewhat naïvely advertised the evening as featuring Hugh Thompson, "the hero of My Lai." I got a flood of

inflammatory emails from those in the greater military community who told me that no service member who gave an order like
his could be called a "hero." I had my examples wrong.

The night of the event came. Thompson gave his talk, followed
by a Q&A. A Vietnam vet, from outside the academy, stood up,
and seething with rage, demanded how Thompson could possibly
have given an order to turn on fellow soldiers. It was treason, he
implied. Thompson kept his calm and gave his reasons. Other
questions followed and Thompson was equally composed. At the
end of the talk, that angry veteran went up to the stage and in tears
embraced Thompson, with the words: "Welcome home, bro." We
all watched. We didn't know how it was going to play out.

Reconciliations of that sort don't always happen. Thompson was
a hunted and haunted man for a long time. The Army wanted to
forget him and blot out the stain of the atrocities. It took 30 years,
that same spring, for the Army finally to recognize Thompson
and his crew's moral courage with the Soldier's Medal awarded to
Thompson and his crew at the Vietnam War Memorial.

Would Thompson's example figure among the exemplars in
a modern Stoicism? Would an updated, retold tale of *Seneca's
Letters to Lucilius* include Thompson? It's an odd thought experiment. How would you recreate the sort of motives that prompt
Seneca's own selection of examples—driving home a point, emulation, deterrence, but also flattery and rhetorical ornament? Still, I
reflected on something similar when I came to write *Stoic Warriors*
about my years at the Naval Academy and the Stoic culture of the
military.

I was struggling with the Stoic view of anger. It was an emotion,
Seneca argued, that would run rampant if given license. It was too

dangerous an emotion to allow in any form. There were better ways to motivate justice than through anger, he insisted. Whetting a warrior's appetite with anger can unleash payback and revenge, precisely the sort of venom that motivated the GIs of the Charlie Company who carried out the My Lai massacre. They wanted payback for buddies who had been killed by mines and booby-traps. It was time to get even.

That may be, but Thompson's courage that morning in March 1968 stood as a vivid counterexample to me. Here was someone whose anger set him in motion, but who then acted with restraint and justice and courage to stop the atrocity. Nonviolent resistance is not a part of armed warfare. But restraint is. Thompson exited his helicopter with only a sidearm. He was not looking for payback, but a way to rescue innocent civilians who were being murdered.

I kept thinking about Thompson as I was writing *Stoic Warriors* and so invited him to speak again, at Georgetown this time. It was now 2002, four years after we had first met. Would he be willing to be interviewed by me before the talk? He was fine with that, and so we settled down to talk in my office for an hour or so before the lecture. As he started recalling that morning in My Lai, tears welled up in his eyes, "Don't make me break down," he said softly. I insisted several times that we could stop. But he wanted to keep talking. It was important, he told me. He relived the morning of March 16, 1968.

He couldn't make sense of his initial impressions as he hovered over the village during routine reconnaissance. Earlier in the morning, there had been no sign of enemy action and no reports of Americans hurt. But now just an hour later, flying over the same site, he and his crew began to see a swath of devastation and a ditch piled high with bodies. His mind began to go places it didn't want to go.

"I guess I was in denial," he said to me. "You've got to understand, we were ready to risk our lives to save these American guys on the ground." And so, he began to construct alternative scenarios for what he was seeing. Maybe the carnage was from an earlier morning aerial artillery. But why then the ditch? He tried out another scenario: Maybe "when the artillery started coming, the enemy ran out into the ditch and a lucky artillery round got them." But every house has a bomb shelter. When artillery is coming, "why are you going to leave this safe bomb shelter and take a walk in the park?" Maybe the Americans did the humane thing, he thought to himself. They dug a mass ditch for the enemy dead caught in the artillery raid. But then he looked again at the ditch. "Everybody isn't dead. Wait a minute. We don't put the living with the dead in a grave." He then settled on what he was afraid to think: "These people were marched down in that damn ditch and murdered." And then he saw the Americans marching out others from their shelters into the ditch. At this point, he radioed for help but got little uptake on the other end. His pleas for help had somehow gotten garbled and were misconstrued as warnings about a threat, and so resulted in delay and more killings, though in hindsight, he now knows better: the messages weren't mangled but ignored.

As he witnessed killings, the anger started to brew. "I was hot. I'll tell you that. I was hot." "I had had enough. Dammit, it ain't gonna happen. They ain't gonna die." I could still see and hear traces of the outrage. He was controlled but emotional. But he also didn't forswear the anger that motivated him then to stop the slaughter.

The time for the lecture came. We walked to the auditorium, filled with Georgetown students and some young cadets and midshipmen from the D.C. area. He told them about My Lai, what he saw, and how he viewed GIs on the ground that morning as the real enemy. He then told them about returning to Vietnam some years back. He went to the village that was the site of the killing field. A frail, aging women rushed up to meet him. She had survived the massacre by playing dead in the ditch. He remembered her. He smiled gently as she looked up at him, imploring, "Why didn't the people who committed the murder come back with you. . . ." She finished her thought without pause but the interpreter's translation lagged behind. ". . . so that we could forgive them?" This was not at all how Thompson thought the sentence would end. "How could this woman have compassion in her heart for someone who is so evil? She's a better person than I am." Mercy, compassion, the possibility of reining in anger, all were on display at that moment in this survivor's question. And this as told to us by a man who had earlier said what motivated him to rescue that women and others like her was fury. Call it moral indignation, call it moral outrage. It was still anger.

Would a Stoic permit it? The Stoics don't believe that injuries others inflict are serious wrongs. Anger is always mistaken as a motive, so they can't really help us here. Acting on principle is what they offer instead. But clearly that won't do. It would be hard to imagine Thompson remaining calm once he accepted the true horrors of what he saw. Perhaps we should give his anger a special term, "transitional anger" as the philosopher Martha

Nussbaum does, to mark the fact that Thompson wasn't focused on retaliation but amelioration—rescue of innocents. He wasn't wishing ill on the offenders. If anger comes with the idea of payback, then that isn't what motivated Thompson's actions. Still, Thompson came to view what Calley and his unit did that day as evil. And he wasn't ready to forgive them without atonement on their part.

Teaching by example, on its own, is always inadequate. It is a jumping-off point for analysis and context, question and examination. We are inspired by examples, but we need to know what we are emulating and why. And in the case of Stoic models of courage, we need to be ready to question Stoicism's own account of moral motivation. Anger may sometimes take us down the right path and one we might not otherwise go down if we accept with calm what we see.

A DANCE AND A GAME OF CATCH

Ancient and modern Stoics can seem far too self-absorbed. As daily meditation, the art of Stoic living is a way of looking inward to control what's outward. Examine yourself morning and night, pre-rehearse, set your fears, arm yourself for the assault of life's challenges. Be prepared. Anticipate. These are lessons we've been exploring. But it can sound like fortress-building. Learn to be undisturbed not just by knowing what you can and can't control, but by fortifying the boundary between you and what's outside. And yet, we've argued throughout, the Stoics urge a socially engaged and connected life. They urge a fellowship of moral learners and a view of humanity as deeply shared and cooperative. That is key to our resilience. And it is key to our flourishing. But if that's so, then how is meditation and the mental effort of noticing and being aware not just about me, but about others and the give and take of our relationships?

The question is at the heart of Seneca's explorations in *On Favors*. Exchanges of goodwill and gratitude depend on noticing attitude and the emotional overlays of the exchange. "Is there any virtue which we Stoics respect more or do more to stimulate? Is there anyone better fitted to encourage it than we are with our stress on the sanctity of human fellowship?" His essay is aptly addressed to one "Liberalis." But we soon learn that "liberality" or generosity doesn't depend on grandeur or magnificence. The attitude expressed, and not the size or glitter of the gift, is key. "The mind is what raises small things high, casts lustre on dingy things, discredits things that are great and valued."

Attitude is expressed, Seneca goes on to tell us, through emotions. And so, the art of Stoic living, not surprisingly, includes lessons in emotional expression—how to show feelings, including how to fake them at times. And how to detect them in others. This is a strange preoccupation for a Stoic, we might muse. But not really. The Stoics are counselors of the emotions and emotional behavior—teaching how to shift cognitive focus to begin to loosen disappointment and grief, or, in the case at hand, express and read generosity or its absence. The Stoics see strong shades of will in what we show on our faces or express in the intonations in our voice. By paying heed to the nuances of emotional expression, we become better in taking on the many roles (*personae*) we play in life. Sometimes, like good actors, we get to choose the plays that "are most suited" to our talents, Cicero notes. Other times, we have to work with whatever roles we are given.

In gift-giving, says Seneca, we should watch how others see us. The "gift was great—but he hesitated, he put it off, he groaned as he gave it, he gave it haughtily, he flaunted it about; it was not the beneficiary he wished to please; he did it for his ambition, not for me." We "spoiled" a favor "by silence," or "with a look of reluctance." Premeditate, next time, on the impressions we leave and what we pick up in others' comportment. Cicero gives similar advice: We can judge fitting actions "from a glance of the eyes, from the relaxation or contraction of an eyebrow . . . from a raising or lowering of the voice, and so on." These views about emotional signaling are precursors to theories that would come some two thousand years later, in Darwin's seminal work on the expression of emotions and more contemporary research on facial expression by Erving Goffman, Paul Ekman, and Wallace Friesen, among others.

Conferring gifts, Seneca teaches, requires emotions expressed aptly, and attunement to the responses. Gift-giving and gratitude are a kind of dance, he says, pointing to the three Graces or muses, who joining hands in a circle, give, accept, and return in a smooth, coordinated movement: "There is a sequence of kindness, passing from one hand to another, which comes back none the less to the giver, and that the beauty of the whole is lost if the sequence is anywhere interrupted." Think of dancers in a *corps de ballet*, say in *Swan Lake*. The ensemble moves as one mass as each dancer's sequenced movement undulates from one body to another. There's connectivity. No gap. We have seen that the Stoics, and especially Marcus in his visceral battlefield image of body parts, appeals to the ideal of organic human connection.

Exchanges of goodwill are like a game of catch, Seneca illustrates with a different image: "a good player needs to send it off differently to a tall partner than to a short one." If you want the ball to be caught, you gauge the pitch to the catcher, so it has a better chance of being caught and returned. If you are a coach, or a parent in the playground teaching your child, you tailor the game not only to the height of the young catcher, but to the skill level, and from there nudge progress along. If a game of catch is not just about skill, but all the other things that go into play—fun, frustration, and the need for encouragement and support, then the game is also a moment for the parent, to read emotions, and for the child, to manage them.

Contemplating the subtle contours of emotional exchange is not the usual fare of modern Stoic practice. Modern Stoics talk more about lifehacks to beat fear or disappointment, rejection or grief. "Self-improvement," "personal development," is what I hear often from those who turn to Stoicism for spiritual guidance. But the ancient Stoics always viewed doing well or flourishing as a social project, both in how it is achieved and what its content is. Living virtuously is how we live well with others. Seneca's claim is that social fellowship is finely textured, a matter of noticing a furrowed brow, an air of arrogance, a groan, hesitation, or on the positive side, the warmth of a smile or a shared laugh.

We now know from developmental psychologists that from early infancy onward we track gestures and teach ourselves resilience, trust, and mutual love through them. We orient ourselves in the world to what's safe or dangerous by being exquisite readers of countless muscles in the face. (The blind track through other senses.) Part of being "at home in the world" (*oikeiōsis*), that basic Stoic notion of lifelong development and social orientation, Seneca is now saying, requires reading the signs of goodwill and when it's missing. We are "mind readers," reading intention through emotional signs and signals: "You cannot have a favour if the best part of it is missing—the judgment that went into it." The modern philosopher P. F. Strawson echoes the point: "We should consider in how much of our behavior the benefit or injury resides mainly or entirely in the manifestation of attitude itself." Seneca's teaching is that the presentation of attitude may itself have an element of practice: Attitude is manifest in emotions, some candid, some performed, some nursed so that we might come to feel what we show. It may take labor.

Seeing emotions is another way of noticing and paying attention. It is a form of attention directed not inward, but outward at others with whom we share the world.

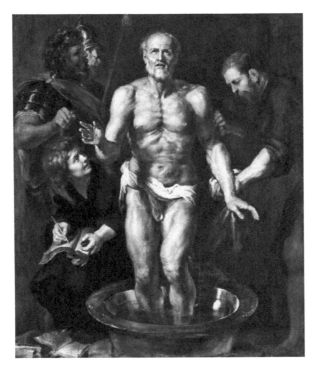

Peter Paul Rubens, *The Dying Seneca*, 1612/1613, oil on panel.

———— ✦ ————

A HEALTHY
MODERN
STOICISM

A FINAL MOST UNLIKELY TEST

"Cyclist vs. Deer." That was the heading on the medical report the nurse handed me. A final test had come as I was finishing this book, and I hadn't exactly pre-rehearsed this event. My husband Marshall was cycling in Rock Creek Park not far from our home when a deer couldn't make up its mind which way to cross the road. It started one way, got almost to the other side, saw a car coming, and then turned back and crossed the road again. My husband and the deer collided. The deer got away injury-free. My husband ended up with seven broken ribs, a collapsed lung, and a dislocated shoulder. He took a "really bad beating," an ER doc told me, as I became faint hearing the news. "We're going to have to take him to a trauma center in D.C."

Covid was raging here. My husband and I had taken all precautions and were essentially in lockdown for five months. And now we were headed to a big city hospital.

What should I think, as a Stoic? Epictetus was whispering in my ear: "It's only his body."

You've got to be joking, I'm thinking. His brain is his body. We have friends who are doctors, helping me understand "flailed chests," pneumonia threats, pulmonary functions, neurological issues, what to watch out for cognitively. Any cognitive deficits, they're asking? "Only his body?" Stockdale may have had his leg pummeled as a downed Navy aviator now in enemy hands, and then was tortured as a POW for more than seven years. He found his salvation in Epictetus, a once enslaved Stoic and fellow cripple. But my husband wasn't a POW. And the enemy I had been worried about of late was a vicious virus that we were doing our best to smartly fight. I wasn't thinking about his body taking a hit from an indecisive deer.

"A bad beating" kept racing through my head. I had been focused all week in thinking about brutal beatings of enslaved Romans and Stoic commentary. The Stoics famously minimize pain of the body. But they also blur the distinction between what you suffer due to bad luck and what you suffer due to others' injustice. Getting hit by a deer, when you're a careful and conscientious cyclist, is bad luck. Being flogged or tortured as an enslaved person is nothing other than injustice.

Seneca famously rails against brutality toward enslaved Romans. But it's more self-serving than rooted in a defense of

humanity: those who are enslaved can turn on those who en-
slave them; better to have them be grateful than afraid; do them
a favor, and they may return one, including the favor of taking
your place in death: "Suppose I show you someone fighting for his
master's safety without regard for his own, riddled with wounds
yet pouring out from his very entrails what blood is left there and
seeking, so as to give his master time to escape, a respite for him at
the cost of his own life." The moral lesson is that enslaved persons
are capable of benevolence. The political lesson for the intended
audience, the elite who are Seneca's peers, is that it pays to curb
your anger when contemplating flogging your servant. The body,
its integrity and its pain, a person and the respect due their humanity, were not part of either lesson.

We are all enslaved to external powers, the Stoics teach. But
they also teach that some of us have more worldly power than others. Morality is one thing; legality and social reality another. The
Stoics never challenge the institution of enslavement.

This sets us up for a final reckoning. How do we build a healthy
modern Stoicism on the foundation of ancient Greek and Roman
culture? In the current "cancel culture" with monuments of oppression toppling, why consort with ancient philosophers who
not only condoned enslavement but celebrated inner freedom as
the most noble kind of liberation?

Diogenes the Cynic, an iconic figure for the Stoics, may have
cross-dressed, showed off body parts in public, and spurned marriage as a convention, but however unconventional, he didn't
argue against the convention of enslavement, even though himself enslaved. He looked for a different kind of freedom and mastery. Hence, his brazen quip on the auction-block as he pointed

to a Corinthian in the crowd: "Sell me to this man; he needs a master." Inner mastery was the real liberation. Epictetus, the most famous of enslaved Stoics, became well-educated and a teacher with scores of followers, including an emperor. But he never argued against the institution of enslavement; if flogging an enslaved person was morally objectionable, the evil was in the degradation of the person in power, not in the degradation of the person flogged. In a similar vein, his teacher Musonius Rufus taught that the problem with adulterous sex with an enslaved woman is weakness of will on the part of the male adulterer, not any unjust treatment toward the woman. The true power of an enslaved person is spiritual independence of fortune and assault. Weak control of desire is the sin, whether it is consorting with an enslaved woman, or a married or unmarried woman consorting with an enslaved man. There's gender equity here, but the real sin, a weak will, is worse in a man.

Enslavement is universal: we are all hostages to fortune and the cravings of our bodies. Freedom is also universal: we all share in humanity and reason. Contrary to what Aristotle taught, the Stoics took it as near cliché that enslavement has no basis in nature. We are in a community of common origin and common fate.

That may be. But equality of spirit is not equality of everyday social reality. Seneca, for a good part of his life, lived in opulence. His retinue of enslaved house servants would make Downton Abbey look understaffed. The Stoics invest in community and reliance on others for strength. But in practice, that reliance isn't always benign. Your body, preaches Epictetus, is "like a poor overburdened ass" weighted down with its own "pack-saddles" and "bridles." It's a tool that can get "pressed into public service."

"Don't resist or mutter, otherwise you will get a beating." This is the enslaved person's side of the bargain.

So, as we conclude these lessons in modern Stoicism, I show my hand, if it hasn't been already. I teach and write about ancient and modern ethics. I adore texts, I pore over them, I argue with them, and I insist that my students read them carefully and argue hard with them. I am not an orthodox Stoic (whatever that could mean for a modern), or just an expositor of texts. I have put myself in the position of a curious and inquisitive neo-Stoic, capturing the best of ancient Stoicism and lessons worthy of a modern Stoicism.

In building a healthy modern Stoicism, I've implicitly adopted certain principles as background guides:

1. Psychological mastery can't be at the cost of human vulnerability.
2. Reliance on others depends upon building communities of cooperation, respect, and support.
3. Denying pain, whether of a body or mind, is not a permanent solution for grit.
4. Monitoring quick impressions includes watching for distortions and bias produced by fear and anger, as well as desire.

For each of these principles, I have shown how we get footholds in Stoic texts—some to do with the multi-layers of emotions, others with notions of empathy and global human connectedness, still others to do with psychological and moral distress and the role of compassion in healing, and yet others with the role of effortful attention. I have been respectful of the texts. But I also have let them talk to us, and have allowed us to talk to them and question them and consider new applications.

Still, we haven't had a proper reckoning with the Stoics on the institution of enslavement. In a time of our own reckoning with our history of enslavement, we need to. How do we assess a modern Stoicism in the age of Black Lives Matter?

Seneca's remarks are our focus, and in particular, his 47th *Letter*. Although modern scholars once took his remarks there as enlightened and an ancient underpinning of contemporary humanistic thinking, it is now generally regarded as quite the opposite. Seneca may have "pleaded a powerful case for the humane treatment" of those who were enslaved, but more out of expediency than social conscience. The institution of enslavement was critical to the Roman elite. As imperial adviser to Nero, Seneca's emphasis was squarely "on acceptance of the status quo."

"'THEY ARE SLAVES.' NO, THEY ARE HUMAN BEINGS."

So Seneca opens his letter to Lucilius on how to treat enslaved servants in your household. He continues in rapid volley with his alter-ego: "'They are slaves.' No, they are housemates. 'They are slaves.' No, they are lowborn friends." The next salvo delivers the pivotal moral lesson: "'They are slaves.' Fellow slaves, rather if you keep in mind that fortune has its way with you just as much as with them." You are "born of the same seeds." Disasters can lay "highborn nobles" low. Shared fortune and shared humanity are equalizers.

Still, the highborn noble employs, and the enslaved is a tool, as Aristotle had said, even if now, for the Stoics, tools by convention and chance only. And a tool for what? To wipe up spit and vomit at banquets, to carve the expensive fowl and carry the cup of wine, to serve drinks in public, but cater to lust in private—"for he is a boy only at the party: in the bedroom he's the man." He knows this highborn's taste, which foods "stimulate his palate," which ones make him "queasy," which ones he has a "hankering for," "which please his eye." He knows with whom he likes to dine, and who is "beneath his dignity." It's an intimate knowledge, now cataloged from the side of power, written for a peer group whose habits and household economy depended on enslaved workers.

Seneca's own list of household functions for servants went on and on: "cook, baker, masseurs, bath attendant, personal trainer, major-domo [chief steward]"; ostentatious households, like his, would have had, in addition, hairdressers, guest-announcers, valets and chamber maids, porters and ushers, litter bearers, those who restrained the sick and insane. You depended on the enslaved help from waking moments to the meditative hours of night. You needed them for the business of a gentrified daily life—inside the house to meet every whim and need and outside the house to tend to the garden and lands. It is no surprise that "fugitive slaves are almost an obsession in the sources. . . . Slaveowners did not suffer such loss of property lightly." To lose an enslaved worker was a major disruption in household lifestyle and economy.

Seneca may be meditating at night on how to curb rage at a household servant, precisely because flogging an enslaved worker who makes too much noise at dinner or who disturbs the landowner when he is working on his household accounts (or, closer to home, his self-account "when the light has been taken away and my wife has fallen silent") was not at all unusual. Rehearsing restraint, at bedtime or morning meditations, might mean the enslaved person won't run away, or turn on you in an inquisition under brutal torture.

This is the social setting of humane treatment of enslaved Romans in Seneca's milieu. It's an accommodation to convention. The moral setting is nobler—we are all enslaved. "Show me who isn't! One person is a slave to lust, another to greed, a third to ambition—and all are slaves to hope; all are slaves to fear." Enslavement is a mental state. And a shared one at that. So don't look "for friends only in the Forum or in the Senate House." They are in your backyard and in your household. A person's "clothing" or "position in life" is no indication of their true freedom. It is the mind that should be free.

This is both the attraction of Stoicism and its pernicious side. Throughout this book, I have tried to turn the modern Stoic outward—realizing the promise of belonging in the world, connectedness, and shared reason and humanity. And I have widened the angle of will and attention so that they monitor a wider range of impressions that affect our well-being, or *eudaimonia*. This is the full promise of Stoicism and its Socratic inheritance: to examine and cross-examine ourselves about what we take to be the goods and bads in the world. For the Stoics, "false" goods and bads have to do with the externals, or indifferents—what is outside the genuine good of rationality and its perfection in virtue.

But the Stoics never make rationality indifferent to external resources. Quite to the contrary, wisdom is in selecting or preferring those goods that are, for the most part, in accord with nature. They are what we would take: health over disease, sufficient material means over penury, good children and friends over those who are evil. Those preferences, and how we express them in the messy world of action, are the concrete manifestation of our virtue. Reason and its excellence or perfection are the genuine good because they are fundamental to our collective well-being. We obviously can't control all outcomes. But we can cultivate reason, curiosity, a respect for the truth, and a belief that everyone deserves adequate resources to cultivate reason. That is the Stoic seed, even if not sown in their own times.

So, in constructing a modern Stoicism, can Stoicism meet the challenge?

Kant, in the European Rational Enlightenment, begins the work. He develops the notion of reason as shared. It becomes the foundation of moral law that we, and not gods or nature or the cosmos, create. It binds us and is the source of moral obligations and duties that hold universally, without exemptions based on expedience or self-interest. Kant crafts a powerful principle of humanity to block treating persons as mere means with price tags, even though his writings, penned almost two millennia after Seneca's, are no pure model for emancipation for all human beings.

TEXTS AND CONTEXTS

So how do we deal with texts that have morally troubling strands? Do we expunge those bits? Do we choose not to teach them or, more radically, banish that author's work as a whole? Or do we try to do what the Stoics themselves teach in their better moments: show judgment and flexibility to meet the challenges? I choose the latter. In the case at hand, the challenges are understanding times different from our own and views influenced (sometimes far too heavily) by those historical frames.

Philosophy is never ahistorical, even if it pretends to be. Even when it takes the view "from nowhere," it's written from the ground, by flesh and blood humans, influenced by and often reacting to their culture and practices and predecessors.

Philosophy prides itself as the discipline of argument. But its practice is never just pure argument. It's a discipline that gathers followers and faithful, disciples, like those who met in Athens, in the cool of a fresco-lined portico, or in the gymnasium of the Lyceum, or the Academy.

Still, the Roman Stoics are a different breed of philosopher from Aristotle and Plato, or even the ancient Greek Stoics who met at that colonnaded portico. They argue, but they also preach and sermonize. That has been part of their enduring historic appeal. And it is again, behind the great Stoic revival. Stoic philosophy can be a secular religion, a spiritual practice focused on goodness and moral progress without the accretions of establishment religion.

Historically, the direction of influence obviously went the other way. Early Judeo-Christian thinkers absorbed some of the pagan philosophy. That, in part, is why Stoicism remains so deeply familiar to many of us. Its theories about emotional control and mustering will to guard against temptation and sudden impulse or impressions—all this appealed to earlier Western religious thinkers. They used Stoicism to interpret sacred texts and guide moral progress.

Stoicism brings, in its own right, a tradition not of worship, but of meditative practice. While Stoic meditation is not the stilling of the chattering mind familiar from Eastern practices, it is meant, in the end, to help find calm in dealing with the big and not so big challenges of everyday life. It's a discipline of prudence, not fear, where prudence, somehow, isn't obsessive. The promise is tranquility.

THE WAY FORWARD

We are living in anxious times. Our conception of politics has become upended. Our democracy is threatened. Our control of disease has been tested. Economic, social, and health inequities rip open the sin of enslavement and the legacy of Jim Crow America. There is moral outrage in the streets. Unemployment is at its highest since the Great Depression. All this makes it hard to know how to go forward. We need leaders, we need education, we need science, and we need greater equity.

The Stoics can't help us with all of that. They can give us solace in some corners—lessons about our mortality, lifehacks for facing fears, ways to manage disabling emotions, better ways to be prepared for sudden shifts in fortune, a sense of connectedness that supports resilience, the place of benevolence and gratitude in our lives. Cultivating humanity, Seneca's rallying call, is an unfinished business. What we need to do is not just soul repair, but social repair. "Some things are up to us and others not." It's not what happens to you, but how you react to it that matters. These are Epictetus's familiar teachings. But we can't accept the historical fact of Epictetus's enslavement to justify our own retreat. That is cowardice, given who we are, our times, and the profound moral and political challenges we face. What we cannot accept, we have to change. And we have to change it by changing not just us, but the institutions and social structures that frame who we collectively are. It is a social project, requiring social grit and a belief in the unity of humanity. That's what Marcus envisioned on the battlefield as he beheld its opposite—human beings torn asunder in strewn body parts. That's what happens, he wrote to himself, when you cut yourself off from the community and the well-being of that whole. You make yourself an "outcast" of humanity.

The Stoics warn about the corruption of values—false glory, greed, excessive materialism. Seneca warns about tyrants who demand loyalty. He knows about speechwriters who paper over palace killings, who write about mercy to calm a worried public that the murder of a rival would be the end, not the beginning of more bloodshed. Seneca is that speechwriter and his hands are dirty. His philosophical writings strain with the tensions of power and the fear of losing it, loyalty and its costs, opulence and abstinence. He writes, in part, as prayers for redemption. He writes for freedom.

Stoicism is a way to endure and cultivate inner virtue when tight control from outside threatens your very being. It was a philosophy suited for the times. It again feels like a philosophy for the times. But we are moderns. We have much to learn from the ancients. But we also have mistakes to avoid. Stoic discipline and resilience, virtue and the bonds of reason and rationality can help unite us to face our individual and shared challenges. But only when empathy and mercy course through the veins of reason. That is a way forward. It is a way forward as a healthy modern Stoic.

ACKNOWLEDGMENTS

THIS BOOK was written during the pandemic, isolated from our children and grandchild, who live in California, and from friends and colleagues. The only silver lining in the quarantine has been the absence of distractions. That, plus a serendipitously timed sabbatical and research leave, made the writing of this book possible. For continued institutional support, I am profoundly grateful to Georgetown University and my wonderful chair, Bill Blattner. He has held our department together with brilliance and good cheer in these trying times. I owe thanks, too, to Georgetown President Jack DeGioia, Provost Bob Groves, and Dean Chris Celenza for their support, especially as we all pivoted to a new way of coming together as a teaching, learning, and research community.

The book got a head start during a graduate seminar on Stoic Ethics in the fall of 2019. It was a vibrant in-person class, text-driven with students and faculty. In the class were ardent Stoic sympathizers and ardent skeptics. I am grateful to everyone in that class for helping breathe new life into the texts. I am especially grateful to philosophy colleagues Rachel Singpurwalla (University of Maryland) and Marcus Hedahl and Michael Good (US Naval Academy) for joining the seminar that term. And I am grateful to the graduate students—Beba Cibralic, Christopher Kochevar, Elisa Reverman, Megan Ritz, Andy Sullivan, Jeffrey Tsoi, and Ari Watson—for their engagement with these strange and hard texts.

I owe a singular debt to Katherine Ward, my research assistant, and now Assistant Professor at Bucknell University. She helped me throughout this project with her usual calm and efficiency, remarkable research skills, and terrific judgment.

I previewed some of the ideas in this book at seminars and lectures here and abroad. I am grateful for the lively conversations and thank all those who extended invitations to me. Among those lectures and institutions are: The McCain Keynote Lecture, US Naval Academy; The Blegen Lecture, Vassar College; Jean Beer Blumenfeld Center for Ethics, Georgia State University; European International Society for Military Ethics (EuroIsme), Vienna; Danish Institute for International Studies, Copenhagen; ARQ National Psychotrauma Center, (Diemen) Amsterdam; Ethics of War and Peace Keynote, West Point Academy; Western-Chinese Ethics of War and Peace, University of Virginia; National Endowment for the Humanities Coming Home Dialogues with New America Foundation; Emerson College, Boston; John Deigh Book Fest, University of Texas School of Law (remarks to appear as "Shame & Guilt: From Deigh to Strawson & Hume, and Now to the Stoics" in *Philosophy and Phenomenological Research* book symposium); Cultural Heritage and the Ethics of War Keynote, Arts and Humanities Research Council (AHRC, UK) (presented in writing only due to pandemic); NIH Department of Bioethics, Joint Bioethics Colloquium, Bethesda.

At the ARQ Trauma Center in Amsterdam, I am especially grateful to Annelieke Drogendijk, Jackie June ter Heide, and Marlene van de Ven. I thank Bart Nauta for his case study with Aart Van Oosten. For conversations about moral injury and its treatment, I am grateful to Shira Maguen and her colleagues at the San Francisco VA Health Care System, and to Brett Litz of the VA Boston Health Care System. At the Danish Institute for International Studies, I am grateful to Robin Schott, Johannes Lang, and Joanna Bourke for the opportunity to think more about resilience and moral injury.

I thank Simon Drew for his interest in modern Stoicism and for introducing me to Bob Cymber, Dobbie Herrion, Jeff Loesch, and Shammi Sheth. I also thank the BBC World Service for inviting me to participate in their radio Forum: *Calm in the Chaos: The Story of the Stoics* with other guests Massimo Pigliucci and Donald Robertson. The program set me thinking again about Stoicism and my complicated relationship with it.

Stoic Wisdom owes an enormous debt to my editor at Oxford University Press, Peter Ohlin. He was enthusiastic from the beginning and an astute and quick reader, lesson by lesson, line by line. The mistakes are all mine, but I owe him much for helping me avoid many more. It was a great pleasure to work with him so closely, especially during this time of isolation. I also owe thanks to my agent Jim Levine, who saw promise in this book from its inception. His keen judgment at critical moments has been invaluable.

I am indebted to Emily Bang, editorial assistant at OUP, for her work in preparing the manuscript for copyediting.

Seneca teaches that how we show gratitude matters. My husband Marshall Presser is a very funny and witty man. I wish I had one fraction of his humor. If I did, I would have just the right joke to tell right now to express my gratitude and love. But telling jokes is his thing, not mine. So, Marshall, I thank you for the life we have shared since we met while living abroad in Edinburgh, and I thank you for the family we have created—our amazing children, Kala and Jonathan, their wonderful partners, Jonathan's Elaine and Kala's Austin, and Jonathan and Elaine's adorable little Max.

Nancy Sherman
Kensington, Maryland
August 27, 2020

NOTES

LESSON 1

Page 1 **It's the right "operating system"**: https://www.wired.co.uk/article/susan-fowler-uber-sexism-stoicism.

Page 6 **That's what "man makes of himself"**: See Aurelius (2011, 8.34).

Page 6 **"I am a citizen of the world"**: See Laertius (1925, 6.63).

Page 8 **Emerson . . . Stoic notion of self-mastery**: See Woelfel (2011).

Page 11 ***Hercules Furens* (*Hercules Raging*)**: For a minority view that the plays were not written by Seneca the philosopher, see Thomas (2003). I am grateful to Margaret Graver, Martha Nussbaum, and Amy Richlin for correspondence about this.

Page 15 **Philo captures the Stoic paradox with a pair of treatises**: See Garnsey (1996, p. 157).

LESSON 2

Page 18 **He could take in good food and wine**: Wilson (2007, p. 72ff.).

Page 18 **Aristophanes satirizes him**: Using Wilson trans. Wilson (2007, p. 73) quoting *The Clouds* (362–363).

Page 19 **a snub nose "doesn't put a barricade between the eyes"**: Xenophon (2013, 5.4–5.7).

Page 19 **Socratic irony**: Vlastos calls it "complex irony" Vlastos (1991, p. 31).

Page 19 **"I do not think I know what I do not know."**: Plato (1978, 21d).

Page 19 **The irony isn't feigned ignorance**: Vlastos (1991, p. 36). See end of *Symposium* for Alcibiades's yearning for a bit of Socrates's virtue (Plato, 1997a).

Page 20 **Nature must have so constructed us**: See Frede (1987, pp. 151–153).

Page 20 **Zeno was the first head of the Stoa**: See Long (1999, p. 623).

Page 20 **he is often part of a duo with Socrates**: See Long (1999, p. 623).

Page 20 **he rolled the tub over hot sands**: Laertius (1970, 6.22–24). For a wonderful portrait, see Gérôme (1860).

Page 20 **Following the Cynic rule on dress**: Laertius (1970, 6.22).

Page 21 **brings to mind Abbie Hoffman**: Boissoneault (2017).

Page 21 **"he was at home nowhere—except in the universe"**: Schofield (1999b, p. 64).

Page 21 **He spurned marriage**: Laertius (1970, 6.29).

Page 21 **he championed unisex clothing and liberally showing off body parts**: Laertius (1970, 7.32–34).

Page 22 **"demagogues the lackeys of the people"**: Laertius (1970, 6.41; 6.74).

Page 22 **get rid of errors of conduct**: Laertius (1970, 6.42).

Page 22 **"An ignorant rich man"**: Laertius (1970, 6.48).

Page 22 **Philip freed him**: Laertius (1970, 6.43).

Page 22 **"The great thieves are leading away the little thief"**: Laertius (1970, 6.46).

Page 22 **"Socrates gone mad."**: Laertius (1970, 6.54).

Page 23 **the substance of his teachings**: Laertius (1970, 6.63).

Page 23 **teaching by a strenuous mental training**: Laertius (1970, 6.70–71).

Page 23 **"capable of outright victory over anything"**: Laertius (1970, 6.71).

Page 24 **Others . . . also set up schools**: For a wonderful introduction to the changing milieu of ancient philosophy in the agora, see Long and Sedley's introduction (Long & Sedley, 1987b).

Page 24 **Malcom Schofield**: Schofield (1999b). Also, Schofield (1999a).

Page 24 **Zeno . . . an ideal cosmopolitan city**: Plutarch (1034F) as quoted in Schofield (1999b, p. 25).

Page 24 **"beneficent, kind, well-disposed" to humans**: Arius Didymus in Eusebius as quoted in Schofield (1999b, p. 67). Also, see Cicero *De Natura Deorum* 2.3 in Schofield (1999b, p. 67).

Page 25 **We are by nature social and political animals**: Aristotle (1984a, NE 1097b11); Laertius (1970, 7.24).

Page 25 **"take on the complexion of the dead."**: Laertius (1970, 7.2).

Page 26 **no one was a more hapless youth**: Laertius (1970, 7.21).

Page 26 **central in Greek Stoic thought: logic, physics, and ethics**: For debate about how connected these areas of study are, see the symposium on Julia Annas's *The Morality of Happiness* (Annas, 1995; Cooper, 1995; Sherman, 1995a).

Page 26 **"prevents us from seeing the situation as a whole"**: Laertius (1970, 7.111–112).

Page 27 **"he alone was strong enough to carry the load of Zeno"**: Laertius (1970, 7.171).

Page 28 **"In industry," Chrysippus "surpassed everyone,"**: Laertius (1970, 7.171).

Page 28 **The unruliness of emotions . . . encrusted parts of modern thought**: In his ethical writings Immanuel Kant, the preeminent philosopher of the Rational Enlightenment, aligns with the Stoics in his normative view that emotions can be excessive and irrational and so, unreliable moral motivators on their own. For a critique of what Kant learns from the Stoics on the emotions and a piecing together of his often unappreciated and complex views on how emotions figure in the moral life, see Sherman (1997b).

Page 29 **His works, *On Moral Ends* and *On Duties* indispensable in European political thought**: I am indebted to Miriam Griffin's introduction to Cicero (1991) and King's introduction to Cicero (1927).

Page 29 **The tension is a recurrent theme**: Seneca (2015, 108.15–16). See Wilson (2019) for a lively biography of Seneca to which I am indebted in this capsule biography. Also, I have learned enormously from the classic M. Griffin (1976).

Page 31 **he showed her limited gratitude**: Wilson (2019).

Page 31 **the mirror sometimes turns outward**: Wilson (2019).

Page 32 **Seneca is a pragmatist**: See esp. *Letters* 102 and 79.13. In the latter essay, "glory is the shadow of virtue" (Seneca, 2015). I am indebted here to the excellent discussion of Seneca's quest for revised glory in Edwards (2017).

Page 32 **he has fallen into recent obscurity**: Despite an important translation by Cora Lutz in 1947 (Rufus, 1947). For recent translations, see C. King (2011). See Nussbaum's translations in the appendix to her superb essay (Nussbaum, 2002).

Page 32 **"waiting quietly through the wild riot"**: Tacitus *Annales*, xvi.32, Tac. Hist. i.14; 17 as quoted in Parker (1896).

Page 33 **Epictetus was among them.**: Parker (1896).

Page 33 **"the Same Excellence . . . Belongs to a Man and a Woman."**: Nussbaum (2002, p. 287).

Page 33 **The writings are informal**: See Margaret Graver's excellent *Stanford Encyclopedia of Philosophy* entry on Epictetus (Graver, 2017).

Page 34 **Though a popularizer**: I am indebted in this brief biography to Tony Long's superb work on Epictetus, especially in his introduction in Epictetus (2018) and Long (2002).

Page 34 **the gifted ones couldn't be easily repelled**: Epictetus (1995, 3.6.10).

Page 35 **equestrian statue**: One of the few, if not the only, equestrian statues from antiquity to have survived. Relevant here is a note from Walters

Art Museum in Baltimore regarding a reduction of the monumental statue that they hold in their collection: Of the original, they note: "dedicated in AD 176—the only equestrian statue from antiquity to have survived. It escaped being melted down for cannon because it was thought to represent Constantine, the first Christian emperor. In the early 1500s, the rider was correctly re-identified as the Roman Emperor Marcus Aurelius" ("Equestrian Statue of Marcus Aurelius").

Page 35 **His view of interdependence**: Inwood (1999, p. 676).

Page 36 **caught himself before he gave in to wailing**: Philo (1953, 4.16–19; 4.73).

Page 36 **We can nip them in the bud.**: Seneca, around the same time, will develop a parallel account of threshold emotions, presumably drawing from common earlier Stoic sources (Graver, 1999). Also, see Sorabji (2000).

Page 37 **the boundary extends outward beyond the *polis***: As discussed and quoted in Schofield (1999b, p. 108). See Aristotle (1984a, NE I.7 1097b7–11) for the source passage.

Page 37 **intermediate degrees of sin**: Sorabji (2000, pp. 8–9).

Page 37 **bad angels or the devil could induce the agitation**: For the complex route from "Stoic agitation to Christian temptation," see Sorabji (2000). Sorabji notes that pagan sources, such as Porphyry, concur that bad demons can stir up agitations (Sorabji, 2000, p. 348).

Page 38 **a "perfect wise man should lack" ordinary "motions"**: Erasmus (1501/1905, pp. 10, 88–119).

Page 38 **It is also a critical lesson in policing**: See Stoughton (2015).

Page 39 **it is not undiluted asceticism**: Montaigne (1957/1595, 1.14); Schaefer (2001). On Montaigne's own manner of living, see Montaigne (1957/1595, 3.13). For Montaigne on drunkenness, see Montaigne (1957/1595, 2.2).

Page 39 **He also famously ushers in the doubt and fallibilism of the modern era**: Schneewind (1990, pp. 224–236). I am grateful to conversations with Huaping Lu-Adler about Descartes and Stoic influences.

Page 39 **Kant's famous idea that all persons are due respect as ends in themselves**: For more on the Stoic influences on Kant, see Sherman (1997b, esp. Ch. 3, "Stoic Interlude").

Page 40 **a "garment that dresses virtue to advantage"**: Kant (1974, p. 147). These remarks are brief. For a more comprehensive study of Kant on the emotions, see Sherman (1990, 1995b, 1995c, 1997a, 1997b, 1998).

Page 40 **the American founding fathers**: See Montgomery (1936).

LESSON 3

Page 44 **the chief infectious disease doctor of the National Institutes of Health**: Specifically, US National Institute of Allergy and Infectious Diseases.

Page 44 **"we want to be where the infection is going to be"**: Baker (2020).

Page 44 **learning how "to dwell in advance"**: Cicero (2002, p. 222).

Page 44 **The warnings were not heeded**: Sanger, Lipton, Sullivan, & Crowley (2020). According to a disclosure of the draft report, "confusion" was cited throughout the report, with messages and lack of agency coordination (Lipton et al., 2020). Note headline: "He Could Have Seen What Was Coming: Behind Trump's Failure on the Virus."

Page 45 **Some put the stress note on self-reliance**: Epictetus (1925, 1.6.30). See Donald Robertson, for example: (D. J. Robertson). He interprets the passage this way: "We should not wait for help from others but learn to be self-reliant and to take action where necessary."

Page 45 **Whose dignity we don't always properly respect**: This raises issues as to whether the Stoics, like Aristotle, defended the institution of enslavement. I discuss the issue in Lesson 9. For a review of Stoic texts, see D. Robertson (2017). For a groundbreaking treatment, see Finley (2017, originally published in 1980).

Page 45 'I am a member of the system made of reasonable beings.': Aurelius (2011, 7.13), translation slightly emended.

Page 46 a recognition of our interdependence: Luna, St. John, Wigglesworth, Lin II, & Shalby (2020).

Page 46 "woven together" by a "common bond": Aurelius (2011, 7.9).

Page 46 compatible with "being asleep": Aristotle (1984a, NE 1.5 1095b33ff).

Page 47 entrust to chance: Aristotle (1984a, NE 1.9 1099b24).

Page 47 happy tortured on the rack: Aristotle (1984a, NE 1.10 1101a5–7). For a pioneering study of the fragility of happiness and goodness in Aristotle's ethics, see Nussbaum (1986).

Page 47 "The decision rests with perception": Aristotle (1984a, NE 1109b22, 1094b25, 1094b21). For a more extensive discussion of Aristotle's ethics, see Sherman (1989, 1997b).

Page 47 wanting more precision and brighter stripes: Long (1968). Note, Zeno was a student of Polemo, the third head of the Academy where Aristotle studied for 20 years before founding the Lyceum. He would, thus, likely be familiar with Aristotle's view (Rist, 1983).

Page 48 They are "preferred." Their opposites are . . . dispreferred": "In general," in that not all tokens of these two types are things we prefer or disprefer. In addition, there are things that are neither preferred nor dispreferred but unqualifiedly indifferent in that nature doesn't dispose us one way or another—such as "having an odd or even number of hairs on one's head" (Long & Sedley, 1987b, 58B; Diogenes Laertius 7.104–5, SVF 3.119).

Page 48 the striving critical to stabilizing that new value scheme: See Gill's helpful remarks on aspiration (Gill, 2019, Ch. 2). His view overlaps with my own focus on the life of the moral progressor as itself an important way of life and not just preparation for some idealized life of the sage.

Page 48 the human turned divine: That is a worry Aristotle voices often in his ethics, especially in (1984a, 10.7–8). See Sherman (1989, pp. 94–106).

Page 49 **death toll . . . more American lives . . . than lost in battle in all of World War Two?**: https://www.washingtonpost.com/history/2020/11/19/ranking-covid-deaths-american-history/; https://www.businessinsider.com/more-americans-dead-covid-19-us-battle-deaths-wwii-2020-12

Page 49 **"Some things in the world are up to us, while others are not"**: Epictetus (2018, Encheiridion 1).

Page 50 **"Anger is undoubtedly set in motion by an impression received of a wrong."**: Seneca (1995a, 2.3–4).

Page 51 **Emotion, is thus, a kind of voluntary action.**: Seneca (1995a, 2.4).

Page 51 **"It is not things themselves that trouble people"**: Epictetus (2018, *Encheiridion* 5).

Page 51 **"epistemic standpoint"**: For a wonderful discussion with insight into the current philosophical literature, see Ward (2020). For critical work in this area, see Fricker (2007).

Page 51 **we are not always free to choose those standpoints**: Philo emphasizes time as an important aspect of mental control of assent to impressions. So in explaining Abraham's running to meet the three men (in Genesis 18.2) who promise that they will return next year and Sarah will bear a son, Philo says, "it gives us warning to those who without reflexion and taking thought rush upon whatever happens to be there, without first thinking and looking, and it teaches them not to rush out before they clearly see and grasp what the matter is" (Philo, 1953, 4.3).

Page 51 **"hidden persuaders"**: Vance Packard's prescient term from his 1957 book with that title (Packard, 1957).

Page 52 **to live as a Stoic in the most extreme conditions**: For more on my discussion and interviews with Adm. Stockdale, see Sherman (2005b). I return to Stockdale's Stoicism in greater detail in Lesson 6.

Page 52 **he knows well the cost of voluntary retreat**: For Seneca as public servant and retirement, see M. Griffin (1976, pp. 315–366).

Page 52 **Retirement . . . needs justification**: Seneca (1935, On Leisure 4.1).

Page 53 **"wholly dominated by evil"**: Seneca (1935, On Leisure 3.3).

Page 53 **"the hindrance is not in the doer, but in the things to be done"**: Seneca (1935, On Leisure 6.3).

Page 53 **we are constrained by access to input**: On Stoic notions of intellectual virtue, see Sherman & White (2007).

Page 54 **"What a great person!"**: Epictetus (1995, 3.12.16).

Page 55 **"I learned this from a wise man"**: Cicero (2002, 3.29).

Page 55 **regularly rehearse potential future evils**: Cicero (2002, 3.30).

Page 56 *Prosphatos* **connotes . . . "rawness,"**: Cicero (2002, 3.52); Long & Sedley (1987a, 65B; Andronicus, *On Passions* 1, *SVF* 3.391, part).

Page 56 **"Dwelling in advance"**: Cicero (2002, p. 222).

Page 56 **immersion in imagination**: That is the traditional and educative role of ancient tragedy—a *mimēsis*, or imitation of life. See reflections on this and tragic accidents in Aristotle's *Poetics* (Sherman, 1992).

Page 57 **Pre-rehearsal . . . a form of pre-exposure**: Cicero (2002, 3.58).

Page 57 **(CBT, itself with roots in Stoicism)**: Both Albert Ellis and Aaron Beck, founders of an early version of CBT, acknowledge the debt (Beck, 1975; Ellis, 1962). Note, there has been a move within the military community to use the term "post-traumatic stress (PTS)," dropping the "D" for "disorder," which many find stigmatizing. One argument often made is that servicemembers don't come home from war with "limb disorders," but "limb injuries." Psychological injuries should be viewed with parity. Others argue that insofar as post-traumatic stress is a *normal* response to an *abnormal* situation of overwhelming life threat, the notion of a "disorder" gets the response wrong. I have used "PTSD" in the preceding discussion for consistency, because the literature I go on to cite on pre-exposure uses the term. Elsewhere in this book, I drop the "D."

Page 58 **Through repeated approach . . . the fear response is deconditioned**: Hendriks, de Kleine, Broekman, Hendriks, & van Minnen (2018).

Page 58 **"Attention bias"**: Badura-Brack et al. (2015); Lazarov et al. (2019); Ilan Wald et al. (2013).

Page 58 **Israeli Defense Force . . . "attention bias modification training"**: I. Wald et al. (2016, p. 2633).

Page 59 **"might have been able to prevent"**: Cicero (2002, 3.58).

Page 59 **take moral responsibility . . . to make sense of what seems senseless**: I call this "accident guilt" in Sherman (2010). See also Sherman (2011).

Page 59 **Moral Injury**: For extended discussion of this, see Sherman (2010, 2015a).

Page 61 **"If you go out to bathe"**: Epictetus (2018, 4).

Page 61 **"if at the outset" I say to myself**: Epictetus (2018, 4).

Page 62 **"When you kiss your little child"**: Epictetus (2018, 3).

Page 62 **if my foot had a mind . . . ". . . impulse to get muddy"**: Epictetus (1925), using trans. by Long & Sedley (1987b, 58J).

Page 62 **"Seeing that we do not know beforehand what is going to happen"**: Epictetus (1925, 2.10.5–6), following J. Klein (2015, pp. 267–268), emendation of Oldfather trans.

Page 64 **"if nothing happens to prevent it"**: The Greek term is *huperairesis*. Often *exceptio* in Latin. See Inwood (1985, pp. 119–126). For a contrary view that reservation does not involve conditional impulses and that there may not be evidence for the synergy of Stoic logic and psychology, see Brennan (2000).

Page 64 **"My business will be successful *unless*"**: Seneca (1932b, 13.2–3); italics added.

Page 64 **"And use only impulse and aversion, but lightly"**: Epictetus (2018), emended trans. following Brennan (2000, p. 151).

Page 64 **"because he does all such things with reservation"**: Long & Sedley (1987b, 65E; 65W, *SVF*3.564); Stobaeus (1999, 2.115.5–9).

Page 65 **The idea seems a bit too good to be true**: For an eloquent and careful elaboration of the critique, see Brennan (2000).

Page 66 **The sage doesn't assent to future . . . contingents**: Brennan (2000, p. 164).

Page 66 **"foes to tranquility"**: Seneca (1932b, 13.3–14.1).

Page 67 **an analogy with archery**: Cicero (2001, 3.22) and Annas and Woolf's note. For a discussion of the difference between objectives (or targets) and ends (or goals), see Inwood (1986).

Page 68 **the accidents of bad luck may frustrate our objectives . . . but not the overall end**: This is at the crux of the Stoic break with Aristotle. The Stoics, unlike Aristotle, hold that external goods and the cooperation of a hospitable world for realizing our objectives are not necessary for the overall end of good living or a happy life. Virtue is sufficient.

Page 68 **Psychotrauma Center in Amsterdam**: Known as ARQ, National Psychotrauma Center in Diemen (Amsterdam), Netherlands. I am grateful to ARQ and colleagues there for the opportunity to give the keynote.

Page 68 **Firefighter Aart van Oosten**: I am indebted to Bart Nauta for his abbreviated and translated version of his interview with Aart (which I have here emended slightly). For the original interview, see Nauta (2019).

Page 70 **virtue is a skill like being a good doctor**: The idea is familiar from Aristotle. Certain skills are like medicine, "for the job of medicine is not to produce healthy things, but to advance as far as is possible in that direction" (Aristotle, 1984c, Rhetoric 1355b10–13). They are "stochastic" skills, those in which achievement of objective is distinct from practicing the skill perfectly; we may practice the skills perfectly even when we fail to bring about the desired objectives. For discussion, see Inwood (1986).

Page 71 **Boston's Brigham and Women's Hospital**: Lamas (2020).

Page 72 **Dr. Anthony Fauci**: Barbaro (2020a) reflecting on his podcast interview with Fauci.

Page 72 **"art of living"**: Von Arnim (1964, *SVF* 2.117, *SVF* 3.95 [Stobaeus *Eclogae*] 2.58).

LESSON 4

Page 76 **"All of the above are appropriate"**: Egan (2020).

Page 76 **the fear of infecting their families**: As in this account (Editorial Board, 2020).

Page 76 **three distinct layers of emotional experience**: As we outline a general view, keep in mind that this is a simplification. Stoic thought spans at least 500 years and is marked by considerable internal debate and greater or less sympathy with competing schools with whom individual Stoics are in dialogue.

Page 77 **These emotions and their subtypes**: For one list of the subspecies of this fourfold classification, see Long & Sedley (1987b, 65E); Stobaeus (1999, 2.90, 19.9; *SVF* 3.394, part).

Page 77 **Impressions that you assent to**: Brennan (2005) for helpful elaboration.

Page 77 **"Anger is set in motion by an impression"**: Seneca (1995a, 2.1.3–4).

Page 78 **a two-tiered evaluative judgment**: Cicero (2002, 3.75–76). Sherman (2005b, pp. 143–149) for further discussion.

Page 78 *perverted* **cognitions**: *tou logou diastrophas* (Von Arnim, 1964; *SVF* 1.208). Also Seneca (1995a, 3.15): "a departure from reason."

Page 78 **by analogy with a runner**: Long & Sedley (1987b, 65J, Galen, *On Hippocrates' and Plato's doctrines* 4.2.10–18; *SVF* 3.462, part).

Page 79 **a body "in free fall"**: Seneca (1995a, 1.74; 2015, 3.14; also 3.16.2).

Page 79 **"rational joy,"** . . . **"exhilaration"**: Graver notes that Seneca speaks of joy as "exhilaration," "an uplift of the mind" affectively similar to an ordinary person's delight in the birth of a child or in winning an election. See Graver, "Ethics II: Action and Emotion" in Damschen (2014, 272.3).

Page 80 **"rational caution"**: Long & Sedley (1987b; 65F Diogenes Laertius 7.116; *SVF* 3.431).

Page 80 "**The wise person is companionable**": Stobaeus, 2.7.11M, as quoted in Graver (2007, p. 179), with slight modification.

Page 80 **attitudes of mutual goodwill:** As Margaret Graver notes, the emotions mentioned here—*eunoia, agapāsis,* and *aspasmos*—are among the cultivated eupathic (or good) emotions of the sage, and specifically, species of the genus of rational wish—*boulēsis*—directed at and sensitive to pursuit of the good, or virtue (Graver, 2007, pp. 179, 58).

Page 81 "**They come unbidden and depart unbidden.**": Seneca (2015, 11.7).

Page 82 "**. . . even the bravest man often turns pale**": Seneca (1995a, 2.3.2–3).

Page 82 **Sarah when she laughed:** Philo (1953, 4.16).

Page 82 "**The wise person conquers all adversity, but still feels them.**": Seneca (2015, 9.3).

Page 82 **That a skipper blanches white:** Gellius (1927, Vol. 3, 19.1).

Page 83 For the view that pre-emotions (*propatheiai*) may be akin to what neurobiologist Joseph LeDoux (LeDoux, 1996, 2015) in the earlier work called "low road emotions," or rapid-process amygdala responses, see Sorabji (2000, pp. 145–150), referring to LeDoux (1996, pp. 138–178). For some well-placed skepticism about the exact parallels, given the motley variety of Seneca's full list of examples, see Graver (2007, p. 97).

Page 83 **a cognitive theory in which emotions are appraisals:** The leading emotion theory among both philosophers and psychologists is a cognitive theory. For cognitive emotion theories in philosophy, see Roberts (2009); Deigh (1994); Nussbaum (2001). For cognitive emotion theories in psychology, see the work of Nico Frijda (N. H. Frijda, 1986) and those influenced by his work: Ortony (1988); Oatley (1992); Scherer (2005).

Page 84 "**Eyes ablaze and glittering**": Seneca (1995a, 1.1.4).

Page 84 "**harm to himself, first of all**": Seneca (1995a, 3.4.4).

Page 85 **"that man without a shred of decency"**: Homer (1999, 22.398–405; 24.64–65).

Page 85 **"an animal, struggling against the noose"**: Seneca (1995a, 3.16.1; 3.27–26; 2.34.1).

Page 85 **the "bad" breast that withholds milk**: M. Klein (1984, p. 68).

Page 86 **reactive attitudes and their emotional bite**: Strawson (1962). See Sherman (2010, 2015a) on reactive attitudes to do with moral injury.

Page 86 **brutal killing of George Floyd**: Hill et al. (2020). Relatedly, see the place of anger in Ta-Nehisi Coates's plea for reparations in his *Atlantic* essay on redlining practices that have kept African Americans from being able to buy and own homes (Coates, 2014). For an early discussion of clashing views on the place of anger in African-American protest (specifically, the debate between Booker T. Washington and W. E. B. Dubois), see Boxill (1976).

Page 86 **"good trouble."**: Lewis (2020).

Page 86 **anger in political justice**: Nussbaum (2015, 2016).

Page 87 **"People in academic . . . focusing only on reputation and status"**: Nussbaum (2015, p. 49).

Page 87 *eudaimonia* **will hang on . . . retaliatory rebalance**: Nussbaum (2015, p. 49).

Page 87 **intrinsic goods that from a modern perspective**: For her list of 10 central capabilities that are a bare minimum for a life worthy of human dignity, see Nussbaum (2011, pp. 31–35).

Page 88 **strive to make selections . . . promoting dignity rationally and constructively**: Nussbaum preserves this impetus in her notion of "transitional anger" (Nussbaum, 2015).

Page 88 **Navy Captain Brett Crozier**: Gafni & Garofoli (2020); also Ismay (2020).

Page 89 **"commander of a ship like this."**: Garland (2020).

Page 89 **"stands up for anger" as "the spur to virtue."**: Seneca (1995a, 3.3.1–5). Aristotle takes up anger in *Nicomachean Ethics* (Aristotle, 1984a, 2.9 and 4.5). At 2.9 he argues that determining how much and what sort of anger is appropriate in a given situation is a matter of practical wisdom: "the judgment rests in perception" (1109b15–25).

Page 89 **"hit the mean."**: Aristotle (1984a, 2.9 1109b15–25).

Page 90 **"sober and wineless days,"**: Plutarch (2000, 464c–d; 453d); Seneca (1995a, 2.12.3–4).

Page 90 **proto "worry, annoyance, mental pain, vexation."**: Long & Sedley (1987b, 65E, Stobaeus 2.90, 19–91, 9, *SVF* 3.394, part).

Page 90 **Dr. Christine Blasey Ford**: I have benefited from a private lecture given by attorney Debra Katz, who represented Christine Blasey Ford before Congress. The lecture was on April 26, 2020, to a group in Washington, D.C.

Page 91 **fear warning system**: "Ford Cites Hippocampus in Recollection of Alleged Assault" (2018).

Page 91 **my civic responsibility**: Zhouli (2018).

Page 91 **"100 percent."**: Associated Press (2018).

Page 91 **"belligerent and aggressive,"**: As some of his college friends said he became when inebriated (*New York Times*, 2018).

Page 91 **his voice loud, his face contorting at times, defensive bite-backs**: See especially his remarks to Sen. Amy Klobuchar when she asked if he experienced "black outs" after drinking ("Kavanaugh challenges notion that he was 'belligerent' while drinking," 2018).

Page 92 **residual feelings of fear and anger**: "that first mental jolt which affects us when we think ourselves wronged." It can "happen to the very wisest of persons" (Seneca, 1995a, 2.2.2).

Page 92 **anger itself . . . impetus for . . . constructive action**: But even if we stick with anger as a pre-emotion, it may be more cognitively robust than just a mental or physical *frisson*. Seneca offers a motley collection of preliminary affects: There are the kind we mentioned earlier—pallor, tears, blanching, blushing, knee-knocking, erections, "mental jolts" and "bodily agitations." But then there are more cognitively rich "emotional preludes." So he asks his contemporaries to imagine reading about events from the last decades of the *Republic*: "We often have a sense of being angry with Clodius as he drives

Cicero into exile or with Antony as he kills him. Who remains un-
provoked by the arms which Marius took up or by Sulla's proscrip-
tions? Who would not feel furious with Theodotus and Achillas or
with the boy himself who undertook such an unboyish crime?" These
are emotional preludes, because they are "motions of mind with no
positive wish to be in motion" (Seneca, 1995a, 2.2.3–5). What is
truncated about the emotion is not so much the thought process,
but the absence of what psychologists now call "action tendencies"
(Nico H. Frijda, 1987).

Page 92 **emotion is a choice**: For Cicero on reforming the second evaluative judgment—in the case of grief to do with mourning behavior—
see Cicero (2002, 3.76).

Page 92 *Unorthodox*: Winger (2020).

Page 93 **hollowed out, "contracted" feeling**: The Stoic model of the
mind is physical. Emotions are sometimes described as changes in
"tensions" of reason manifest by "contractions, cowerings, tearings,
swellings, and expansions" (Long & Sedley, 1987b, 65K, Galen, *On
Hippocrates' and Plato's doctrines* 4.3.2–5; Posidonius fr. 34, part).

Page 94 **The need to grieve**: On hospital nurses not being able to grieve
because they don't know the names of those fallen in duty, see Jewett
& Szabo (2020).

Page 94 **"For my mind was swollen"**: Cicero (2002, 3.76).

Page 94 *Tusculan Disputations*: Cicero (2002, p. xv). As always, I am
deeply indebted to Margaret Graver's introduction, translation and
important commentary on this work.

Page 94 **"the comforter has one responsibility"**: Cicero (2002, 3.76).

Page 95 **"not the right moment for such a lesson"**: Cicero (2002, 3.77).

Page 95 **"It's a big task to persuade a person"**: Cicero (2002, 3.79).

Page 96 **"we may be forgiven our tears,"**: Seneca (2015, 63.1).

Page 96 **twinge . . . an emotional scar . . . without culpability**: At
Seneca (2015, 99.14), Seneca uses the Stoic term *morsus*, a biting:
"What you feel is not grief but only a biting: It is you who are making
it into grief."

Page 96 **The tears "are squeezed out of us"**: Seneca (2015, 99.18–19).

Page 96 **"These [preliminary] tears are shed"**: Seneca (2015, 99.18–19).

Page 97 **nursing the tears**: Seneca (2015, 99.21). For insightful clinical research on persistent distress in prolonged grief reactions, see Boelen (2019). He points to the importance of the first six months for early identification and early treatment of those at risk, and notes the prevalence among those at risk to continue to yearn to see the lost one. The yearning and clinging are attitudes that the Stoics pinpoint as unravelling control.

Page 97 **"Replacing the friend is better than crying."**: Seneca (2015, 63.11).

Page 97 **"As if birth order determined our fate!"**: Seneca (2015, 63.14).

Page 98 **"I am sick myself."**: Seneca (2015, 27.1).

Page 98 **"not a doctor but a patient."**: Seneca (2015, 68.9).

LESSON 5

Page 102 **The story is Tara Westover's . . . in** *Educated.*: Westover (2018).

Page 102 **"If you want anything good, get it from yourself,"**: Epictetus (1995), 29.4.

Page 103 **In contemporary psychological writing, resilience**: for example, Bonanno (2004); Fleming & Ledogar (2008); Konnikova (2016); Reivich & Shatte (2002).

Page 105 **social support from the ground up**: See Stanton (1968).

Page 105 **"a horse runs, a hound tracks,"**: Aurelius (2011, 5.6, 5.30, 6.7, 7.74; 5.6, 6.42). The picture is organic, and organic communities, rooted in local cultures and national differences, don't always promote an expansive humanism. This is a modern debate, not taken up in Marcus's own political reflections. For our own contemporary debate, see Nussbaum & Cohen (1996/2002).

Page 105 **'I am a member of the system made of reasonable beings.'**: Aurelius (2011, 7.13).

Page 106 **sharing the dance floor**: For reflections on motor resonances and synchronies in both dance and battle, see Sherman (2018, 2020).

Page 106 **"mutually intertwined movements,"** . . . **even sleepers**: Aurelius (2011, 7.9; 6.42).

Page 106 **"Whenever you desire to cheer yourself"**: Aurelius (2011, 6.48). See Caston (2016) and Gill's chapter (2016).

Page 107 **I should be "a disciple of Antonius . . .**: Aurelius (2011, 6.30).

Page 107 **the right reply was not by "carping,"**: Aurelius (2011, 1.1–17).

Page 108 **even owe the existence of our cities not to social contracts,**: Aristotle (1984b, 1.1–2); Annas (1993, pp. 148–149).

Page 109 **The developmental story is complex**: For an excellent overview, see J. Klein (2016).

Page 109 **"one comes to value that person more highly . . . "**: Cicero (2001, 3.23). More generally, 3.20–23. On sociality as natural, see Cicero (2001, 3.66–70).

Page 109 **"in virtuous activity that strains every nerve"**: Aristotle (1984a, 9.8, 1168b29–69a11).

Page 109 **"nothing is more his own than . . . the whole human race."**: Seneca (2015, 73.7–8).

Page 110 **the concrete and emotional bonds that connect us**: So, for example, the Enlightenment philosopher Immanuel Kant, deeply influenced by the Stoics, famously constructs the ideal moral commonwealth through principles of practical reason. He doesn't fully develop how we rally each other in supportive affiliations or grow strong through reciprocal and compassionate care. Still, he gives many hints for how to fill out a more complete picture, which I undertake in Sherman (1997b).

Page 110 **"When I devote myself to friends,"**: Seneca (2015, 62.2).

Page 111 **The demigod Hercules:** Fitch (1987).

Page 111 **sage rises only as often as the phoenix**: Seneca (2015, 42.1).

Page 111 **anxiety about a most improbable and dangerous birth**: Philo (1953, 4.16).

Page 112 **"Every time a letter comes"**: Seneca (2015, 67.2). Also, see Graver and Long's *Introduction* for the epistolary relationship.

Page 112 **"been the cause of good"**: Seneca (2015, 102.18).

Page 112 **"I swell—I exult— . . . from your letters"**: Seneca (2015, 67.2, 34.1).

Page 112 **"We get joy . . . even in their absence."**: Seneca (2015, 35.3).

Page 112 **"not only . . . but see that one as you want him to be."**: Seneca (2015, 35.3).

Page 114 **late adolescence . . . most need outside counsel**: Cicero (1991, 1.107–125); Epictetus (1983, 17). See Gill (1988).

Page 114 **thin crust of good manners**: For more on this, see Sherman (2005b, Ch. 3, "Of Manners and Morals").

Page 114 **giving is reciprocated in the teacher's own growth**: Seneca (2015, 36.4).

Page 115 **"You made a lot of mistakes, Mr. Cohen,"**: Baltimore Sun Staff (2019).

Page 117 **"Our children are the messages for a future"**: See CNN Politics (2019). Also C-Span (2019).

Page 118 **"We keep zealously transferring those from the enclosing circles"**: Long & Sedley, (1987b, 57G; Hierocles [Stobaeus 4.671], 7-673, 11).

Page 118 **Calling all women . . . "my mother"**: Plato (1997a, *Republic* 5); Aristotle (1984d, *Politics* 2.1, 1262b16).

Page 119 **We catch . . . as if by contagion**: Hume (1968, 579).

Page 120 **"By the imagination we place ourselves in his situation,"**: Smith (2000, 1.1., pp. 3–4; 1.2., p. 23).

Page 121 **"Stamp out his great ambition!"**: Seneca (2010, 75–108)

Page 122 **"If I had wished to rule the underworld"**: Seneca (2010, 610).

Page 122 **"More labours for me."**: Seneca (2010, 635).

Page 122 **"hordes of ghosts."**: Seneca (2010, 1148).

Page 122 **"Bad luck is not your fault."**: Seneca (2010, 1200).

Page 122 **"Who has ever called an accident a crime?"**: Seneca (2010, 1236–1238).

Page 123 **"Forgive yourself"**: Seneca (2010, 1265).

Page 123 **"Use your heroic courage"**: Seneca (2010, 1275).

Page 123 **"Grant me the joy of . . . touching you"**: Seneca (2010, 1248–1250).

Page 125 **Sifting through the emotional residue**: I am grateful to Jackie June ter Heide for her presentation of this case at the ARQ National Psychotrauma Center in Amsterdam and in subsequent correspondence.

LESSON 6

Page 130 **"Five years down there, at least."**: "Courage Under Fire," in James B. Stockdale (1995, p. 189).

Page 131 **seven and a half years as the senior prisoner of war**: Yablonka (2006).

Page 133 **in their own way and together indomitable forces**: For an earlier account of Stockdale's Stoicism, see Sherman (2005b, especially Ch. 1, "A Brave New Stoicism" and notes). For Sybil and Jim's memoir, see James B. Stockdale & Stockdale (1990).

Page 133 **Throw "a bit of glory"**: Epictetus, (1995, 2.22.11).

Page 134 **moral injury . . . "a syndrome of shame, self-handicapping,"**: Litz, Lebowitz, Gray, & Nash (2016, p. 21). See also Litz, Stein, Delaney, Lebowitz, Nash, et al. (2009); Maguen & Litz (January 13, 2012). I am deeply grateful for conversations over the years and shared symposia with Bill Nash, Brett Litz, and Shira Maguen.

Page 135 **"If you do this, I'll own you forever."**: The story is retold in "The Body of an American," a play by Dan O'Brien. I saw the play at Theater J in Washington, D.C., in March 2016.

Page 137 **Layne McDowell was meant for a cockpit**: Chivers (2018, pp. 6–24, 119–121). I am grateful for correspondence and conversation with Chris Chivers about this account in the *The Fighters*. For a conversation at Georgetown with myself, Chivers, and others (including

James Fallows of the *Atlantic*) on moral injury (on the occasion of the publication of *Afterwar* 2015), watch Sherman (2015b).

Page 138 **But shunting . . . military moral injury to psychological overreach**: For an extensive treatment of moral injury from a philosophical perspective, see Sherman (2015a).

Page 141 **"Socrates . . . made me feel shame"**: Plato (1989, 216a–b). See the insightful study of Graver (2007, pp. 191–211).

Page 141 **Alcibiades . . . not an ordinary weak-willed person**: See Callard (2018) for a reconstruction of Alcibiades on weakness of will and aspiration.

Page 142 **Cicero reminds his readers of the *Symposium* passage**: Cicero (2002, 3.77, 34–35).

Page 142 **"Suppose a person is upset about his own lack of virtue"**: Cicero (2002, 4.61–62).

Page 144 **taking considerable risk onto himself . . . to minimize the risk to the child**: Following Walzer (1977) on permissible collateral killings: "Double effect is defensible . . . only when the two outcomes are the product of a *double intention*: first, that the 'good' be achieved; second, that the foreseeable evil be reduced as far as possible" (pp. 155–156).

Page 145 **It is a way they hold themselves accountable**: Compare the attitude of ex-SEAL petty chief officer Eddie Gallagher and the rightful moral disgust of some of his teammates of his love of killing. See Dave Philipps's coverage of the story (Philipps, 2019).

Page 145 **"Use your heroic courage"**: Seneca (2010, p. 1275).

Page 145 **so the burden they bear is fairer.**: I am grateful for the opportunity to have participated in a keynote panel on moral injury at West Point, Fall 2019, with Tessman (2019). Lisa Tessman discussed the notion of fitting but unfair reactive attitudes which I refer to here. Also, see Sherman (2015a, 2010) for more on service members' own stories of the invisible wounds of war and the challenges of healing once home.

Page 146 **Mercy . . . "leniency in exacting punishment."**: Seneca (1985, 2.6.3–7.1).

Page 146 **"We have all sinned"**: Seneca (1985, 1.7).

Page 147 **The Stoic moral tutor, like the good farmer (or vintner)**: Seneca (1985, 2.4.4; 2.7.4–5).

Page 148 **Just put a yoke on his "royal neck."**: Seneca (2010b, 748).

Page 148 **"I wish I could be merciful. I cannot,"**: Seneca (2010b, 764).

Page 150 **The benevolence of the benevolent spectator ... part of self**: And this is not lost on clinicians working on therapeutic moral repair, especially in a technique called "adaptive disclosure" (Litz, Lebowitz, Gray, & Nash, 2016; Griffin, Worthington, Davis, Hook, & Maguen, 2018; Griffin, Cornish, Maguen, & Worthington, Jr., 2019; Purcell, 2018). Again, thanks to Brett Litz, Bill Nash, Shira Maguen, Brandon Griffin, and Natalie Purcell for conversation on self-forgiveness and the work of adaptive disclosure at the VA.

LESSON 7

Page 153 **Zeno from Citium was a dye merchant**: Laertius (1970, 7.2).

Page 153 **The Stoic marketer is Ryan Holiday**: I was interviewed by Ryan Holiday a number of years back (Holiday). I started thinking about Stoics and lifehacking death when a tech reporter for *Medium*, Jeff Bercovici, approached me for an interview for his story "Silicon Valley's Latest Lifehack Death" (Bercovici, 2018).

In this lesson, I draw on these other stories that track Silicon Valley's interest in Stoicism: Alter (2016); Benzinga (2020); Bowles (2019); Carr & McCracken (2018); Dowd (2017); Fowler (2017); Goldhill (2016); Margolis (2019); Richards & Feloni (2017); Rosenberg (2020); Schein (2019).

Page 154 **"Hack: 1. n."**: Raymond (1991, p. 189).

Page 155 **By 2011 "lifehack" ... added to ...** *Oxford Dictionaries Online.*: "Lifehack" (2020).

Page 155 **In his 2017 TED talk**: Ferriss (2017). See also Western, D.

Page 156 **"stamp out an image,"**: Cicero (2002, p. 222), quoting Galen, *Precepts of Hippocrates and Plato*, referring to either Chrysippus or Posidonius.

Page 156 **"Some things are up to us"**: Epictetus (1983, p. 1).

Page 157 **Ferriss's net worth**: Western, D.

Page 158 **"finer and more godlike to attain it for a *polis*,"**: Aristotle (1984a, 3.7; 1.2).

Page 159 **a new virus has laid bare . . . an old virus**: Racism is a social determinant of health, pediatric researchers have shown, with profound effects on the health status of children, adolescents, young adults, and their families. See Trent, Dooley, & Dougé (2019).

Page 159 **Philip Ozuah . . . Montefiore Health System**: Ozuah (2020).

Page 159 **"an African American is threatening my life,"**: Maslin Nir (2020).

Page 160 **Cory Booker**: Corasaniti (2020).

Page 160 **Facial recognition systems**: Timberg (2016).

Page 161 **"habituation and constant attention may lessen"**: Seneca (1995a, 2.4).

Page 161 **"the knees of even the fiercest soldier tremble"**: Seneca (1995a, 2.3).

Page 161 **space for more "deliberate decision."**: Seneca (1995a, 2.3).

Page 161 **"thinking fast and slow,"**: Kahneman (2011).

Page 162 **only to have them talk through our bodies**: For endocrinal, neural, and immune bi-directional pathways forming part of a gut-brain axis, see Clapp et al. (2017).

Page 163 **Simon Drew's, *The Practical Stoic***: Drew (2020a, 2020b, 2020c).

Page 164 **functional and dysfunctional families.**: For an important reminder, see Salvador Minuchin's pathbreaking work on families (Minuchin, 1974).

Page 164 **For Shawn, running track feels like freedom**: This story was on NPR's Morning Edition with Noel King (N. King, Kwong, Westerman, & Doubek, 2020).

Page 166 **"respectfulness . . . suited to bonding humans together."**: Cicero (1991, 1.99).

Page 167 **neuropathways that make you more resilient**: Benzinga (2020).

Page 167 **"Try Toronto in the winter, sir."**: Braun (2019).

Page 167 **Twitter's mission . . . global conversation**: Twitter (2020).

Page 167 **"Overton Window,"**: For discussion, see Astor (2019).

Page 167 **Megaphones create noise**: Warzel (2020).

Page 168 **8.8 million tweets . . . #BlackLivesMatter hashtag**: M. Anderson, Barthel, Perrin, & Vogels (2020).

Page 168 **racial confrontation in Central Park**: See Maslin Nir (2020). Note, Christian Cooper's reflections that the Twitter "frenzy" that led to "canceling" Amanda Cooper and her being fired from her job at an investment company left him very uneasy: "I'm uncomfortable with defining someone by a couple of seconds of what they've done. No excusing that it was a racist act, because it was a racist act. But does that define her entire life? I don't know. Only she can tell us if that defines her entire life by what she does going forward, and what she's done in the past. I can't answer that. So the frenzy is what makes me uncomfortable." Archived transcript from the NYT podcast *The Daily* (Barbaro, 2020c).

Page 168 **complicit in helping to create**: To be sure, there are evils that the digital services themselves create through the social behavior they incentivize. For Jack Dorsey's reflections on Twitter's mistakes, see his interview with Michael Barbaro on *The Daily* podcast (Barbaro, 2020b). And for an insightful case study on trying to stem social media outrage on Twitter and then getting co-opted into it, see Barbaro (2020d). As this book is going to press, Twitter and Facebook have shut down President Trump's accounts following his role, through the use of those platforms, in inciting the Capitol siege on January 6, 2021.

Page 168 **"I live by the principle of everything is connected,"**: Cuccinello (2020).

Page 168 **public Google spreadsheet**: Schleifer (2020).

Page 169 **"frayed and crushed by continual reminders of service rendered"**: Seneca (1995b, 2.10–11).

Page 169 **"books to a country bumpkin"**: Seneca (1995b, 1.11.6; 1.12.3).

Page 169 **Gift giving . . . central to social cohesion**: Seneca (1995b, 1.4.2).

Page 169 **goodwill . . . in material and emotional conveyances**: Seneca (1995b, 2.18). For fuller discussion of Seneca on giving gifts, see Sherman (2005a, Ch. 3, "Manners and Morals").

Page 169 **"Scan the contents of your mind."**: Cicero (2001, 2.118).

Page 170 **"manifestation of attitude itself"**: Strawson (1993, p. 49).

Page 170 **beating death**: For an insightful piece, see Bercovici (2018).

Page 170 **"The person who fears death . . ."**: Seneca (1932, 11.6).

Page 170 **"Philosophy is practice for dying and death,"**: Plato (1997b, 64a).

Page 171 **"We too are extinguished; we too are lighted."**: Seneca (2015, 54.5).

Page 171 **"Present time is very brief."**: Seneca (1932a, 10–12).

Page 171 **"Yeah. I'd like to live forever."**: Recode Staff (2017).

Page 172 **"Choice cannot relate to impossibles,"**: Aristotle (1984a, 3.2 1111b20ff), with slight emendation of translation.

Page 172 **the fasting billionaires**: Dave Esprey, a tech investor turned biohacking entrepreneur is also a Stoic proponent (Garfield, 2016).

Page 172 **make ourselves adaptable (*faciles*)**: Seneca (1932b, 14).

Page 172 **bulletproof against death**: Indeed, one biohacker who wants to cheat death names his product "Bulletproof" (Garfield, 2016).

Page 173 **"rational departure" from life**: I am indebted in this discussion of Stoic suicide to Miriam Griffin's superb two-part article (M. Griffin, 1986a, 1986b).

Page 173 **"a rational exit from life"**: Laertius (1925, 7.130).

Page 174 **a person bitten by a mad dog**: Kant (1964, 6:424).

Page 174 **Zuckerberg rightly laments**: Zuckerberg (2018, p. 48).

Page 175 **Curtis Dozier**: Dozier (2017).

Page 175 **educating reason ought to be open to all**: I am grateful here for discussion by Grahn-Wilder (2018, pp. 245–246).

Page 176 **Musonius Rufus . . . teaching women as well as men**: Using Martha Nussbaum trans. in Nussbaum (2002, pp. 316–317). In the same article, Nussbaum argues compellingly that Musonius has an "incomplete feminism."

LESSON 8

Page 181 **Seneca . . . bedtime meditation is to "interrogate" himself**: Seneca (1995a, 3.36).

Page 181 **Carl Reiner**: Martin (2020).

Page 182 **"Bring an accusation against yourself"**: Seneca (2015, 28.10), with slight emendation of Graver & Long translation, substituting "be harsh with yourself" for the more literal, "offend yourself," in *te offende*.

Page 182 *Prosokhē*: Sorabji (2000, p. 13).

Page 182 **"Is it possible to be altogether faultless?"**: Epictetus (1995, 4.12).

Page 182 **Contrary to current psychological findings**: For a review of some psychological studies on "cognitive load" and weakened self-control, see Kahneman (2011, esp. Ch. 3, "The Lazy Controller," pp. 31–49).

Page 182 **"I scan the day . . ."** : Seneca (1995a, 3.36–38). With slight emendations to the translation.

Page 184 **"Think of the sleep that follows . . ."** : Seneca (1995a, 3.36.2; 3.37.3).

Page 185 **What "oozed out"**: Seneca (1995a, 2.36). See Sorabji (2000, p. 213).

Page 185 **"costs you great anxiety (*sollicitudine*)"**: Seneca (2015, 59.15). "*Anxietas*" is also in the Stoic vocabulary with roots in the Greek, *angh*, meaning burdened or troubled, but in the verb form, "to choke" or "strangle" or "squeeze," as preserved in the medical term "angina," a sense of tightness or squeezing in the chest. For a lively discussion of the history of the notion of anxiety, see Le Doux (2015).

Page 186 **"consistent, virtuous, error-free view of the world"**: Brennan (2005, p. 71). For more on the sage's epistemic invincibility and the role of what the Stoics call "strong assent" to *kataleptic* impressions, see esp. pp. 69–73.

Page 186 **"ethical and epistemic super-being,"**: Brennan (2005, p. 73).

Page 186 **"superlunary heaven,"**: Seneca (2015, 59.16).

Page 187 **"Better to be Socrates dissatisfied"**: Mill (1979, Ch. 2).

Page 187 **cognitive and behavioral therapy**: The founders of the earliest forms of modern cognitive behavioral therapy, Albert Ellis (in the 1950s) and Aaron Beck (in the 1960s), were influenced by the Stoic cognitive view of emotions and viewed it as a precursor of the modern cognitive approach in therapy. Their view was called "Rational Emotive Psychotherapy" (Beck, 1975; Ellis, 1962). For contemporary review of the connections, see Donald Robertson's work (D. J. Robertson, 2019).

Page 188 **Stoic meditation, through talk . . . a therapy** (*therapeia*): The Stoics were interested in exhortation and not just exploration. Most contemporary psychotherapists are keen not to pile on to the guilt or distress that often brings their patients to them. For a discussion of self-knowledge and the moral perspective within psychoanalysis, see Sherman (1995d).

Page 189 **supporting medical and neurobiological science**: There's some empirical science regarding long-standing effectiveness of Vedic meditation in reducing stress. See Hartley, Mavrodaris, Flowers, Ernst, & Rees (2014); Walton, Schneider, & Nidich (2004). For mindfulness and trauma research, and a model of Mindfulness-based Fitness Training for the military, see Stanley (2019). There is considerable research in complementary medicine and brain imaging aimed at understanding the mental states, processes, and functions of various kinds of meditation. But there is ambiguity in use of terminology in the studies, and not clear crossovers with what is being investigated and measured and what long-term meditators of various traditions are practicing. For a good overview, see Dam NTV (2018).

Page 190 **Shammi Sheth**: From an interview by zoom with Shammi Sheth, May 20, 2020. I am grateful to Simon Drew for the introduction.

Page 190 **"the art of living."**: Von Arnim (1964, *SVF* 2.117; 1964, *SVF* 3.95 [Stobaeus *Eclogae*] 2.58).

Page 191 *The Tibetan Book of Living and Dying*: Rinpoche (1992). See also Thurman (1984); Guenther (1989).

Page 191 **"personal selflessness" or "emptiness"**: Thurman (1984, pp. 245–246).

Page 191 **assenting is forming beliefs and emotions**: For a more detailed discussion of impressions as states of mind and beliefs and emotions as events see Brennan (2005, pp. 65–69).

Page 192 **Dobbie Herrion**: From an interview by zoom with Dobbie Herrion and Bob Cymber, June 3, 2020. I am grateful to Simon Drew for the introduction.

Page 193 **Walter Mischel's . . . "Marshmallow Test"**: Mischel & Ebessen (1970), conducted at Stanford's Bing Nursery School. The original test used five little pretzel sticks as the immediate reward and five pretzel sticks plus two cookies as the deferred reward. The Behavior Mod simulation brings to mind, also, the legend of Gyges's ring, retold by Glaucon in the opening books of Plato's *Republic* (2.359dff). Would the just and unjust person act any differently, one from the other, if each had a ring, which when twisted around their fingers, made them invisible? How would they act unobserved without, as Glaucon asks, "the compulsion" of rewards and sanctions?

Page 193 **longer a child could wait, the better she would fare later in life**: Mischel, Ayduk, et al. (2011); Murray (2016); Konnikova (2014); Healy (2018).

Page 194 **"The first mental agitation"**: Seneca (1995a, 2.4.2).

Page 194 **"assent to an evaluative impression"**: See Brennan (2005, p. 87) for useful unpacking of Stoic impulses and emotions.

Page 194 **System 1**: Kahneman (2011, p. 21).

Page 194 **"a sudden glint in the eyes"**: Seneca (1995a, 2.2–4).

Page 195 **"When System 1 runs into difficulty,"**: Kahneman (2011, p. 24).

Page 195 **"If you need a model, take Socrates."**: Seneca (2015, 104.26–33; 98.17).

Page 195 **Romans far outstrip the Greeks in their exemplars**: Cicero (1991, 3.47; 2001, 2.62); Mayer (2008, p. 302).

Page 195 **Romans "produce more striking examples of moral performance."**: Quintilian, 12.2.30.

Page 196 **"If wisdom were given to me with this proviso"**: Seneca (2015, p. 6).

Page 196 **a Pompey or a Caligula**: Seneca (2015, 4.6–7).

Page 196 **"if it can happen at all it can happen today."**: Seneca (2015, 63.15).

Page 197 **My Lai Massacre**: I interviewed Hugh Thompson several times between 1998 and 2004 and have written about him at length in Sherman (2005b). I was reminded of Thompson's example in thinking about police brutality and the blue wall of silence that protects police from standing up to each other. On this, see Ackerman (2020).

Page 198 **the Soldier's Medal awarded to Thompson**: Associated Press (1998).

Page 201 **returning to Vietnam**: For Thompson's return to My Lai, see Mike Wallace's *60 Minutes* interview with Thompson (T. Anderson, 1998). Also, see the important investigative journalism in Bilton (1992). Also, Angers (1999).

Page 202 **rescue of innocents**: Nussbaum (2015, 2016). See her discussion of the Stoics and payback (Nussbaum, 2016, esp. pp. 35–38).

Page 202 **Thompson . . . wasn't ready to forgive them without atonement.**: Calley made his first public apology only in 2009. Hugh Thompson died in January 2006. I learned of his death, sadly, shortly after my book *Stoic Warriors* (2005) came out.

Page 203 **"Is there any virtue which we Stoics respect more?"**: Seneca (1995b, 1.15.2).

Page 203 **"The mind is what raises small things high"**: Seneca (1995b, 1.6.2).

Page 204 **plays that "are most suited" to our talents**: Cicero (2001, 1.114). Also, 1.124–46 for the subtleties of gesture important in fitting action. For an insightful discussion of Cicero on roles in life, see Gill (1988).

Page 204 **The "gift was great—but he hesitated,"**: Seneca (1995b, 1.6-7).

Page 204 **We "spoiled" a favor "by silence,"**: Seneca (1995b, 2.3).

Page 204 **"from a glance of the eyes"**: Cicero (2001, 1.146).

Page 204 **on the expression of emotions**: Darwin (1872); Ekman (1982); Ekman & Friesen (1980); Goffman (1959). For philosophical work on emotional expression, see Glazer (2014, 2016, 2017).

Page 204 **"sequence of kindness, passing from one hand to another"**: Seneca (1995b, 1. 3.2).

Page 205 **like a game of catch**: Seneca (1995b, 2.17.3–7).

Page 205 **developmental psychologists**: Emde, Gaensbauer, & Harmon (1976); Greenspan (1989); Stern (1985).

Page 206 **"You cannot have a favour if the best part of it is missing"**: Seneca (1995b, 1.15.6).

Page 206 **"the manifestation of attitude itself."**: Strawson (1993, p. 49).

Page 206 **It may take labor.**: Arlie Russell Hochschild's (Hochschild, 1983) insightful notion of "emotional labor" may come to mind here, though her original concept had to do with women's work and accepting emotional management that profits commercial interests at great personal cost. The stress and anxiety that are the result of this "surface acting" pose a challenge the ancient Stoics clearly don't take up.

LESSON 9

Page 211 **"Suppose I show you someone fighting for his master's safety"**: Seneca (1995b, 3.19).

Page 212 **"Sell me to this man; he needs a master.":** Laertius (1970, 6.74).

Page 212 **the evil was in the degradation of the person in power, not . . . flogged**: Epictetus (1995, 4.1.119).

Page 212 **Musonius Rufus**: Rufus (1947, Fragment 12).

Page 212 **the Stoics took it as near cliché**: M. Griffin, (1976, p. 257); Seneca (1995b, 3.28); Griffin presents an overall cautious and balanced view of Seneca on the institution of enslavement (pp. 256–285).

Page 212 **not equality of everyday social reality**: For an insightful view of Seneca's humanitarian remarks on enslavement in the context of the social realities of Roman hierarchical structures and elite household economies, see Bradley (2008).

Page 212 **"like a poor overburdened ass"**: Epictetus (1995, 4.1.79–80).

Page 214 **once . . . an ancient underpinning of . . . humanistic thinking**: Bradley (2008, p. 335); Finley (2017, p. 189).

Page 214 **"on acceptance of the status quo"**: M. Griffin (1976, pp. 256, 284). Both Miriam Griffin's classic work on Seneca in the court of Nero and Moses Finley's (Finley, 2017) landmark study (originally published in 1980) of ancient institutions of enslavement are indispensable. Bradley's work (Bradley, 2008) makes abundantly clear the perils of ignoring social context.

Page 214 **" 'They are slaves.' "**: Seneca (2015, 47.1).

Page 214 **"born of the same seeds."**: Seneca (2015, 47.10), emending translation slightly.

Page 215 **the enslaved person is a tool**: Aristotle (1984b, 1253b32–54a9). Seneca counters the idea of enslaved persons as natural tools this way: "Jobs are assigned by chance. Character is something each person gives himself" (Seneca, 2015, 47.15).

Page 215 **To wipe up spit and vomit**: Seneca (2015, 47.6–7).

Page 215 **"cook, baker, masseurs,"**: Bradley (2008, p. 346).

Page 215 **"[F]ugitive slaves are almost an obsession"**: Finley (2017, p. 179).

Page 216 **"my wife has fallen silent"**: Seneca (2015, 122.15).

Page 216 **"all are slaves to fear"**: Seneca (2015, 47.17).

Page 216 **A person's "clothing" or "position in life"**: Seneca (2015, 47.16).

Page 217 **his writings . . . no pure model for emancipation**: Recent attention has focused on Kant's views on colonialism and his hierarchical account of the human races. For a discussion of his remarks on colonial practices and enslavement, see Flikschuh (2014).

Page 219 **"Some things are up to us and others not."**: Epictetus (1983, 1,5).

Page 220 **an "outcast" of humanity**: Aurelius (2011, 8.34).

BIBLIOGRAPHY

Ackerman, E. (2020, June 4). The Police Will Be Part of the Solution, Too. *New York Times*. Retrieved from https://www.nytimes.com/2020/06/04/opinion/police-violence-reform-protests.html.

Alter, A. (2016, December 6). Ryan Holiday Sells Stoicism as a Life Hack, Without Apology. *New York Times*. Retrieved from https://www.nytimes.com/2016/12/06/fashion/ryan-holiday-stoicism-american-apparel.html?smid=em-share.

Anderson, M., Barthel, M., Perrin, A., & Vogels, E. A. (2020, June 10). #BlackLivesMatter surges on Twitter after George Floyd's death. *Pew Research Center*. Retrieved from https://www.pewresearch.org/fact-tank/2020/06/10/blacklivesmatter-surges-on-twitter-after-george-floyds-death/.

Anderson, T. (1998). Back to My Lai. *60 Minutes* (M. Wallace). New York, NY.

Angers, T. (1999). *The Forgotten Hero of My Lai*. Lafayette, LA: Acadia House.

Annas, J. (1993). *The Morality of Happiness*. New York, NY: Oxford University Press.

Annas, J. (1995). Reply to Cooper. *Philosophy and Phenomenological Research*, 55(3), 599–610. doi:10.2307/2108441.

Aristotle. (1984a). Nicomachean Ethics (NE) (W. D. Ross & J. O. Urmson, Trans.). In J. Barnes (Ed.), *The Complete Works of Aristotle: The Revised Oxford Translation* (Vol. 2). Princeton, NJ: Princeton University Press.

Aristotle. (1984b). Politics. In J. Barnes (Ed.), *The Complete Works of Aristotle: The Revised Oxford Translation* (Vol. 2). Princeton, NJ: Princeton University Press.

Aristotle. (1984c). Rhetoric. In J. Barnes (Ed.), *The Complete Works of Aristotle: The Revised Oxford Translation* (Vol. 2). Princeton, NJ: Princeton University Press.

Aristotle. (1984d). *The Complete Works of Aristotle: The Revised Oxford Translation* (J. Barnes, Ed.). Princeton, NJ: Princeton University Press.

Associated Press. (1998, March 7). 3 Honored for Saving Lives at My Lai. *New York Times*. Retrieved from https://www.nytimes.com/1998/03/07/us/3-honored-for-saving-lives-at-my-lai.html.

Associated Press. (2018, September 27). Christine Blasey Ford Says She Is "One Hundred Percent" Certain Kavanaugh Assaulted Her. *New York Times*. Retrieved from https://www.nytimes.com/video/us/politics/100000006131149/sexual-assault-kavanaugh-ford.html.

Astor, M. (2019, February 26). How the Politically Unthinkable Can Become Mainstream. *New York Times*. Retrieved from https://www.nytimes.com/2019/02/26/us/politics/overton-window-democrats.html.

Aurelius, M. (2011). *Meditations* (R. Hard, Trans.). New York, NY: Oxford University Press.

Badura-Brack, A. S., Naim, R., Ryan, T. J., Levy, O., Abend, R., Khanna, M. M., . . . Bar-Haim, Y. (2015). Effect of Attention Training on Attention Bias Variability and PTSD Symptoms: Randomized Controlled Trials in Israeli and U.S. Combat Veterans. *The American Journal of Psychiatry*, 172(12), 1233–1241. doi:10.1176/appi.ajp.2015.14121578.

Baker, S. (2020, March 10). Fauci: We Can't Be Doing the Kinds of Things We Were Doing a Few Months Ago. *Axios*. Retrieved from https://www.axios.com/anthony-fauci-coronavirus-risk-containment-1f8aca36-f190-4f4d-aa2e-4d69408fdd33.html.

Baltimore Sun Staff. (2019, February 28). Full transcript: Rep. Elijah Cummings' Closing Statements at Michael Cohen Hearing. *Baltimore Sun*. Retrieved from https://www.baltimoresun.com/politics/bs-md-cummings-transcript-20190228-story.html.

Barbaro, M. (2020a, April 4). Calling Dr. Fauci. *New York Times*, p. 2. Retrieved from https://www.nytimes.com/2020/04/03/podcasts/daily-newsletter-fauci-coronavirus.html?searchResultPosition=5.

Barbaro, M. (2020b, August 7). *Jack Dorsey on Twitter's Mistakes*. Retrieved from https://www.nytimes.com/2020/08/07/podcasts/the-daily/Jack-dorsey-twitter-trump.html.

Barbaro, M. (2020c). *The Daily*. Retrieved from https://www.nytimes.com/2020/08/10/podcasts/the-daily/cancel-culture.html?showTranscript=1.

Barbaro, M. (2020d, August 11). *The Daily*. Retrieved from https://www.nytimes.com/2020/08/11/podcasts/the-daily/cancel-culture.html.

Beck, A. (1975). *Cognitive Therapy and the Emotional Disorders*. Madison, CT: International Universities Press.

Benzinga, S. M. W. (2020, January 24). The Silicon Valley Stoic: A Glimpse into Jack Dorsey's Bizarre Morning Routine. *Yahoo Finance*. Retrieved from https://finance.yahoo.com/news/silicon-valley-stoic-glimpse-jack-163022397.html.

Bercovici, J. (2018, July 18). Silicon Valley's Latest Lifehack: Death. Retrieved from https://onezero.medium.com/game-over-bf20324ba420.

Bilton, M., & Sim, K. (1992). *Four Hours in My Lai*. New York, NY: Penguin.

Boelen, P. A., & Lenferink, L. I. M. (2019). Symptoms of Prolonged Grief, Posttraumatic Stress, and Depression in Recently Bereaved People:

Symptom Profiles, Predictive Value, and Cognitive Behavioural Correlates. *Social Psychiatry and Psychiatric Epidemiology*, 55, 765–777. doi:https://doi.org/10.1007/s00127-019-01776-w.

Boissoneault, L. (2017, August 24). How the New York Stock Exchange Gave Abbie Hoffman His Start in Guerrilla Theater. *Smithsonian Magazine*. Retrieved from https://www.smithsonianmag.com/history/how-new-york-stock-exchange-gave-abbie-hoffman-his-start-guerrilla-theater-180964612/.

Bonanno, G. A. (2004). Loss, Trauma, and Human Resilience: Have We Underestimated the Human Capacity to Thrive after Extremely Aversive Events? *American Psychologist*, 50(1), 20–28.

Bowles, N. (2019, March 26). Why Is Silicon Valley So Obsessed with the Virtue of Suffering? *New York Times*. Retrieved from https://www.nytimes.com/2019/03/26/style/silicon-valley-stoics.html?smid=em-share.

Boxill, B. R. (1976). Self-Respect and Protest. *Philosophy & Public Affairs*, 6(1), 58–69.

Bradley, K. R. (2008). Seneca and Slavery. In J. Fitch (Ed.), *Seneca: Oxford Readings in Classical Studies* (pp. 335–347). New York, NY, and Oxford, UK: Oxford University Press.

Braun, L. (2019, May 12). Silicon Valley Billionaires Adopt Fasting as a Way of Life. *Toronto Sun*. Retrieved from https://torontosun.com/news/local-news/braun-silicon-valley-billionaires-adopt-fasting-as-a-way-of-life.

Brennan, T. (2000). Reservation in Stoic Ethics. *Archiv für Geschichte der Philosophie*, 82, 149–177.

Brennan, T. (2005). *The Stoic Life*. Oxford, UK: Oxford University Press.

C-Span (Producer). (2019, October 17). House Leadership Tributes to Representative Elijah Cummings. Retrieved from https://www.c-span.org/video/?465290-5/house-leadership-tributes-representative-elijah-cummings.

Callard, A. (2018). *Aspiration*. New York, NY: Oxford University Press.

Carr, A., & McCracken, H. (2018, April 4). "Did We Create This Monster?" How Twitter Turned Toxic. *Fast Company*.

Retrieved   from   https://www.fastcompany.com/40547818/
did-we-create-this-monster-how-twitter-turned-toxic.

Caston, R. R. (2016). *Hope, Joy, and Affection in the Classical World.*
New York, NY: Oxford University Press.

Chivers, C. J. (2018). *The Fighters: Americans in Combat in Afghanistan
and Iraq.* New York, NY: Simon & Schuster.

Cicero. (1927). *Tusculan Disputations* (J. E. King, Trans. Vol. 8).
Cambridge, MA, and London, UK: Harvard University Press.

Cicero. (1991). *On Duties* (E. M. Atkins, Trans.; M. T. Griffin, E. M.
Atkins, Ed.). Cambridge, UK: Cambridge University Press.

Cicero. (2001). *On Moral Ends* (R. Woolf, Trans.; J. Annas, Ed.).
Cambridge, UK: Cambridge University Press.

Cicero. (2002). *Cicero on the Emotions: Tusculan Disputations 3 and 4*
(M. Graver, Ed.). Chicago, IL: University of Chicago Press.

Clapp, M., Aurora, N., Herrera, I.., Bhatia, M., Wilen, E., & Wakefield,
S. (2017). Gut Microbiota's Effect on Mental Health: The Gut-Brain
Axis. *Clinics and Practice, 7*(4), 987–987. doi:10.4081/cp.2017.987.

CNN Politics (Producer). (2019, February 27). Rep. Cummings Makes
Fiery Speech in Defense of Democracy. Retrieved from https://www.
cnn.com/videos/politics/2019/02/27/elijah-cummings-closing-
michael-cohen-testimony-sot-vpx.cnn.

Coates, T.-N. (2014, June). The Case for Reparations. *The Atlantic.*
Retrieved   from   https://www.theatlantic.com/magazine/archive/
2014/06/the-case-for-reparations/361631/.

Cooper, J. M. (1995). Eudaimonism and the Appeal to Nature in the
Morality of Happiness: Comments on Julia Annas, The Morality of
Happiness. *Philosophy & Phenomenological Research, 55*(3), 587–598.

Corasaniti, N. (2020, June 13). Cory Booker on Newark Pride, Black
Lives Matter and "This Distraught Present." *New York Times.*
Retrieved from https://www.nytimes.com/2020/06/13/us/politics/
cory-booker-racism-black-lives-matter.html.

Cuccinello, H. C. (2020, April 15). Jack Dorsey, Bill Gates and at Least
75 Other Billionaires Donating to Pandemic Relief. *Forbes.* Retrieved

from https://www.forbes.com/sites/hayleycuccinello/2020/04/15/jack-dorsey-bill-gates-and-at-least-75-other-billionaires-donating-to-pandemic-relief/?sh=4792c9cb21bd.

Dam NTV, v. V. M., Vago, D. R., Schmalzl, L., Saron, C. D., Olendzki, A., Meissner, T., Lazar, S. W., Kerr, C. E., Gorchov, J., et al. (2017). Mind the Hype: A Critical Evaluation and Prescriptive Agenda for Research on Mindfulness and Meditation. *Perspectives on Psychological Science, 13*(1), 36–61.

Damschen, G. A. H. (Ed.). (2014). *Brill's Companion to Seneca: Philosopher and Dramatist.* Leiden, the Netherlands, and Boston, MA: Brill.

Darwin, C. (1872). *The Expression of the Emotions in Man and Animals.* London, United Kingdom: John Murray.

Deigh, J. (1994). Cognitivism in the Theory of Emotions. *Ethics: An International Journal of Social, Political, and Legal Philosophy, 104*(4), 824–854.

Dowd, M. (2017, October 21). With . . . Susan Fowler. She's 26, and Brought Down Uber's C.E.O. What's Next? *New York Times.* Retrieved from https://www.nytimes.com/2017/10/21/style/susan-fowler-uber.html?smid=em-share.

Dozier, C. (2017). White Supremacists Use Parthenon for Logo. Retrieved from https://pages.vassar.edu/pharos/2017/11/21/white-supremacists-use-parthenon-for-logo/.

Dozier, C. (2020a, June 3). *The Practical Stoic.* Retrieved from https://practicalstoicpodcast.podbean.com/e/prof-nancy-sherman-the-life-teachings-of-seneca/.

Dozier, C. (2020b, March 6). *The Practical Stoic.* Retrieved from https://www.simonjedrew.com/nancy-sherman-on-stoic-emotion-and-senecas-humanity/.

Dozier, C. (2020c). *The Practical Stoic.* Retrieved from https://podcasts.apple.com/us/podcast/the-practical-stoic-with-simon-j-e-drew/id1278694631.

Editorial Board. (2020, April 23). A Breath of Fresh Air. *New York Times.* Retrieved from https://www.nytimes.com/2020/04/23/opinion/coronavirus-fresh-air-fund.html?searchResultPosition=2.

Edwards, C. (2017). Seneca and the Quest for Glory in Nero's Golden Age. In S. Bartsch, K. Freudenburg, and C. Littlewood (Ed.), *The Cambridge Companion to the Age of Nero* (pp. 164–176). Cambridge: Cambridge University Press.

Egan, E. (2020, January 2). Writing a Book Is a Solitary Endeavor: Publishing One Is a Group Effort. *New York Times.* Retrieved from https://www.nytimes.com/2020/01/02/books/review/inside-the-list-the-making-of-a-bestseller.html.

Ekman, P. (1982). *Emotion in the Human Face* (2nd ed.). Cambridge, UK; New York, NY; Paris, France: Cambridge University Press; Editions de la Maison des Sciences de l'Homme.

Ekman, P., & Friesen, W. (1980). Relative Importance of Face, Body, and Speech in Judgments of Personality and Affect. *Journal of Personality and Social Psychology, 38*(2), 270–277.

Ellis, A. (1962). *Reason and Emotion in Psychotherapy.* Oxford, UK: Lyle Stuart.

Emde, R., Gaensbauer, T. J., & Harmon, R. J. (1976). Emotional Expression in Infancy: A Biobehavioral Study. *Psychological Issues, 10*(1).

Epictetus. (1925). *The Discourses as Reported by Arrian, The Manual, and Fragments* (W. A. Oldfather, Trans.). Cambridge, MA, and London, UK: Harvard University Press.

Epictetus. (1983). *Handbook of Epictetus* (N. White, Trans.). Indianapolis, IN: Hackett.

Epictetus. (1995). *The Discourses* (R. Hard, Trans.; C. Gill, Ed.). London, UK: Everyman.

Epictetus. (2018). *How to Be Free: An Ancient Guide to Stoic Life. Encheiridion and Selections from Discourses* (A. A. Long, Trans.). Princeton, NJ: Princeton University Press.

Equestrian Statue of Marcus Aurelius. Retrieved from https://art.
thewalters.org/detail/20970/equestrian-statue-of-marcus-aurelius/.

Erasmus. (1501/1905). *The Manual of a Christian Knight* (A Book
Called in Latin Enchiridion Militis Christiani and in English the
Manual of the Christian Knight Replenished with Most Wholesome
Precepts Made by the Famous Clerk Erasmus of Rotterdam to
the which is Added a New and Marvellous Profitable Preface ed.).
London: Methuen.

Ferriss, T. (2017, April). *Why You Should Define Your Fears Instead of
Your Goals* [Video]. TED Conferences. https://www.ted.com/talks/
tim_ferriss_why_you_should_define_your_fears_instead_of_your_
goals.

Finley, M. I. (2017). *Ancient Slavery and Modern Ideology* (Expanded
Edition, Brent Shaw, Ed.). New York, NY: Marcus Weiner Publications.

Fitch, J., Trans. (1987). *Seneca, Hercules Furens: A Critical Text with
Introduction and Commentary*. Ithaca, NY: Cornell University Press.

Fleming, J., & Ledogar, R. J. (2008). Resilience, an Evolving Concept: A
Review of Literature Relevant to Aboriginal Research. *Pimatisiwin*,
6(2), 7–23.

Flikschuh, K., & Ypi, L. (Eds.). (2014). *Kant and Colonialism: Historical
and Critical Perspectives*. New York, NY, and Oxford, UK: Oxford
University Press.

Ford Cites Hippocampus in Recollection of Alleged Assault. (2018). In:
ABC News. Retrieved from https://abcnews.go.com/Politics/video/
ford-cites-hippocampus-recollection-alleged-assault-58123603.

Fowler, S. (2017). Reflecting on One Very, Very Strange Year at Uber.
Retrieved from https://www.susanjfowler.com/blog/2017/2/19/
reflecting-on-one-very-strange-year-at-uber.

Frede, M. (1987). Stoics and Skeptics on Clear and Distinct Impressions.
In *Essays in Ancient Philosophy* (pp. 151–176). Minneapolis:
University of Minnesota Press.

Fricker, M. (2007). *Epistemic Injustice: Power and the Ethics of Knowing*.
New York, NY: Oxford University Press.

Frijda, N. H. (1986). *The Emotions.* Cambridge, UK: Cambridge University Press.

Frijda, N. H. (1987). Emotion, Cognitive Structure, and Action Tendency. *Cognition and Emotion, 1*(2), 115–143. doi:10.1080/02699938708408043.

Gafni, M., & Garofoli, J. (2020, March 31). Captain of Aircraft Carrier with Growing Coronavirus Outbreak Pleads for Help from Navy. *San Francisco Chronicle.* Retrieved from https://www.sfchronicle.com/bayarea/article/Exclusive-Captain-of-aircraft-carrier-with-15167883.php#.

Garfield, L. (2016, October 9). The Founder of Bulletproof Coffee Plans to Live to be 180 Years Old—Here's His Daily Routine. *Business Insider.* Retrieved from https://www.businessinsider.com/dave-asprey-bulletproof-coffee-routine-2016-10#:~:text=The%20founder%20of%20Bulletproof%20Coffee,old%20%E2%80%94%20here's%20his%20daily%20routine&text=Dave%20Asprey%20wants%20to%20cheat,for%20a%20very%20long%20time.

Garland, C. (2020, April 6). In Speech to USS Roosevelt Crew, Modly Calls Fired Captain Either "Stupid" or Knowingly Negligent. *Stars and Stripes.* Retrieved from https://www.stripes.com/news/in-speech-to-uss-roosevelt-crew-modly-calls-fired-captain-either-stupid-or-knowingly-negligent-1.625061.

Garnsey, Peter. (1996). *Ideas of Slavery from Aristotle to Augustine.* Cambridge, UK: Cambridge University Press.

Gellius, A. (1927). *The Attic Nights* (J. C. Rolfe, Trans.). Cambridge, MA, and London, UK: Loeb Classical Editions.

Gill, C. (1988). Personhood and Personality: The Four Personae Theory in Cicero, De Officiis I. *Oxford Studies in Ancient Philosophy, 6,* 169–199.

Gill, C. (2016). Positive Emotions: Are They Enough? In R. Caston & R. Kaster (Ed.), *Hope, Joy, and Affection in the Classical World.* New York: Oxford University Press.

Gill, C. (2019). *Stoic & Modern Ethics*. Unpublished

Glazer, T. (2014). Can Emotions Communicate? *Thought: A Journal of Philosophy*, 3(3), 234–242.

Glazer, T. (2016). Looking Angry and Sounding Sad: The Perceptual Analysis of Emotional Expression. *Synthese*, 194(9), 1–25.

Glazer, T. (2019). Epistemic Violence and Emotional Misperception. *Hypatia*, 34(1), 59–65.

Goffman, E. (1959). *The Presentation of Self in Everyday Life*. New York, NY: Anchor Random House.

Goldhill, O. (2016, December 17). Silicon Valley Tech Workers Are Using an Ancient Philosophy Designed for Greek Slaves as a Life Hack. *Quartz*. Retrieved from https://qz.com/866030/stoicism-silicon-valley-tech-workers-are-reading-ryan-holiday-to-use-an-ancient-philosophy-as-a-life-hack/.

Grahn-Wilder, Malin. (2018). *Gender and Sexuality in Stoic Philosophy*. Cham, Switzerland: Palgrave Macmillan.

Graver, M. (1999). Philo of Alexandria and the Origins of the Stoic "propatheiai". *Phronesis: A Journal of Ancient Philosophy*, 44(4), 300–325.

Graver, M. (2007). *Stoicism and Emotion*. Chicago: University of Chicago Press.

Graver, M. (2017). Epictetus. *The Stanford Encyclopedia of Philosophy*. https://plato.stanford.edu/entries/epictetus/.

Greenspan, S. I. (1989). *The Development of the Ego: Implications for Personality Theory, Psychopathology, and the Psychotherapeutic Process*. Madison, CT: International Universities Press.

Griffin, B., Cornish, M., Maguen, S., & Worthington, E. L., Jr. (2021). Forgiveness as a Mechanism of Repair Following Military-Related Moral Injury. In J. Currier, K. Drescher, & J. Nieuwsma (Ed.), *Addressing Moral Injury in Clinical Practice* (pp. 71–86). Washington, DC: APA Publishing.

Griffin, B., Worthington, E., Davis, D., Hook, J., & Maguen, S. (2018). Development of the Self-Forgiveness Dual-Process Scale. *Journal of Counseling Psychology*, 65(6), 715–726.

Griffin, M. (1976). *Seneca: A Philosopher in Politics*. Oxford: Oxford University Press.

Griffin, M. (1986a). Philosophy, Cato, and Roman Suicide: I. *Greece & Rome, 33*(1), 64–77.

Griffin, M. (1986b). Philosophy, Cato, and Roman Suicide: II. *Greece & Rome, 33*(2), 199–202.

Guenther, H. (1989). *Tibetan Buddhism in Western Perspective*. Berkeley, CA: Dharma Publishing.

Hartley, L., Mavrodaris, A., Flowers, N., Ernst, E., & Rees, K. (2014). Transcendental Meditation for the Primary Prevention of Cardiovascular Disease. *Cochrane Database of Systematic Reviews* (12), Cd010359. doi:10.1002/14651858.CD010359.pub2.

Healy, M. (2018, June 26). The Surprising Thing the "Marshmallow Test" Reveals about Kids in an Instant-Gratification World. *Los Angeles Times*. Retrieved from https://www.latimes.com/science/sciencenow/la-sci-sn-marshmallow-test-kids-20180626-story.html.

Hendriks, L., de Kleine, R. A., Broekman, T. G., Hendriks, G.-J., & van Minnen, A. (2018). Intensive Prolonged Exposure Therapy for Chronic PTSD Patients Following Multiple Trauma and Multiple Treatment Attempts. *European Journal of Psychotraumatology, 9*(1), doi:10.1080/20008198.2018.1425574.

Hill, E., Tiefenthäler, A., Triebert, C., Jordan, D., Willis, H., & Stein, R. (2020, May 31). How George Floyd Was Killed in Police Custody. *New York Times*. Retrieved from https://www.nytimes.com/2020/05/31/us/george-floyd-investigation.html.

Hochschild, A. R. (1983). *The Managed Heart: Commercialization of Human Feeling*. Berkeley: University of California Press.

Holiday, R. Stoicism in the Military: An Interview with Professor Nancy Sherman. Retrieved from https://dailystoic.com/nancy-sherman/.

Homer. (1999). *The Iliad* (R. Fagles, Trans.). New York, NY: Penguin.

Hume, D. (1968). *A Treatise of Human Nature*. London, UK: Oxford University Press.

Inwood, B. (1985). *Ethics and Human Action in Early Stoicism*. Oxford, UK: Oxford University Press.

Inwood, B. (1986). Goal and Target in Stoicism. *Journal of Philosophy*, *83*(10), 547–556.

Inwood, B. (1999). Stoic Ethics. In K. Alglra, J. Barnes, J. Mansfeld, & M. Schofield (Eds.), *The Cambridge History of Hellenistic Philosophy* (pp. 675–705). New York, NY: Cambridge University Press.

Ismay, J. (2020, April 5). Navy Captain Removed from Carrier Tests Positive for Covid-19. *New York Times Magazine*. Retrieved from https://www.nytimes.com/2020/04/05/magazine/navy-captain-crozier-positive-coronavirus.html.

Jewett, C., & Szabo, L. (2020, April 15). Coronavirus Is Killing Far More US Health Workers Than Official Data Suggests. *The Guardian*. Retrieved from https://www.theguardian.com/us-news/2020/apr/15/coronavirus-us-health-care-worker-death-toll-higher-official-data-suggests.

Kahneman, D. (2011). *Thinking, Fast and Slow* (1st ed.). New York, NY: Farrar, Straus and Giroux.

Kant, I. (1964). *The Doctrine of Virtue, Part II of the Metaphysics of Morals* (M. J. Gregor, Trans.). Philadelphia: University of Pennsylvania Press.

Kant, I. (1974). *Anthropology from a Pragmatic Point of View* (M. J. Gregor, Trans.). The Hague, NL: Nijoff.

Kavanaugh Challenges Notion That He Was "Belligerent" While Drinking. (2018). In *PBS NewsHour*: PBS.

King, C. (2011). *Musonius Rufus*: William Irvine at CreateSpace. com. Retrieved from https://www.youtube.com/watch?v=qsVtXJtl7lw&ref=hvper.com&utm_source=hvper.com&utm_medium=website.

King, N., Kwong, M., Westerman, A., & Doubek, J. (2020, June 3). How a Mother Protects Her Black Teenage Son from the World. *NPR*. Retrieved from https://www.npr.org/2020/06/03/868173915/how-a-mother-protects-her-black-teenage-son-from-the-world.

Klein, J. (2015). Making Sense of Stoic Indifferents. *Oxford Studies in Ancient Philosophy*, 49, 227–281.

Klein, J. (2016). The Stoic Argument from *Oikeiosis*. *Oxford Studies in Ancient Philosophy*, 50, 143–199. doi:10.1093/acprof:oso/9780198778226.001.0001.

Klein, M. (1984). *Envy and Gratitude and Other Works: 1946–1963*. New York, NY: Free Press.

Konnikova, M. (2014, October 9). The Struggles of a Psychologist Studying Self-Control. *The New Yorker*. Retrieved from https://www.newyorker.com/science/maria-konnikova/struggles-psychologist-studying-self-control.

Konnikova, M. (2016, February 11). How People Learn to Become Resilient. *The New Yorker*. Retrieved from https://www.newyorker.com/science/maria-konnikova/the-secret-formula-for-resilience.

Laertius, D. (1925). *Lives of Eminent Philosophers* (R. D. Hicks, Trans., Vol. 2). London, UK, and Cambridge, MA: Harvard University Press.

Laertius, D. (1970). *Lives of Eminent Philosophers* (Vol. 2). Cambridge, MA: Loeb Classical Library, Harvard University Press.

Lamas, D. J. (2020, April 3). Who Gets a Ventilator? *New York Times*, p. 27. Retrieved from https://www.nytimes.com/2020/04/02/opinion/coronavirus-ventilator-shortage.html.

Lazarov, A., Suarez-Jimenez, B., Abend, R., Naim, R., Shvil, E., Helpman, L., . . . Neria, Y. (2019). Bias-Contingent Attention Bias Modification and Attention Control Training in Treatment of PTSD: A Randomized Control Trial. *Psychological Medicine*, 49(14), 2432–2440. doi:10.1017/S0033291718003367.

LeDoux, J. (1996). *The Emotional Brain*. New York, NY: Simon & Schuster.

Le Doux, J. (2015). *Anxious: Using the Brain to Understand and Treat Fear and Anxiety*. New York, NY: Viking.

Lewis, J. (2020, July 30). Together, You Can Redeem the Soul of Our Nation. *New York Times*. Retrieved from https://www.nytimes.com/2020/07/30/opinion/john-lewis-civil-rights-america.html.

Life hack. (2020). In *Wikipedia*. https://en.wikipedia.org/wiki/Life_ hack.

Lipton, E., Sanger, D. E., Haberman, M., Shear, M. D., Mazzetti, M., & Barnes, J. E. (2020, April 11). He Could Have Seen What Was Coming: Behind Trump's Failure on the Virus. *New York Times*. Retrieved from https://www.nytimes.com/2020/04/11/us/politics/ coronavirus-trump-response.html.

Litz, B., Lebowitz, L., Gray, M. J., & Nash, W. (2016). *Adaptive Disclosure: A New Treatment for Military Trauma, Loss, and Moral Injury*. New York, NY, and London, UK: Guilford Press.

Litz, B., Stein, N., Delaney, E., Lebowitz, L., Nash, W. P., et al. (2009). Moral Injury and Moral Repair in War Veterans: A Preliminary Model and Intervention Strategy. *Clinical Psychology Review*, *29*(8), 695–706.

Long, A. A. (1968). Aristotle's Legacy to Stoic Ethics. *Bulletin of the Institute of Classical Studies*, *15*, 72–85.

Long, A. A. (1999). The Socratic Legacy. In K. Algra, J. Barns, J. Mansfeld, & M. Schofield (Ed.), *The Cambridge History of Hellenistic Philosophy* (pp. 617–641). Cambridge: Cambridge University Press.

Long, A. A. (2002). *Epictetus: A Stoic and Socratic Guide to Life*. Oxford, UK: Oxford University Press.

Long, A. A., & Sedley, D. N. (1987a). *The Hellenistic Philosophers* (Vol. 2). Cambridge, UK: Cambridge University Press.

Long, A. A., & Sedley, D. N. (1987b). *The Hellenistic Philosophers* (Vol. 1: Translations of the Principal Sources with Philosophical Commentary). Cambridge, UK: Cambridge University Press.

Luna, T., St. John, P., Wigglesworth, A., Lin II, R.-G., & Shalby, C. (2020, March 20). L.A. County Confirms 61 New Coronavirus Cases, Says Median Age among All Patients Is 47. *Los Angeles Times*. Retrieved from https://www.latimes.com/california/story/2020-03-19/gavin-newsom-california-1-billion-federal-aid-coronavirus.

Maguen, S., & Litz, B. (2012, January 13). Moral Injury at War. Retrieved from http://www.ptsd.va.gov/professional/pages/moral_injury_at_ war.asp.

Margolis, R. (2019, April 17). Why Are Silicon Valley Billionaires Starving Themselves? *The Week*. Retrieved from https://theweek.com/articles/835226/why-are-silicon-valley-billionaires-starving-themselves.

Martin, S. (2020, July 9). Carl Reiner, Perfect. *New York Times*. Retrieved from https://www.nytimes.com/2020/07/09/movies/steve-martin-carl-reiner.html.

Maslin Nir, S. (2020, June 14). How 2 Lives Collided in Central Park, Rattling the Nation. *New York Times*. Retrieved from https://www.nytimes.com/2020/06/14/nyregion/central-park-amy-cooper-christian-racism.html.

Mayer, R. G. (2008). Roman Historical Exempla in Seneca. In J. Fitch (Ed.), *Seneca: Oxford Readings in Classical Studies* (pp. 299–315). New York, NY, and Oxford, UK: Oxford University Press.

Mill, J. S. (1979). *Utilitarianism*. Indianapolis, IN: Hackett.

Minuchin, S. (1974). *Families and Family Therapy*. Cambridge, MA: Harvard University Press.

Mischel, W., Ayduk, O., et al. (2011). "Willpower" over the Life Span: Decomposing Self-Regulation. *Social Cognitive and Affective Neuroscience*, 6(2), 252–256.

Mischel, W., & Ebessen, E. B. (1970). Attention in Delay of Gratification. *Journal of Personality and Social Psychology*, 16(2), 329–337.

Montaigne. (1957/1595). *Essays* (D. Frame, Trans.). Stanford, CA: Stanford University Press.

Montgomery, H. C. (1936). Washington the Stoic. *The Classical Journal*, 31(6), 371–373.

Murray, J., Theakston, A., & Wells, A. (2016). Can the Attention Training Technique Turn One Marshmallow into Two? Improving Children's Ability to Delay Gratification. *Behavior Research and Therapy*, 77, 34–39.

Nauta, B. (2019). Hoe gaan we de kinderen eruit halen? Aart van Oosten—brandweerman. In B. Nauta, H. Te Brake, & I. Raajimakers (Ed.), *Dat ene Dilemma: Persoonlijke verhalen over morel keuzes op de werkvloer* (pp. 31–39). Amsterdam: Amsterdam University Press with ARQ National Pyschotrauma Centrum.

New York Times. (2018, September 30). Chad Ludington's Statement on Kavanaugh's Drinking and Senate Testimony. *New York Times.* Retrieved from https://www.nytimes.com/2018/09/30/us/politics/chad-ludington-statement-brett-kavanaugh.html.

Nussbaum, M. C. (1986). *The Fragility of Goodness: Luck and Ethics in Greek Tragedy and Philosophy.* Cambridge and New York: Cambridge University Press.

Nussbaum, M. C. (2001). *Upheavals of Thought: The Intelligence of Emotions.* Cambridge, UK: Cambridge University Press.

Nussbaum, M. C. (2002). The Incomplete Feminism of Musonius Rufus, Platonist, Stoic, and Roman. In M. C. Nussbaum & J. Sihvola (Ed.), *The Sleep of Reason* (pp. 283–326). Chicago, IL, and London, UK: University of Chicago Press.

Nussbaum, M. C. (2011). *Creating Capabilities: The Human Development Approach.* Cambridge, MA: Harvard University Press.

Nussbaum, M. C. (2015). Transitional Anger. *Journal of the American Philosophical Association, 1*(01), 41–56. doi:10.1017/apa.2014.19.

Nussbaum, M. C. (2016). *Anger and Forgiveness: Resentment, Generosity, Justice.* New York: Oxford University Press.

Nussbaum, M. C., & Cohen, J. (Eds.). (1996/2002). *For Love of Country.* Boston: Beacon Press.

Oatley, K. (1992). *Best Laid Schemes: The Psychology of Emotions.* New York, NY: Cambridge University Press.

Ortony, A., G. L. Clore, & A. Collins. (1988). *The Cognitive Structure of Emotions.* New York, NY: Cambridge University Press.

Ozuah, P. O. (2020, June 9). I Fought Two Plagues and Only Beat One. *New York Times.* Retrieved from https://www.nytimes.com/2020/06/09/opinion/coronavirus-racism-montefiore-medicine.html.

Packard, V. (1957). *The Hidden Persuaders.* New York, NY: D. McKay.

Parker, C. (1896). Musonius the Etruscan. *Harvard Studies in Classical Philology, 7,* 123–137.

Philipps, D. (2019, December 27). Anguish and Anger from the Navy SEALs Who Turned in Edward Gallagher. *New York Times*. Retrieved from https://www.nytimes.com/2019/12/27/us/navy-seals-edward-gallagher-video.html.

Philo. (1953). *Questions and Answers on Genesis* (R. Marcus, Trans.). Cambridge, MA, and London, UK: Loeb Classical Library.

Plato. (1978). Apology (G. M. A. Grube, Trans.). In *The Trial and Death of Socrates*. Indianapolis, IN: Hackett.

Plato. (1989). *Symposium*. Indianapolis, IN: Hackett.

Plato. (1997a). *Complete Works*. Indianapolis, IN: Hackett.

Plato. (1997b). Phaedo (G. M. A. Grube, Trans.). In J. M. Cooper & D. S. Hutchinson (Eds.), *Complete Works*. Indianapolis, IN: Hackett.

Plutarch. (1976). *De Stoicorum repugnantiis*. In *Moralia* (H. Cherniss, Trans., Vol. 13, Part 2). Cambridge, MA: Harvard University Press.

Plutarch. (2000). *Moralia: On the Control of Anger* (W. C. Hembold, Trans., Vol. 1). Cambridge, MA: Harvard University Press.

Purcell, N., Burkman, K., Keyser, J., Fucella, P., & Maguen, S. (2018). Healing from Moral Injury: A Qualitative Evaluation of the Impact of Killing Treatment for Combat Veterans. *Journal of Aggression, Maltreatment & Trauma, 27*(6), 645–673.

Quintilian. Institutio oratoria. Retrieved from https://ryanfb.github.io/loebolus-data/L124N.pdf.

Raymond, E. (1991). *The Hacker's Dictionary*. Cambridge, MA: MIT Press.

Recode Staff. (2017, September 12). CEO Geoff Woo Answers Biohacking Questions on Too Embarrassed to Ask. *Vox*. Retrieved from https://www.vox.com/2017/9/12/16296408/transcript-hvmn-ceo-geoff-woo-answers-biohacking-questions-too-embarrassed-to-ask.

Reivich, K., & Shatte, A. (2002). *The Resilience Factor*. New York, NY: Broadway Books.

Richards, D., & Feloni, R. (2017, November 18). "The 4-Hour Workweek" Author Tim Ferriss Reveals What He's Learned after a Difficult Year of Introspection, and How He Built a Passionate

Fanbase of Millions. *Business Insider*. Retrieved from https://onezero. medium.com/game-over-bf20324ba420.

Rinpoche, S. (1992). *The Tibetan Book of Living and Dying*. San Francisco, CA: Harper Collins.

Rist, J. (1983). Zeno and Stoic Consistency. In J. P. Anton, & A. Preus (Ed.), *Essays in Ancient Greek Philosophy* (Vol. 2, pp. 465–476). Binghamton, NY: SUNY Press.

Roberts, R. (2009). Emotions and the Canons of Evaluation. In P. Goldie (Ed.), *The Oxford Handbook of Philosophy of Emotion*. Oxford, UK: Oxford University Press.

Robertson, D. (2017, November 5). Did Stoicism Condemn Slavery? Retrieved from https://donaldrobertson.name/2017/11/05/did-stoicism-condemn-slavery/.

Robertson, D. J. The Stoicism of Thomas Jefferson. *Medium*. Retrieved from https://medium.com/stoicism-philosophy-as-a-way-of-life/ the-stoicism-of-thomas-jefferson-e9266ebcf558.

Robertson, D. J. (2019). *How to Think like a Roman Emperor: The Stoic Philosophy of Marcus Aurelius*. New York, NY: St. Martin's Press.

Rosenberg, J. (2020, January/February). Why Silicon Valley Fell in Love with an Ancient Philosophy of Austerity. *Mother Jones*. Retrieved from https://www.motherjones.com/media/2020/01/silicon-valley-stoicism-holiday/.

Rufus, M. (1947). *Musonius Rufus, The Roman Socrates* (C. Lutz, Trans.). Retrieved from https://philocyclevl.files.wordpress.com/2016/09/ yale-classical-studies-10-cora-e-lutz-ed-musonius-rufus_-the-roman-socrates-yale-university-press-1947.pdf.

Sanger, D. E., Lipton, E., Sullivan, E., & Crowley, M. (2020, March 19). Before Virus Outbreak, a Cascade of Warnings Went Unheeded. *New York Times*, p. 1. Retrieved from https://www.nytimes.com/2020/ 03/19/us/politics/trump-coronavirus-outbreak.html.

Schaefer, D. L. (2001). Montaigne and the Classical Tradition. *International Journal of the Classical Tradition*, 8(2), 179–194.

Schein, M. (2019, January 17). Tim Ferriss Is Everything That's Wrong with the Modern World (and Why You Should Follow His Lead). *Forbes*. Retrieved from https://www.forbes.com/sites/michaelschein/2019/01/17/tim-ferriss-is-everything-thats-wrong-with-the-modern-world-and-why-you-should-follow-his-lead/#19026ad93f3d.

Scherer, K. R. (2005). What Are Emotions? And How Can They Be Measured? *Social Science Information, 44*, 695–729. doi:10.1177/0539018405058216.

Schleifer, T. (2020, June 11). Inside Jack Dorsey's Radical Experiment for Billionaires to Give Away Their Money. *Vox*. Retrieved from https://www.vox.com/recode/2020/6/11/21287395/jack-dorsey-start-small-billionaire-philanthropy-coronavirus-twitter-square-kaepernick-rihanna.

Schneewind, J. B. (1990). *Moral Philosophy from Montaigne to Kant* (Vol. 1). New York, NY: Cambridge University Press.

Schofield, M. (1999a). Social and Political Thought. In K. Alglra, J. Barnes, J. Mansfeld, & M. Schofield (Eds.), *The Cambridge History of Hellenistic Philosophy* (pp. 739–770). New York, NY: Cambridge University Press.

Schofield, M. (1999b). *The Stoic Idea of the City*. Chicago, IL: University of Chicago Press.

Seneca. (1932a). On the Shortness of Life. In J. W. Basore (Ed.), *Moral Essays*. Cambridge, MA, and London, UK: Loeb Classical Library, Harvard University Press.

Seneca. (1932b). On Tranquility of Mind (J. W. Basore, Trans.). In *Moral Essays* (Vol. 2). Cambridge, MA, and London, UK: Harvard University Press.

Seneca. (1935). On Leisure (J. W. Basore, Trans.). In *Moral Essays*. Cambridge, MA, and London, UK: Harvard University Press.

Seneca. (1985). *On Mercy* (J. W. Basore, Ed., Vol. 1). Cambridge, MA: Harvard University Press.

Seneca. (1995a). On Anger (J. M. Cooper & J. F. Procope, Trans.). In *Moral and Political Essays*. New York, NY: Cambridge University Press.

Seneca. (1995b). On Favours (J. M. Cooper & J. F. Procopé, Trans.). In *Moral and Political Essays*. New York, NY: Cambridge University Press.

Seneca. (2010). Hercules Furens. In E. Wilson (Ed.), *Seneca: Six Tragedies*. Oxford, UK, and New York, NY: Oxford University Press.

Seneca. (2015). *Letters on Ethics to Lucilius* (M. Graver & A. A. Long, Trans.). Chicago, IL, and London, UK: University of Chicago Press.

Sherman, N. (1989). *The Fabric of Character: Aristotle's Theory of Virtue*. Oxford, UK: Oxford University Press.

Sherman, N. (1990). The Place of Emotions in Kantian Morality. In O. Flanagan & A. O. Rorty (Eds.), *Character, Psychology and Morality* (pp. 158–170): Cambridge, MA: MIT Press.

Sherman, N. (1992). Hamartia and Virtue. In A. O. Rorty (Ed.), *Essays on Aristotle's Poetics* (pp. 177–196). Princeton, NJ: Princeton University Press.

Sherman, N. (1995a). Ancient Conceptions of Happiness. *Philosophy and Phenomenological Research*, 55(4), 913–919. doi:10.2307/2108341.

Sherman, N. (1995b). *Kant on Sentimentalism and Stoic Apathy*. Paper presented at the Proceedings of the Eighth International Kant Congress.

Sherman, N. (1995c). Reason and Feeling in Kantian Morality, discussion review of Paul Guyer, Kant and the Experience of Freedom. *Philosophy and Phenomenological Research*, 55(2), 369–377.

Sherman, N. (1995d). The Moral Perspective and the Psychoanalytic Quest. *The Journal of the American Academy of Psychoanalysis*, 23(2), 223–241.

Sherman, N. (1997a). Kantian Virtue: Priggish or Passional? In A. Reaths, B. Herman, and C. Korsgaard (Ed.), *Reclaiming the History of Ethics: Essays for John Rawls* (pp. 270–296). Cambridge, UK: Cambridge University Press.

Sherman, N. (1997b). *Making a Necessity of Virtue: Aristotle and Kant on Virtue*. New York, NY: Cambridge University Press.

Sherman, N. (1998). Concrete Kantian Respect. *Social Philosophy and Policy, 15*(1), 119–148.

Sherman, N. (2005a). Stoic Warriors: On Modern Soldiers and Ancient Wisdom. *TPM: The Philosopher's Magazine, 32*, 34–38.

Sherman, N. (2005b). *Stoic Warriors: The Ancient Philosophy behind the Military Mind*. New York, NY: Oxford University Press.

Sherman, N. (2010). *The Untold War: Inside the Hearts, Minds, and Souls of Our Soldiers*. New York, NY: W. W. Norton & Company.

Sherman, N. (2011). War and the Moral Logic of Survivor Guilt. *New York Times*. Retrieved from https://opinionator.blogs.nytimes.com/2011/07/03/war-and-the-moral-logic-of-survivor-guilt/.

Sherman, N. (2015a). *Afterwar: Healing the Moral Injuries of Our Soldiers*. New York, NY: Oxford University Press.

Sherman, N. (2015b). Afterwar: Healing the Moral Wounds of Our Soldiers. Retrieved from https://www.youtube.com/watch?reload=9&v=PhYmCFgwfmM&feature=youtu.be.

Sherman, N. (2018). Dancers and Soldiers Sharing the Dance Floor: Emotional Expression in Dance. In J. McMahon (Ed.), *Social Aesthetics and Moral Judgment: Pleasure, Reflection and Accountability* (pp. 121–138). London, UK: Routledge.

Sherman, N. (2021). Trenches, Cadences, and Faces: Social Connection and Emotional Expression in the Great War and After. In A. L. LaCroix, J. S. Masur, M. C. Nussbaum & L. Weinrib (Ed.), *Cannons and Codes: War, Literature, and America's Wars* (p. 1). New York, NY: Oxford University Press.

Sherman, N., & White, H. (2007). Intellectual Virtue: Emotions, Luck, and the Ancients. In M. DePaul & L. Zagzebski (Ed.), *Intellectual Virtue: Perspectives from Ethics and Epistemology* (pp. 34–54). Oxford and New York: Oxford University Press.

Smith, A. (2000). *The Theory of Moral Sentiments*. New York, NY: Prometheus.

Sorabji, R. (2000). *Emotion and Peace of Mind: From Stoic Agitation to Christian Temptation*. Oxford, UK, and New York, NY: Oxford University Press.

Stanley, E. A. (2019). *Widen the Window*. New York, NY: Avery, Penguin.

Stanton, G. R. (1968). The Cosmopolitan Ideas of Epictetus and Marcus Aurelius. *Phronesis: A Journal of Ancient Philosophy*, *13*(2), 183–195.

Stern, D. (1985). *The Interpersonal World of the Infant*. New York, NY: Basic.

Stobaeus, A. D. (1999). *Epitome of Stoic Ethics (Eclogae)* (A. Pomeroy, Trans. and Ed.). Atlanta, GA: Society of Bibical Literature.

Stockdale, J. B. (1995). *Thoughts of a Philosophical Fighter Pilot*. Stanford, CA: Hoover Press.

Stockdale, J. B., & Stockdale, S. (1990). *In Love and War: The Story of a Family's Ordeal and Sacrifices during the Vietnam Years*. Annapolis, MD: Naval Institute Press.

Stoughton, S. (2015). Law Enforcement's "Warrior" Problem. *Harvard Law Review*, *128*, 225–234.

Strawson, P. F. (1962). Freedom and Resentment. *Proceedings of the British Academy*, *48*, 1–25.

Strawson, P. F. (1993). Freedom and Resentment. In J. Fischer & M. Ravizza (Eds.), *Perspectives on Moral Responsibility* (pp. 45–66). Ithaca, NY: Cornell University Press.

Tessman, L. (2019). *Moral Injury and Moral Failure*. Paper presented at the West Point War, Fall 2019.

Thomas, D. K. (2003). Who Wrote Seneca's Plays? *The Classical World*, *96*(3), 271–280. doi:10.2307/4352761.

Thurman, R. (1984). *The Central Philosophy of Tibet: A Study and Translation of Jey Tsong Khapa's Essence of True Eloquence*. Princeton, NJ: Princeton University Press.

Timberg, C. (2016, October 18). Racial Profiling, by a Computer? Police Facial-ID Tech Raises Civil Rights Concerns. *Washington*

Post. Retrieved from https://www.washingtonpost.com/business/economy/face-recognition-tech/2016/10/17/986929ea-41f0-44a2-b2b9-90b495230dce_story.html.

Trent, M., Dooley, D. G., & Dougé, J. (2019). The Impact of Racism on Child and Adolescent Health. *Pediatrics, 144*(2), e20191765. doi:10.1542/peds.2019-1765.

Twitter. (2020). Investor Relations FAQ [Press release]. Retrieved from https://investor.twitterinc.com/contact/faq/default.aspx#:~:text=What%20is%20Twitter's%20mission%20statement%3F,a%20free%20and%20global%20conversation.

Vlastos, G. (1991). *Socrates, Ironist and Moral Philosopher.* Ithaca, NY: Cornell University Press.

Von Arnim, J. H. (1964). *Stoicorum Veterum Fragmenta (SVF).* Stuttgart: B. G. Teubner.

Wald, I., Degnan, K. A., Gorodetsky, E., Charney, D. S., Fox, N. A., Fruchter, E., . . . Bar-Haim, Y. (2013). Attention to Threats and Combat-Related Posttraumatic Stress Symptoms: Prospective Associations and Moderation by the Serotonin Transporter Gene. *JAMA Psychiatry, 70*(4), 401–408. doi:10.1001/2013.jamapsychiatry.188.

Wald, I., Fruchter, E., Ginat, K., Stolin, E., Dagan, D., Bliese, P. D., . . . Bar-Haim, Y. (2016). Selective Prevention of Combat-Related Post-Traumatic Stress Disorder Using Attention Bias Modification Training: A Randomized Controlled Trial. *Psychological Medicine, 46*(12), 2627–2636. doi:10.1017/s0033291716000945.

Walton, K. G., Schneider, R. H., & Nidich, S. (2004). Review of Controlled Research on the Transcendental Meditation Program and Cardiovascular Disease: Risk Factors, Morbidity, and Mortality. *Cardiology in Review, 12*(5), 262–266. doi:10.1097/01.crd.0000113021.96119.78.

Walzer, M. (1977). *Just and Unjust Wars: A Moral Argument with Historical Illustrations.* New York, NY: Basic Books.

Ward, K. (2020). *Standpoint Phenomenology.* (Ph.D.). Georgetown University.

Warzel, C. (2020, June 10). The Floyd Protests Show That Twitter Is Real Life. *New York Times*. Retrieved from https://www.nytimes.com/2020/06/10/opinion/sunday/twitter-protest-politics.html.

Western, D. Tim Ferriss Net Worth. *Wealthy Gorilla*. Retrieved from https://wealthygorilla.com/tim-ferriss-net-worth/.

Westover, T. (2018). *Educated: A Memoir*. New York, NY: Random House.

Wilson, E. (2007). *The Death of Socrates*. Cambridge, MA: Harvard University Press.

Wilson, E. (2019). *The Greatest Empire: A Life of Seneca*. New York, NY: Oxford University Press.

Winger, A. (Writer). (2020). Unorthodox. In: Netflix. Retrieved from https://www.netflix.com/title/81019069.

Woelfel, J. (2011). "The Beautiful Necessity": Emerson and the Stoic Tradition. *American Journal of Theology and Philosophy*, *32*(2), 122–138.

Xenophon. (2013). *Symposium* (O. J. Todd, Trans., J. Henderson, Rev.). Cambridge, MA, and London, UK: Harvard University Press.

Yablonka, M. (2006, August). Vice Admiral James Bond Stockdale: Vietnam War Hero and Indomitable Spirit at the Hanoi Hilton. *Vietnam*. Retrieved from https://www.historynet.com/vice-admiral-james-bond-stockdale-vietnam-war-hero-and-indomitable-spirit-at-the-hanoi-hilton.htm.

Zhouli, L. (2018, September 16). Christine Blasey Ford's Letter Detailing Sexual Assault Allegations against Brett Kavanaugh. *Vox*. Retrieved from https://www.vox.com/2018/9/16/17867706/christine-blasey-ford-brett-kavanaugh-sexual-assault-allegations.

Zuckerberg, D. (2018). Social Media Has Elevated Misogyny to New Levels of Violence/Interviewer: N. Iqbal. Retrieved from https://www.theguardian.com/books/2018/nov/11/donna-zuckerberg-social-media-misoyny-violence-classical-antiquity-not-all-dead-white-men.

CREDITS

LESSON 1: THE GREAT STOIC REVIVAL

Eduardo Rosales, *Seneca*, 1836–1873, painting.
Permissions: Public domain.

LESSON 2: WHO WERE THE STOICS?

Zeno of Citium.
Permissions: Photograph by Paolo Monti, 1969, Naples. Courtesy of Biblioteca europea di informazione e cultura.
Cleanthes from the title page of *L. Annaei Senecae philosophi Opera.*
Permissions: Public domain.

Chrysippus of Soli.
Permissions: Courtesy of The British Museum.
Portrait of Cicero, Musei Capitolini.
Permissions: Photo by José Luiz licensed under https://creative-commons.org/licenses/by-sa/3.0/deed.en.
Philo of Alexandria from André Thevet, *Les vrais pourtraits et vies des hommes illustres grecz, latins et payens.*
Permissions: Public domain.
Seneca, part of double-herm of Socrates and Seneca in Antikensammlung Berlin.
Permissions: Photo by Calidius licensed under https://creative-commons.org/licenses/by-sa/3.0/deed.en.
Gaius Musonius Rufus.
Permissions: Public domain.
Illustration of Epictetus.
Permissions: Public domain.
Portrait of the emperor Marcus Aurelius, 2nd century, marble, Archaeological Museum of Istanbul, Turkey.
Permissions: Photo by Eric Gaba licensed under https://creative-commons.org/licenses/by-sa/3.0/deed.en.

LESSON 3: FINDING CALM

Doctors and nurses operating on a patient.
Permissions: Photo by J. C. Gellidon, courtesy of Unsplash.
Aart van Oosten, Firechief Arnemuiden.
Permissions: Courtesy of Aart van Oosten.

LESSON 4: MANAGING YOUR EMOTIONS

Boxer of Quirinal.
Permissions: Photo by Carole Raddato licensed under https://creativecommons.org/licenses/by-sa/3.0/deed.en.

LESSON 5: STOIC GRIT AND RESILIENCE

Terracotta Panathenaic prize amphora.
Permissions: Public domain.
Hercules and Centaur Nessus.
Permissions: Photo by Carlo Raso. Public domain.

LESSON 6: HEALING THROUGH SELF-COMPASSION

Stockdale emerging from his plane one week before he was shot down.
Permissions: Courtesy of Jim and Sybil Stockdale, from their *In Love and War.*
Stockdale as prisoner, 1966.
Permissions: Courtesy of Jim and Sybil Stockdale, from their *In Love and War.*

LESSON 7: LIFEHACKS

Marcus Aurelius.
Permissions: Photo by Heinz Klier, courtesy of Pexels.

LESSON 8: THE ART OF STOIC LIVING

Seneca, engraving.
Permissions: Courtesy of Art Institute Chicago.
Dhyani Buddha Vairocana sculpture.
Permissions: Photograph by H. Bongers, courtesy of Tropenmuseum, part of the National Museum of World Cultures. Licensed under https://creativecommons.org/licenses/by-sa/3.0/deed.en.

LESSON 9: A HEALTHY MODERN STOICISM

The Dying Seneca.
Permissions: Public domain.

INDEX

For the benefit of digital users, indexed terms that span two pages (e.g., 52–53) may, on occasion, appear on only one of those pages.

Figures are indicated by *f* following the page number